International Technology Law & Business

A Practical Glossary

Colm MacKernan

BOOK IDEA SUBMISSIONS

If you are a C-level executive or senior lawyer interested in submitting a book idea or manuscript to the Aspatore editorial board, please e-mail authors@aspatore.com. Aspatore is especially looking for highly specific book ideas that would have a direct financial impact on behalf of a reader. Completed books can range from 20 to 2,000 pages—the topic and "need to read" aspect of the material are most important, not the length. Include your book idea, biography, and any additional pertinent information.

SPEAKER SUBMISSIONS FOR CONFERENCES

If you are interested in giving a speech for an upcoming ReedLogic conference (a partner of Aspatore Books), please e-mail the ReedLogic Speaker Board at speakers@reedlogic.com. If selected, speeches are given over the phone and recorded (no travel necessary). Due to the busy schedules and travel implications for executives, ReedLogic produces each conference on CD-ROM, then distributes the conference to bookstores and executives who register for the conference. The finished CD-ROM includes the speaker's picture with the audio of the speech playing in the background, similar to a radio address played on television.

INTERACTIVE SOFTWARE SUBMISSIONS

If you have an idea for an interactive business or software legal program, please e-mail software@reedlogic.com. ReedLogic is specifically seeking Excel spreadsheet models and PowerPoint presentations that help business professionals and lawyers accomplish specific tasks. If idea or program is accepted, product is distributed to bookstores nationwide.

Published by Aspatore Inc.

For corrections, company/title updates, comments, or any other inquiries, please e-mail store@aspatore.com.

First Printing, 2006
10 9 8 7 6 5 4 3 2 1

ISBN 1-59622-405-3
Library of Congress Control Number: 2006920211

Material in this book is for educational purposes only. This book is sold with the understanding that neither any of the authors nor the publisher are engaged in rendering legal, accounting, investment, or any other professional service. Neither the publisher nor the authors assume any liability for any errors or omissions, or for how this book or its contents are used or interpreted, or for any consequences resulting directly or indirectly from the use of this book. For legal advice or any other, please consult your personal lawyer or the appropriate professional.

The views expressed by the individuals in this book (or the individuals on the cover) do not necessarily reflect the views shared by the companies they are employed by (or the companies mentioned in this book). The employment status and affiliations of authors with the companies referenced are subject to change.

Aspatore Books is the largest and most exclusive publisher of C-level executives (CEO, CFO, CTO, CMO, partner) from the world's most respected companies and law firms. Aspatore annually publishes a select group of C-level executives from the Global 1,000, top 250 law firms (partners and chairs), and other leading companies of all sizes. C-Level Business Intelligence™, as conceptualized and developed by Aspatore Books, provides professionals of all levels with proven business intelligence from industry insiders—direct and unfiltered insight from those who know it best—as opposed to third-party accounts offered by unknown authors and analysts. Aspatore Books is committed to publishing an innovative line of business and legal books, those which lay forth principles and offer insights that when employed, can have a direct financial impact on the reader's business objectives, whatever they may be. In essence, Aspatore publishes critical tools—need-to-read as opposed to nice-to-read books—for all business professionals.

Dedication

To Eugenia, for being my lodestar and for putting up with the jet-lagged midnight "tapping" of this book into my laptop.

Table of Contents

Introduction

This glossary started as a plain English guide for colleagues, clients, and some analyst and journalist friends as to the meaning of the legal jargon that permeated their professional lives. Many of the entries deal with subjects that could, and indeed have, justified entire articles and frequently treatises; space considerations have forced much more abbreviated treatments. However, this is intended to be a practical glossary for managers and executives working in an international environment rather than dictionary primarily for lawyers, and as such seeks to identify and explain terms and where appropriate, alert the reader to the issues they can raise. Perhaps the best introduction is to try to explain some of its history.

Sixteen years ago or so, as a law student and legal intern, I found myself presented with the question of what sort of law I wanted to practice. Rather than making a straightforward choice, I picked (or vacillated between) three to match my interests—intellectual property law, international law, and litigation. Today, if this can be called a legal specialty, it is probably international technology law. The problem with this description is that in practice it encompasses a broad array of legal fields, ranging from intellectual property, international trade, commercial law, export controls, finance, venture capital, corporate governance and competition, and antitrust law. To make this issue worse, someone working in international technology needs to have at least a practical understanding of the ways in which these laws can vary from country to country.

Every legal and business field has its own jargon and catchphrases. One result of combining so many is that one sometimes spends time in meetings wondering what people are talking about. This presents a classic professionals' quandary: does one ask, and appear naïve or nod sagely and try to guess? In my case, one such moment was the negotiation of a software development agreement in which the participants struggled for a while regarding the mysterious subject of avoiding "Easter bunnies," which was resolved by a decision to "let Colm deal with it!" On another occasion, I found myself belabored by a senior board director to determine what the mythical Greek Sisyphus would think of an acquisition. Additionally, a regular part of international technology practice is explaining to colleagues, in plain and non-legalistic language, what another jurisdiction or field's jargon means and what issues are being discussed.

How important is this jargon? The share prices of successful consumer products, pharmaceutical, and high technology companies are typically a large multiple of the book value of their assets, in fact usually between 10 and 30 times tangible book value. What this means in practice, is that over 90 percent of the value of these businesses is intangible, the value of their goodwill, intellectual property, and contractual rights, all assets primarily defined by law. There is danger in this situation, in that these intangible assets are often poorly understood—people find it easier to contemplate the value of bricks, mortar, and physical plant. Moreover, at least published comment on these subjects, be it from journalists and analysts, albeit with some honorable exceptions, is typically bad-to-awful. To give a simple example, more often than not when a new company is described as having a patented technology, it will only have pending patent applications, which might or might not mature into a patent. To be blunt, these industries are international and governed by law; lawyer or not, if you want to work in or with them, you need to understand their language.

Finally, as is traditional, I should thank those who kindly afforded me the opportunity to learn what at least some of this all means, in particular the late Professor Richard Allen Gordon, Professor Jack Schmertz, Ruffin Cordell, Jonathan Faull, Joel Davidow, Takaaki (Taka) Nagashima, Mike O'Keeffe, and of course my clients. Numerous other lawyers and non-lawyers have also helped with reviews and suggestions, for example Jim Wallace, Phillip David, Joe Bial, Jamie Urquhart, Pete Magowan, Lucille Redmond, and especially my partners Peter Langley and Robert Carolina. You can direct any criticisms to them.

Colm MacKernan

3-to-1 Rule: negotiating principle that *at least* three times as much time should go into preparing for any presentation or negotiation as is spent in the negotiation or presentation itself, i.e., in researching the counterparty(ies), planning the proposal, and assembling the materials. The general principle is that preparation and planning will always win over innate ability alone. In contrast, *see* Parking-Lot Briefing.

6-Sigma (6-σ): internal quality control system and standard originally developed by Motorola Corporation and subsequently adopted by General Electric and numerous other companies. 6-σ is a statistically driven method for identifying and correcting sources of quality problems within a manufacturing or service delivery process. Occasionally references to complying or providing data for 6-σ methodologies are found in supply and service contracts. Sigma (σ) is the term or symbol used for a standard deviation (i.e., the margin of error in measuring a quantity). In a standard distribution, 68 percent of results will lie within 1 standard deviation of the mean, while 99.99999998 percent of results lie within 6-σ of the mean; thus in a 6 sigma process the defect rate will, in principle, be 2 per billion (whether it is so low in practice is the subject of some skepticism).

8-K: Securities Law, abbreviation for SEC Form 8-K, a document, which a company that is publicly traded in the United States must file when material facts about the company, which may have an effect on its financial position, change. As with all other SEC filings, Form 8-K filings are available over the Internet from the SEC's EDGAR (Electronic Data Gathering, Analysis, and Retrieval) System.

10b-5, Rule, Violation: U.S. Securities Law rule (regulation) promulgated in 1948 under the Securities Exchange Act of 1934. Rule 10b-5 contains a sweeping prohibition of all forms of deceptive conduct in connection with buying or selling securities [q.v.]. Because of the very broad definition of a "security" in the Act, this means that a broad array of deceptive of misleading statements when raising funds for businesses or selling shares or bonds can be treated as a securities violation. The exact language of Rule 10b-5 is:

> It shall be unlawful for any person, directly or indirectly, by the use of any means or instrumentality of interstate commerce, or of the mails or of any facility of any national securities exchange,
>
> > 1. To employ any device, scheme, or artifice to defraud,
> >
> > 2. To make any untrue statement of a material fact or to omit to state a material fact necessary in order to make the statements made, in the light of the circumstances under which they were made, not misleading, or
> >
> > 3. To engage in any act, practice, or course of business which operates or would operate as a fraud or deceit upon any person,
>
> in connection with the purchase or sale of any security.

Rule 10b-5 has been supplemented by Rules 10b5-1 and 10b5-2 to encompass share dealings using "material non-public information," i.e., insider trading.

10-K: Securities Law, abbreviation for SEC Form 10-K, a detailed document setting forth key aspects of a company's business results and prospects, which U.S. publicly traded companies are required to file once a year with the United States Securities and Exchange Commission containing annual results. The Form 10-K is a rich source of relatively un-spun information about a company, which is much underused by other business. As with all other SEC filings, Form 10-K filings are available over the Internet from the SEC's EDGAR (Electronic Data Gathering, Analysis, and Retrieval) System [q.v.]. The equivalent to a 10-K for foreign companies traded on the U.S. exchanges (e.g., through ADRs or American Depository Receipts [q.v.]) is a Form 20-F.

10-Q: Securities Law, abbreviation for SEC Form 10-Q, a less-detailed document than the annual 10-K setting forth key aspects of a company's business results and prospects which U.S. publicly traded companies are required to file 45 days after the close of each quarter with the United States Securities and Exchange Commission. Information in the 10-Q is not usually audited, but is more up to date than that in a 10-K. As with all other SEC filings, Form 10-Q filings are available over the Internet from the SEC's EDGAR (Electronic Data Gathering, Analysis, and Retrieval [q.v.]) System.

12b Motion, Rule: short form for a Motion-to-Dismiss under the Federal Rules of Civil Procedure. Rule 12, subsection b sets forth a list of grounds under which a defendant can move to have a case dismissed because the complaint is facially deficient (such a motion is also known as a *demurrer,* though strictly a demurrer can also be filed at the end of a trial). The grounds set forth in Rule 12(b) are: (1) lack of jurisdiction over the subject matter; (2) lack of jurisdiction over the person; (3) improper venue (i.e., wrong courthouse); (4) insufficiency of process (i.e., the papers filed are not complete in some manner); (5) insufficiency of service of process (the defendant(s) was(were) not properly served); (6) failure to state a claim upon which relief can be granted; (7) failure to join a necessary party. Of the Rule 12(b) motions, Rule 12(b)(5) and Rule 12(b)(6) motions are probably the most common. Rule 12(b)(6) usually arises when a plaintiff brings a claim that requires it to show a set of factual elements to succeed, but the factual assertions made by the plaintiff are incomplete, i.e., they lack one of the elements. Normally in response to a Rule 12(b)(4)-(7) motion the court will offer the plaintiff the opportunity to re-file its claim, if it can remedy the defects. A Rule 12 motion must usually be filed before the defendant answers the complaint. *See* Motion.

13-D: Securities Law, abbreviation for SEC Form 13-D that must be filed with the United States Securities and Exchange Commission by any investor who acquires 5 percent or more of a U.S. traded public company. These filings can signal a takeover or change of ownership and for this reason, purchasers of blocks of shares in U.S. companies often limit their shareholdings to 4.9 percent to avoid giving up their identity.

20-F: Securities Law, abbreviation for SEC Form 20-F. Equivalent to a 10-K for foreign companies traded in the United States. As with all other SEC filings, Form 20-F filings are available over the Internet from the SEC's EDGAR (Electronic Data Gathering, Analysis, and Retrieval) System.

25 Percent Rule: widely cited basis for royalty rate calculation in patent licensing that is variously described as meaning "taking 25 percent of the profits as a running royalty" or seeking 25 percent of the cost avoided by the use of the invention. The origin of the "rule" is unclear, as is the underlying economic justification.

30(b)(6): refers to Rule 30(b)(6) of the U.S. Federal Rules of Civil Procedure, which allows a party in litigation in U.S. federal courts to take the deposition of a corporation or other entity. The corporation may designate one or more individuals for the various topics that are the subject of the deposition. In essence a 30(b)(6) deponent is an executive, who as a witness speaks for the company.

102: U.S. legal shorthand that refers to §102 of the U.S. Patent Act, 35 U.S.C. §102 which sets forth the novelty requirement for the grant of a U.S. Patent. The various non-novelty grounds are set forth in subsections of §102 which will often also be identified. These are:

> **102(a)** non-novelty because of prior public knowledge or use or described in a printed publication before the priority date of the patent or patent application;
> **102(b)** "time barred" because use or description of the invention in a publication or because it had been placed "on sale" by the inventor, <u>more than one year</u> before the filing date of the patent application (or the date it benefits from under the Patent Cooperation Treaty or Paris Convention);
> **102(c)** abandonment of the invention by the inventor;
> **102(d)** time barred because of the filing of a foreign patent application (i.e., outside the US) more than one year prior to the filing of the U.S. application;
> **102(e)** a prior patent application upon the same invention filed by another before the date of invention of the instant patent;
> **102(f)** derived subject matter, i.e., the wrong inventor has been disclosed "he did not himself invent the subject matter sought to be patented";

102(g) prior invention by another inventor (even where the inventor in the instant patent claim independently created the same invention).

103: U.S. legal shorthand that refers to §103 of the U.S. Patent Act, which requires an invention to be non-obvious "to a person having ordinary skill in the art to which said subject matter pertains." While §102 non-novelty requires that an invention be completely anticipated by a single reference (including technology incorporated by reference) §103 obviousness allows the combination of prior art references.

112 Equivalence: Section 112, paragraph 6 of the United States Patent Act (35 U.S.C. §112) provides:

> "An element in a claim for a combination may be expressed as a means or step for performing a specified function without the recital of structure, material, or acts in support thereof, and such claim shall be construed to cover the corresponding structure, material, or acts described in the specification and ***equivalents thereof***." (emphasis added)

Thus the term denotes equivalents in means-plus-function claims. Section 112 equivalence is a legal doctrine and is different from the equitable doctrine of equivalence [q.v.].

271(f): refers to §271(f) of the United States Patent Act (35 U.S.C. §271(f)), which provides that the supply of un-combined parts of a patented invention to or from the United States constitutes infringement of a U.S. Patent. This clause is designed to make liable U.S.-based companies aiding infringement outside the US.

271(g): provision of United States Patent Act (35 U.S.C. §271(g)) which provides that products manufactured outside the U.S. using a process that is subject to a U.S. process patent infringes that U.S. patent if they are imported into the United States.

301: *See* Special 301.

337: an abbreviation for a type of patent, copyright or trademark action brought before the United States International Trade Commission pursuant to §337 of the Tariff Act of 1930 (19 U.S.C. §1337) for "unfair competition," which usually means violation of intellectual property rights. The ITC cannot award damages, but instead awards an exclusion order directing United States Customs to seize offending imports. ITC cases are run on a fast track—the ITC is normally required to finish the case within twelve to eighteen months. Since §337 is, in principle, a trade protection measure, a plaintiff must show harm to domestic industry, e.g., manufacture by the plaintiff or a licensee in the United States, significant employment of U.S. capital, or U.S. R&D. The European Union has a similar provision, which can also result in an exclusion order, but it is mostly used for trademark protection and infrequently for patent infringement and has recently been amended by Regulation 1383/2003 with a view to making it more effective. 337 cases are heard by an Administrative Law Judge or ALJ, and appeals are to the United States Court of Appeal for the Federal Circuit.

408, FRE Rule: Federal Rules of Evidence Rule 408. *See* Without Prejudice (Rule).

A

A1, A2, A3: *See* Kind-Code.

A-Reference: a classification for prior art references established by WIPO in Standard ST. 14 for search reports. The A classification means that the reference is simply background, i.e., not invalidating prior art. *See* Y-Reference, X-Reference, E-Reference, and P-Reference.

A-Round: colloquial term used to describe the first round of venture capital funding for a startup company. So-called because such investors usually receive shares categorized and numbered "Series A." *See* B-Round.

Abandon, Abandoned, Abandonment: terms used with reference to patent or trademark applications that the applicant has failed to pursue by, for example, not responding within a statutory time limit to an office action or other request from the relevant patent or trademark office or failing to pay fees. It may also be used with respect to a trademark, patent, or other intellectual property right upon which the holder has failed to pay maintenance fees. In either case the applicant or holder usually has a limited time to file a petition and pay a penalty to cure the abandonment, after which the situation becomes final.

Abandonware: a colloquial term used to describe software that the creating entity or company no longer supports or supplies. There is in some quarters a myth that no license is required to use abandonware—this is wrong and dangerous. The copyright owner still has the ability to enforce its rights in such software until the copyright term expires. Some licenses of commercial software likely to be "legacy software," [q.v.] do provide that if it should become abandonware, the licensee has a paid-up license to continue using it for the purposes for which it was supplied.

Ability-Driven Incompetence, Able-Incompetent: a paradoxical problem which may arise with persons of high ability, especially in sales and marketing, when innate capacity induces the person to skimp on or even disdain preparation, resulting in poor performance. The problem can be difficult for managers to identify, since it is camouflaged by the evident ability of the person. *See* 3-to-1 Rule.

Abstract: the preamble to a scientific article, which summarizes the subject matter of an article. There is usually a similar paragraph at the beginning of a patent. The abstract is usually of no significance in patent claim construction and exists primarily to make it easier to find and identify relevant patents.

Abuse of a Dominant Position: *See* Dominant Position.

Abuse-of-Process: means filing, usually in bad faith, a lawsuit, which the plaintiff knows to have no basis in law or fact, with the intent of obtaining information or forcing a nuisance settlement to avoid the complications the suit could cause or otherwise gain unfair or illegal advantages. In most jurisdictions a victim of abuse-of-process can recover some measure of damages.

Abuse of Rights: most civil-code jurisdictions (e.g., Germany, Japan), but not common law jurisdictions (e.g., United States, England) have a general probation on the abusive exercise of legal rights, i.e., the use of a legal right in an anti-social, malicious, or unduly unfair manner. The ability of a judge to refuse to enforce a legal right or contract as abusive is usually set forth in the civil code and can be used with varying frequency. Although abuse of rights is a civil law concept, the decision of a judge to apply the doctrine is likely to be heavily influenced by precedent, i.e., prior decisions, in a manner akin to the common law system.

Access to the File: term used to describe the right of a respondent in a European Competition law proceeding to review the evidence against it. The detailed procedure and limits on such access were set forth in a Commission Notice published in 2004 OJ C 259/8. The legal basis for access to the file is set forth, both in the basic EU competition procedure regulations (i.e., Article 27 of Council Regulation (EC) No 1/2003 (2003 OJ L 1/1) and Article 15 of its implementing regulation (Commission Regulation (EC) No 773/2004 (2004 OJ L 123/18) and Article 18 of the Merger Regulation (Council Regulation (EC) No 139/2004 (2004 OJ L 24/1) and Article 17 of its implementing regulation (Commission Regulation (EC) No 802/2004 (2004 OJ L 133/1 (corrections 2004 OJ L 172/9))).

Accredited Investor: United States Securities Law, specifically the Securities Act of 1933, (15 U.S.C. §77a *et seq.*) provides that an offering of securities to someone in the United States normally must be treated as a "public offering" and that as such, certain things must be done. For example, an offering prospectus must be prepared and various filings made. Further requirements are imposed under state "blue sky" laws. The legal cost of following these procedures can be substantial, typically in the range of hundreds of thousands of dollars. To avoid such costs, the SEC rules define a class of persons as "accredited investors," i.e., people who for various reasons are regarded as sophisticated enough to look after themselves. Such accredited investors can buy securities in a private placement under "Regulation D" (17 CFR §§ 230.501-230.508). Accredited investors are usually institutional investors, venture capital funds, directors, and executive officers of the company and high net worth individuals. At the time of writing, high net worth individuals are persons (and their spouses, or joint income with a spouse in excess of $300,000) with a net worth of $1 million or annual income in excess of $200,000. A detailed definition of accredited investor is published by the SEC, with numerous explanatory examples, and should be consulted by any small company selling shares or securities to persons domiciled in the United States—it is available from the SEC Web site. A company can have an unlimited number of "accredited investors" but is limited to only 35 other investors, who must usually be financially sophisticated. Although early stage capital in technology companies is usually sourced from accredited investors, there are draw-backs, in particular liquidity is limited by the need to find another accredited investor to which to sell any stake, pre-IPO.

Action Estoppel: legal principle that holds that, where a party challenges the validity of a patent, registered design, or trademark in court and loses, that party (except sometimes for revocation actions in the relevant patent or trademark offices) is precluded from challenging validity in a subsequent action concerning the same mark or patent (except for appeals of the original suit).

Acquiescence: when an intellectual property owner knowingly allows a third party to infringe its intellectual property rights. Prolonged acquiescence can give rise to legal defenses in many jurisdictions and with particular respect to a trademark, render it unenforceable. *See* Equitable Estoppel and *Laches*.

Acquired Distinctiveness: *See* Secondary Meaning.

A/D Allowance: *See* Advertising/Display Allowance.

Adaptations: movie industry and entertainment industry jargon for a derivative work, e.g., a screen adaptation of a book, a musical, a play, etc.

Adjusted Gross Participation: movie industry and entertainment industry jargon for a share of the revenue ("participation") generated by a production that consists of gross participation [q.v.] less specified expenses. Great care should be exercised in identifying such deductible expenses, and what can be deducted from "dollar one" [q.v.] or the result will be little better than net participation [q.v.].

ADR: two meanings:

(1)   American Depositary Receipts (also American Deposit*O*ry (Deposit*A*ry) Rights), mechanism for trading shares in non-U.S. companies on U.S. exchanges. Shares in the foreign company are placed in trust with a U.S. bank (the depository/depositary), which issues receipts entitling the holder to a specified number of the shares per Receipt. The Receipts or ADRs are then traded on the U.S. exchanges.

(2)   Alternative dispute resolution, i.e., methods of resolving legal disputes that avoid a courtroom trial, for example mediation, arbitration, or conciliation.

Advance: a term usually arising with respect to copyrightable works such as songs, books, and scripts. It is typically an advance on royalties from the entity to which publication rights have been sold. When the work is published the advance will be deducted from royalties due, possibly with interest or some other uplift. Advances may be non-refundable or refundable. Typically, even a non-refundable advance only becomes non-refundable once the putative author has made certain efforts to deliver the contracted-for work. *See* Certainty/Uncertainty Trade-Off.

Advertising/Display Allowance: a contractual discount to distributors or retailers in exchange for: promoting the product in their own advertising; setting up a product displays; displaying the product prominently; or all of the above.

Advocate General, European Court of Justice: in cases before the European Court of Justice [q.v.], an Advocate-General will, acting as a neutral in the case, render an advisory opinion for the court. Although this opinion is advisory and carries no legal weight as such, it is followed in the majority of cases. There are eight Advocate's General assigned to the ECJ. There is no Advocate-General, as such, for the European Court of First Instance [q.v.], though in important cases one of the 25 judges of that court will act in a similar capacity.

Aesthetic: in intellectual property usually refers to part of what is known as the Aesthetic/Functionality distinction in Design Patents [q.v.] and Registered Designs [q.v.]. These forms of intellectual property can protect the purely aesthetic features of a product, but not the features that are driven by the function for which the product is used.

Affiliate: a term used to describe related companies. Because relationships between corporate entities can be complex, and not just direct parent/subsidiary, many contracts seek to define an affiliate in such a way as to capture the idea of companies which ultimately are under common control, so as to define for example what is an "arms-length" or unrelated (and related) party transaction.

Affiliate Program: a form of Internet-based marketing where a Web site owner receives a commission for referring users to an online merchant's Web site.

Affirmative Defense: a defense that a defendant must assert in its answer, and for which the burden of proof falls on the defendant.

Agence Française de Sécurité Sanitaire des Produits de Santé: the French regulatory agency responsible for the approval of drugs (human and veterinary) and medical devices for sale in France.

Agencia Española de Medicamentos y Productos Sanitarios: the Spanish regulatory agency responsible for the approval of drugs (human and veterinary) and medical devices for sale in Spain.

Agency Directive: the European Commercial Agents Directive caused EU member states to enact certain protections into their national laws governing the relationships between principals and commercial agents appointed in EU member states. A key feature is the requirement that the principal may have to compensate the agent for the loss of the agency. For this reason the retention and termination of commercial agents (and distributors [q.v.]) in EU countries should be approached with care.

Agent: someone who has been granted authority to enter into agreements on behalf of another person, known as the principal. In commercial terms, an agent sells on the supplier's account the goods or services, i.e., the agent never takes title to the goods, and contracts of sale are between the supplier and the customer with the agent usually being paid a commission. An agent is regarded as different from a distributor [q.v.], although in practice it can be difficult to distinguish one from the other. Moreover, even where a party is described as an agent in an agency agreement, courts may consider the facts of the relationship as opposed to the description, applying in effect a duck test [q.v.]. It is also the case that relationships may overtime have evolved from an agency to a distributorship or *vice-versa*. A second area of concern with respect to agency is that courts can imply an agency relationship, where a company allows another party to act with "apparent authority" as its agent, thus making the implied principal liable for the implied agent's activities and promises vis-à-vis third parties. This risk can especially arise where, for example, a local distributor is allowed to trade under the principal's name, an employee engages in unauthorized business, or the putative implied agent is allowed the use of the principal's offices or negligently allowed access to headed paper or other facilities.

Agent, Patent: someone who is a member of a specialized patent prosecution bar but is not necessarily (and frequently is not in fact) a lawyer. Patent agents (Patent Attorneys in the U.K.) are members of a separate profession to lawyers, have specialized training in the drafting and prosecution of patents, usually must have an engineering or science degree, and have passed a special exam. In many jurisdictions, e.g., the United States, only a patent agent may file a patent application on an inventor's behalf, although inventors may (usually unwisely) choose to represent themselves. In Europe, few patent agents are also lawyers (i.e., solicitors or barristers); in the U.S. many, if not the majority of patent agents are also lawyers (i.e., attorneys-at-law). The term patent lawyer is sometimes used in Europe to denote a lawyer who specializes in patent law—but the term does not necessarily denote that the person is a patent agent, and in Europe a patent lawyer is probably not also a patent agent. Whether the agent is, or is not a lawyer, is not simply a matter of legal snobbery; client communications with lawyers as well as the lawyer's internal work product enjoy broad legal privilege [q.v.]. By contrast, communications with a patent agent may not have the same degree of protection.

AIPLA: acronym for the American Intellectual Property Law Association, to which many U.S. and non-U.S. IP lawyers belong and which has many useful publications.

AIPPI: Association Internationale pour la Protection de la Propriété Intellectuelle (International Association for the Protection of Intellectual Property), non-governmental organization promoting international IP protection.

AKZO Procedure: European Competition Law term. As the result of a ruling of a ruling by the European Court of Justice (*AKZO Chemie BV and AKZO Chemie U.K. Ltd v. Commission*, [1986] E.C.R. 1965, the European Commission was forced to implement a special set of procedures to be applied when a party sought access to information submitted to the Commission by a third party. If the party that submitted the information has deemed it a business secret or otherwise confidential, the Commission must first write to that party if the Commission intends to disclose it, affording the submitter an opportunity to object. If the submitter of the information continues to object, and the Commission is still determined to disclose, it must prepare a "reasoned explanation" of its decision, i.e., a statement that explains why the information is not legally protected from disclosure. This reasoned decision may then be challenged to the European Court of First Instance, prior to such disclosure.

Ambush Marketing: advertising vis-à-vis an event in such a way as to benefit from the interest the event creates, without actually participating in the event—for example advertising sporting goods in close proximity to a tournament, without being an "official sponsor" of the tournament. Ambush marketing may be legally risky, depending on applicable trademark law. Jurisdictions hosting major international tournaments may also pass special trademark legislation creating additional liability and legal risk for ambush marketers.

Amendment: in the context of a patent application normally means the changing of the claims of the patent, usually to secure issuance of a patent. Amendments can have significant legal consequences particularly with respect to U.S. patents where they can give rise to "Prosecution History Estoppels [q.v.]" or "File Wrapper Estoppels."

Amicus Curiæ: literally a "friend of the court," refers to third parties to litigation, particularly appellate litigation, who file briefs (memoranda) with the court, urging a particular outcome in the case, usually on public policy grounds. *Amicus Curiæ* are very prevalent in U.S. appellate procedure and also in cases before the European Court of Justice or European Court of First Instance. The effectiveness of such *amicus* briefs is hard to assess, though they may be helpful in obtaining reconsideration *en banc* or writs of *certiorari*. *Amicii* are not supposed to have any direct vested interest in the case, though in reality they are usually approached or encouraged by one party or the other to intervene in this way; if reviewing courts (who are not naïve) suspect that *amicii* are in fact partisans of one party, they may not give much weight to their arguments or briefs.

Amortization Market: term sometimes used by intellectual property practitioners to describe the size of a market necessary before a product can recover its cost of development. In essence, the larger the amortization market, the fewer jurisdictions an inventor needs to apply for a patent in, since as a practical matter, if the remaining markets where no patents subsist are collectively too small to be profitable, the major market patents obtained are enough to guarantee market exclusivity.

Ancillary Restraints: a Competition Law [q.v.] term applied to estrictions on the parties to an agreement or commercial relationship, which, while not core to the purpose of the agreement, are necessary for it to work effectively. An example might be a prohibition on parties to a joint venture competing directly with the joint venture or a post-sale non-compete on the vendor of a business. Ancillary restraints are usually strictly scrutinized and should be limited to what is strictly necessary to make the transaction or business relationship viable.

ANDA: Abbreviated New Drug Application, a form of fast track and simplified application used before the United States Food and Drug Administration (FDA) to secure approval of a drug where a "bioequivalent" compound is already in the marketplace. An ANDA is much faster, less expensive, and more certain than an IND. Typically used for "generic" drugs.

ANSI: acronym for American National Standards Institute, an organization that certifies and consolidates standards developed by other industry groups.

Anticipation: a term used to designate the existence of prior art that describes the invention set forth in a patent or patent application.

Anti-Dilution Clause, Provision: a clause in an investment agreement designed to prevent an early round investor's share of a company being diluted by later down-rounds of investment. Typically, an anti-dilution clause protects an early round investor from having the proportion of the interest in the company their shares represents as a function of the price paid for the shares reduced by the sale of later rounds at a lower subscription price per share (for example if the A round priced shares at $10, the anti-dilution provision would protect against a new round selling each share at $1). A large number of mechanisms can be used to protect against dilution including for example, preference shares that the holder can convert to ordinary shares at a multiple of ordinary shares to each preference shares determined by an anti-dilution provision; and/or forward or reverse stock splits available to the protected party. Anti-dilution clauses are either "full ratchet" or "weighted full ratchet." A full ratchet anti-dilution clause will allow an early round investor to increase the number of its shares to fully match the number of shares it would have received had it paid the later lower price. A "weighted average ratchet" will limit the early round investor to receiving the new shares at the average weighted price of shares issued including the down round (based on various formulae). The weighted average formula may be narrow based, i.e., using only the stock outstanding for the calculation, or broad-based, using all stock, convertible securities, warrants, and options for the calculation.

Antitrust Division: a division of the United States Department of Justice (DOJ) that investigates and prosecutes at a federal level, violations of U.S. Antitrust law, including criminal violations.

Antitrust Guidelines: usually refers to the guidelines promulgated by the two U.S. competition enforcement agencies, the Antitrust Division of the United States Department of Justice (DOJ) and the United States Federal Trade Commission (FTC). Of particular interest in intellectual property are the Antitrust Guidelines for the Licensing of Intellectual Property issued by the DOJ and FTC in 1995. The European Commission has issued "block exemptions" which serve much of the same role as well as various guidelines, in particular the Guidelines on the application of Article 81 of the EC Treaty to technology transfer agreements, 2004 O.J. C 101/2. The Japan Fair Trade Commission (JFTC) has issued guidelines on patent and know-how licensing; joint R&D; patent pooling; franchising; and mergers. The Korean Fair Trade Commission (KFTC) has also issued a guideline with respect to the licensing of intellectual property rights as has the Taiwan Fair Trade Commission which has also issued a guideline on abusive warning letters (as well as advertisements and notices) with respect to patent, trademark and copyright infringement.

Antitrust Law: United States term for Competition Law [q.v.]. United States *Federal* Antitrust law is codified in Title 15 of the United States Code (15 U.S.C.). It finds its origin in the great conglomerates (typically structured through complex networks of interlocking shareholder trusts) that were formed in the United States in the late 19th and early 20th century, for example the Standard Oil Trust which controlled most of the oil industry. Violations of the U.S. antitrust law can be treated as a criminal matter, resulting in fines for companies and individuals, as well as potential prison sentences. Civil claims for violations of U.S. antitrust law can result in Enhanced Damages, i.e., treble damages plus Attorney's Fees for successful claimant(s). Antitrust laws at the state level also exist. *See* Sherman Act, Clayton Act, Robinson Patman Act, Hart Scott Rodino (HSR) Act, Lanham Act.

Antitrust Opinion: an opinion obtained from qualified counsel to the effect that a particular arrangement does not violate, in particular, U.S. Antitrust Law. Such an opinion may be useful to a company or its managers in the event that commercial arrangements are investigated by the United States Department of Justice's Antitrust Division or the FTC, especially in limiting legal liability or criminal culpability.

***Anton Piller* Order**: a court order granted in the U.K., Ireland, and other jurisdictions where English precedents are followed. The order usually permits an agent of the plaintiff to enter the defendant's and related parties' premises to search for and preserve evidence. Anton Piller orders are now known under the English Civil Procedure Rules and Practice Directions as Civil Search Orders. They are difficult to obtain and usually require a strong *prima facie* showing of the quality of the plaintiff's case, the necessity of the order and the likelihood of obtaining evidence that might otherwise be lost or infringing goods that might be sold. They can be applied for on an *ex parte* [q.v.] basis using in England an Application Without Notice [q.v.]. The origin of the term is the case in which the first modern English order was issued, *Anton Piller KG v. Manufacturing Processes Ltd.*, [1976] 1 All E.R. 779 (C.A.).

Apparatus Claim: this refers to a patent claim, which is expressed as a piece of equipment or a device incorporating the invention. Also referred to as a "device claim." By contrast see Method Claim; *see also* Claim.

Appeal as-of-Right, Not-as-of-Right: most legal systems provide for a right of initial appeal to at least a first tier of appellate or reviewing courts without the need to make any special request or application, provided the lower court or agency proceedings are finished. Appeals to higher levels of appeals courts, or more substantial appellate proceedings (e.g., United States *en banc* [q.v.] appeals), and appeals before the lower court or agency proceeding is finished (i.e., interlocutory appeals) may not be as-of-right, but instead may require permission from either the appellate court (e.g., *certiorari* [q.v.]) or from the court from which the appeal is being made. Most notably, in U.S. practice, appeals to the United States Supreme Court are not as-of-right.

API: Application Programming Interface (the P is alternately described as Programming/Programmers'/Processing)—a term used to describe the data format, common functions and address information necessary for various computer applications to exchange information. While APIs provide a way for third parties to write applications compatible with a program, operating system, or suite of programs, APIs are often kept confidential by the owner of the program(s) in order to limit competitors' market access (as well as malicious activities by virus writers and other malign individuals). Much of the Microsoft antitrust and competition cases involved and still involve the issue of access to APIs for Windows®. The term has also come to be more broadly used (albeit not technically accurately) in legal discussion to describe interface information and transfer and communication protocols for a wide array of computing products including hardware. *See* Essential Facilities.

Application Without Notice: a plain English term for an *ex parte* [q.v.] motion, which refers under the new English Civil Procedure Rules, to an application made in court without notice to the defendant, usually for a Civil Search Order (*Anton Piller* Order) [both q.v.] or Freezing (*Mareva*) Injunction [both q.v.]. Applications without notice are supposed to be used only in exceptional circumstances, where it is perceived and can be reasonably argued that prior notice of the motion (referred to usually as an "application") might lead the other party to destroy evidence of remove assets from the court's jurisdiction.

Appreciability Test: European Competition Law [q.v.] principle similar, but not absolutely the same as the Rule of Reason [q.v.]. Appreciability has two parts: (1) for a case to fall within the jurisdiction of the European Competition rules (as opposed to National or member-state competition law) the activities under investigation must have an appreciable impact on trade between the member states of the European Union (and as appropriate the EEA [q.v.]); and, (2) the activity under investigation must constitute an appreciable restriction on competition, i.e., it must have a genuine negative impact on the competitive environment.

Arbitration: a method of dispute resolution involving trying the case before usually one to three arbitrators (i.e., adjudicators paid for by the parties). Arbitration usually requires an agreement between the parties to the arbitral process, which specifies the arbitration rules to be followed, the place of arbitration, the language of the arbitration and the number of arbitrators. Such an agreement can be made when the dispute arises or may be the subject of an arbitration clause in an underlying contract. Arbitration is typically carried out under the auspices of an arbitration organization, such as the American Arbitration Association; International Chamber of Commerce—International Court of Arbitration; the London Court of International Arbitration; CEPANI-CEPINA—the Belgian Centre for the Study and Practice of National and International Arbitration; the Chartered Institute of Arbitrators, and WIPO. In most legal systems, a high standard of review applies to arbitration decisions and so it is quite difficult to appeal one, even if it appears perverse; however, one common exception is decisions relating to areas of law that are regarded as raising public policy issues, e.g., competition law, mandatory rights in employment law or legality of contract. Arbitration is one of a broad group of approaches to legal disputes referred to as alternative dispute resolution or ADR.

Arbitration Clause: a clause in a contract, committing the parties to resolve legal disputes about the contract by arbitration, usually by application of the rules of one of a number of arbitration organizations such as the American Arbitration Association; International Chamber of Commerce—International Court of Arbitration; the London Court of International Arbitration; CEPANI-CEPINA—the Belgian Centre for the Study and Practice of National and International Arbitration; the Chartered Institute of Arbitrators, and WIPO. The exact language of the arbitration clause should usually be similar to specimen language available from each of the organizations. The choice of which arbitration rule to follow, or indeed whether to put arbitration under the rules of any of these bodies depends on the likely circumstances of the case. It is also important to determine what number of arbitrators should be specified, the place of any arbitration and the language of arbitration. Arbitration clauses are almost always enforced by courts, unless the clause seeks to commit certain issues to arbitration, which are in a particular jurisdiction regarded as a public policy matter, and not arbitrable.

Architectural Design: the aesthetic aspects of an architectural design can, in most instances, be protected by copyright law; functional aspects are usually not protected by copyright, though they may potentially be protected by patents. In general, when an architect is commissioned to design a building, the commissioner gets an implied or formal single license to use the designs to build that building—reuse of the design by the commissioner, unless contemplated in the commissioning of the building by both the architect and the commissioner, is generally an infringement of the architect's copyright. Copying of the design by someone other than the commissioner is also a copyright infringement. All of these issues may of course be regulated by the contract between the commissioner and the architect.

Arm's-Length (Arms-Length) Transaction, Sales: a transaction between two unrelated parties, or where the transaction is between related parties, a calculation of price and agreement of terms that is not influenced by the relationship between the parties.

Article 19(3) Notice: European Competition Law term. Notice published in the European Commission's Official Journal [q.v.] (the "O.J.", in which it states its intention to clear or exempt a transaction notified under Article 81 of the Treaty of Rome.

Article 81, 82 (formerly Article 85, 86): the two fundamental European Competition Law provisions are Articles 81 and 82 of the Treaty of Rome, the treaty that founded the European Economic Community (EEC) that evolved into the European Union and remains, though amended, the fundamental EU constitutional document. The drafters of one amending treaty to the Treaty of Rome, the Treaty of Amsterdam, decided it was necessary to renumber the two Articles 81 and 82 from 85 and 86, thus causing wholesale confusion, as many lawyers still habitually use the old numbers as do older published decisions. Article 53 and 54 of the EEA agreement are essentially the same provisions and effectively extend European Competition law to cover the EEA countries, i.e., Norway, Iceland, and Liechtenstein. The titles "Treaty of Rome," "Treaty of Amsterdam," "EC Treaty" as well as the former title "EEC Treaty" are often used and appear in legislation and case-law. Most EU countries have enacted analogues of Articles 81 and 82 in their domestic competition laws and the provisions have also been copied in competition laws around the world. The impact of both provisions is constrained by the *De Minimis* notice [q.v.]. Article 81 provides that agreements, arrangements, and understandings between parties that may reduce competition in the EU are all prohibited in principle, but may be "exempted" if they are on the whole economically beneficial (this exemption system has resulted in the Commission enacting Block Exemptions [q.v.]).

Article 81 reads as follows:

1. The following shall be prohibited as incompatible with the common market: all agreements between undertakings, decisions by associations of undertakings, and concerted practices which may affect trade between Member States, and which have as their object or effect the prevention, restriction, or distortion of competition within the common market, and in particular those that:

(a) directly or indirectly fix purchase or selling prices or any other trading conditions;
(b) limit or control production, markets, technical development, or investment;
(c) share markets or sources of supply;
(d) apply dissimilar conditions to equivalent transactions with other trading parties, thereby placing them at a competitive disadvantage;
(e) make the conclusion of contracts subject to acceptance by the other parties of supplementary obligations which, by their nature or according to commercial usage, have no connection with the subject of such contracts.

2. Any agreements or decisions prohibited pursuant to this Article shall be automatically void.

3. The provisions of paragraph 1 may, however, be declared inapplicable in the case of:

- any agreement or category of agreements between undertakings;
- any decision or category of decisions by associations of undertakings;
- any concerted practice or category of concerted practices;

which contributes to improving the production or distribution of goods or to promoting technical or economic progress, while allowing consumers a fair share of the resulting benefit, and which does not:

(a) impose on the undertakings concerned restrictions that are not indispensable to the attainment of these objectives;

(b) afford such undertakings the possibility of eliminating competition in respect of a substantial part of the products in question.

Article 82 (formerly 86) addresses abuse of a dominant position and states:

Any abuse by one or more undertakings of a dominant position within the common market or in a substantial part of it shall be prohibited as incompatible with the common market insofar as it may affect trade between Member States.

Such abuse may, in particular, consist in:

(a) directly or indirectly imposing unfair purchase or selling prices or other unfair trading conditions;
(b) limiting production, markets, or technical development to the prejudice of consumers;
(c) applying dissimilar conditions to equivalent transactions with other trading parties, thereby placing them at a competitive disadvantage;
(d) making the conclusion of contracts subject to acceptance by the other parties of supplementary obligations, which, by their nature or according to commercial usage, have no connection with the subject of such contracts.

Artists' Resale Rights: provisions that entitle artists the right to a share of the gains on re-sale of their artistic works. Such rights are provided for, in principle, under Article 14(b) of the Berne Convention, but are not mandatory and generally are only present in certain European countries, e.g. France. A recent European directive provides for the uniform provision of such rights in the European Union. The right would apply to works of graphic or plastic art such as pictures, collages, paintings, drawings, engravings, prints, lithographs, sculptures, tapestries, ceramics, glassware, and photographs, provided they are made by the artist or are copies considered to be original works of art according to professional usage (limited productions or signed works, for example) and runs for the life of the artist plus 70 years. There may be a minimum level below which the rights do not apply, not higher than €3,000. The directive makes provision for artists to receive a percentage of the sale price of their works ranging from 4 percent to 0.25 percent in five steps of the sale price, to a ceiling of €12,500. The directive is widely regarded as a bad idea, in part because it does apply to sales made outside the European Union—indeed its effect may be to drive the international art market out of the EU. Because of its French origin, an Artist's Resale Right is often referred to as *droit de suite*.

Assignee Steps in the Shoes of the Assignor, an: *See* Steps in the Shoes of.

Assignment: the transfer of formal record ownership in and title to an intellectual property right. It describes the wholesale transfer of rights as opposed to their licensing. Thus the outright sale of intellectual property, *quasi*-intellectual property, contractual rights including licenses, is carried out by assigning the underlying legal instrument creating the rights, e.g., the patent, copyright, trademark, contract, or license. As compared to an intellectual property license, a license agrees *not to* exercise rights to *prohibit* a licensee from infringing the rights; an assignment *transfers* to the assignee the power to prohibit other from infringement. The extent of the rights conveyed by an assignment will typically be constrained by pre-existing licenses. Certain jurisdictions limit or prohibit the assignment of some intellectual property rights, for example Germany and the Czech Republic prohibit the assignment of copyright, providing that ownership can only be transferred by inheritance or testamentary transfer (i.e., in a will) (e.g., German Law on Copyright and Neighboring Rights, Arts. 28, 29; Czech Republic Copyright Act, Art. 26(1)). However, the author may grant an exclusive or non-exclusive license; since an exclusive license can be drafted in such a way as to grant all the privileges of ownership, the problem is not as serious as it at first sight appears. *See* Steps-In-the-Shoes-of.

Assignment in Gross: *See* Naked License or Assignment

ASP: Average Selling Price, term used in conjunction with running royalties [q.v.] to refer to the average price for arms-length sales [q.v.], or the first sale to an unrelated party.

Attorney: someone granted powers to act on behalf of another and to legally bind the grantor of the power. In the United States, it is common usage for a lawyer, abbreviated from attorney-at-law; in the U.K. and Ireland a Patent Attorney is the equivalent of a Patent Agent, i.e., someone who is a member of a specialized patent prosecution bar, but is not necessarily a lawyer.

Attorneys' Fees: in the United States, the bill from one's lawyers, especially in litigation. The U.S. distinguishes between "legal costs" and "attorneys' fees." The former refers to court expenses such as filing fees, certain expenses related to discovery, and the costs of some witnesses, etc. and in a major suit can be 5-15 percent of the total bill for a litigant. In the U.S. a prevailing party, i.e., the winner of a lawsuit usually receives their legal costs but not their attorneys' fees. Attorneys' fees may be awarded if the statutory provision under which a suit is brought, for example Section 285 of the U.S. Patent Act, provides for the award of attorneys' fees, but even so, such an award only arises in exceptional circumstances, e.g., willful infringement. Certain U.S. statutes, for example civil rights laws can provide for automatic recovery of a winning plaintiff's attorneys' fees. By contrast, most other countries include attorneys' fees in legal costs and will usually award them to the prevailing party, a system known in the U.S. as the English Rule. Defendants, as well as plaintiffs, can receive costs under either system. *See,* Costs, Indemnity Principle. A number of civil law systems, for example Germany, also provide that the winner should receive reimbursement of legal fees.

Attribution, Right of: one of the moral rights provided in many copyright systems. It is the right to be properly identified as the author of a copyrighted work. Although the right of attribution does not usually exist in the non-copyright universe, it can be contractually provided for in the context of technology, in which case it serves as a sort of "box right" [q.v.].

At Will Employee, At Will Employment: the vast majority of the United States has what is known as an "at will" employment system. In effect this means that (absent a written contract that changes the employee's status, e.g., a union agreement) an employee can be dismissed *without cause*, at any time, with only statutory or contractual severance (which has led some commentators to dub it "at *whim* employment.") Indeed, it might be said that having a stated reason for the employee's dismissal is more dangerous, since such a reason may be actionable on grounds of illegal discrimination, whistleblower protection, etc. A key side effect of at-will employment is that it is relatively easy to modify an employee's terms of employment, for example by requiring an existing employee to sign a non-disclosure agreement. By contrast, most of rest of the industrialized world takes the view that an employee, upon completion of a probationary period, has, absent misconduct or incompetence, a right to continued employment, breach of which entitles the employee to compensation. The existence of this right means that employment terms cannot easily be modified by an employer, without effectively changing the contract between the employer and the employee. Moreover, any substantial reduction in the quality of the terms offered to the employee can be considered a "constructive dismissal," i.e., the equivalent of firing the employee, which again could give rise to a claim for compensation. To apply the non-disclosure agreement example, for such an agreement to be effective there must usually be both consent *and* consideration on the part of an already existing employee, i.e., the employee must agree and must be paid some real benefit (consideration) for entering into the additional contractual obligations of the non-disclosure agreement. Failure to understand the impact of the right-to-continued-employment is a major pitfall for U.S. trained managers dealing with personnel issues outside the U.S.

Audit Rights, Auditing: refers to the right of a licensor to audit the licensee to determine whether all sales have been reported. Typically a license will provide that an audit is at the licensor's expense, unless under-reporting is found, at which point the licensee becomes liable for any underpayment plus any audit costs. Auditing is usually done by a third party accounting firm, but occasionally by other IP related consulting companies. Although in theory over-reporting should be as frequent as under-reporting, it is highly unusual to find over-reporting in an audit. Indeed under-reporting is so common that companies that license broadly sometimes use auditing campaigns as a way to rapidly raise short-term revenue. Because such auditing can augment short term revenue (albeit revenue that should have been paid over a long period of time), it can give the erroneous impression that overall license-royalties are rising dramatically, as are future revenues, leading to overvaluation. *See* Metering.

Australia Group: an informal forum through which industrialized nations coordinate their export controls to curb proliferation of chemical and biological weapons. So-called because its first meeting took place at the Australian Embassy in Paris in June 1986. Members include Australia, Canada, Japan, New Zealand, the United States, the members of the European Union, and several other countries. The group has developed a list of precursors useful for chemical weapons development, along with control on certain biological organisms and on equipment useful in producing chemical and biological warfare (CBW) agents. The members of the group also share information concerning the activities of non-member countries where proliferation is a concern, including information on who is seeking chemical precursors and related items for CBW purposes.

Author: the person who created a copyrightable work. *See* Copyright.

Authorized Government Reseller: governments will often negotiate agreements with producers of various goods and services to supply the goods on special, favorable terms, which typically include deep discounts. The producers will then often appoint special distributors as "resellers" so as to facilitate marketing and supply to government agencies as well as tracking sales of products to ensure that they are only supplied on the agreed terms to government agencies. When appointing a distributor in the United States, particularly for software, it is wise to determine the extent of the distributor's experience in acting as an authorized government reseller to the Federal Government's General Services Administration or GSA. *See* GSA Schedule.

Avoidable Transaction: bankruptcy term referring to agreements and contracts that a bankruptcy trustee, receiver, or administrator has the power to cancel unilaterally on behalf of the bankrupt entity. Usually a bankruptcy laws will provide a set of statutory periods during which certain classes of transaction can be cancelled, usually 60 or 90 days, or 1 year depending on the type of transaction. Typically avoidable transactions are preferences (i.e., payments that favor one creditor or class of creditors over others);

gratuitous transfers (i.e., transfers of assets for which no value was received); sales or transfers of assets for less than fair value; and transactions with insiders and parties linked to the bankrupt or its office.

B

B1, B2: *See* Kind-Code.

B-Round: colloquial term used to describe the second round of venture capital funding for a startup company. So-called because such investors might often receive "Series B" shares.

Backdoor Sales: a significant problem with contract manufacturing is the sale of unreported product (or excess factory-rejects) by the contract manufacturer or its employees through the "back door" to illicit channels. This issue is particularly difficult as the backdoor goods are technically counterfeit, but for all practical purposes (except warranty) can usually appear authentic. Backdoor sales can present more issues than just lost revenue—in the case of certain products, especially those with critical safety applications (e.g., aircraft parts) or drugs, such sales can give rise to legal liability for witting or unwitting intermediaries or indeed the manufacturer (for failing to adequately police the disposal of rejects). A copyright, brand, or technology licensee may also find itself liable to the licensor for all backdoor sales. A key way of preventing backdoor sales is an effective method for auditing [q.v.] and metering of production.

Background Intellectual Property: a term usually used and defined in development agreements to describe the intellectual property the parties to the agreement owned prior to the agreement.

Backward Innovation: developing a less sophisticated, de-featured version of a product for a less sophisticated market or to lower price.

Bad Faith: in trademarks refers to an actual intent to deceive or confuse the public by the use of a counterfeit [q.v.] or confusingly similar mark. In many jurisdictions, evidence of bad faith may limit the defenses available to an infringer and may potentially increase damages. In contracts it usually refers to a party entering an agreement, which it had, at the time of the agreement, no intention to honor, or to engage in negotiation with no actual intent to reach an agreement and perhaps an affirmative intent not to do so. In the context of a misstatement by a party, it usually means the actual intent to deceive, not the inadvertent misleading or confusion of another party.

Balancing Fee: a "net royalty" paid in a cross-license [q.v.] situation by the holder of the less valuable IP to the holder of the more valuable IP, i.e., one royalty cancels out most of the other, leaving the balancing fee. There frequently may be tax advantages to such an approach, particularly where one country charges a withholding tax on royalties to licensors in other countries.

Bank of Boeing: nickname for the Export Import (ExIm) Bank of the United States [q.v.] that denotes the historically large proportion of its lending for sales of aircraft by the Boeing Corporation.

Bankruptcy Cascade: when large businesses enter bankruptcy, the pervasiveness of their unpaid bills may cause suppliers to "go bust," taking in turn sub-suppliers and so on *ad infinitum*. Alternately, a supplier that has suffered a large loss may be forced to call in credit granted to other customers, putting pressure on them. In addition, credit agencies may react to a major sector bankruptcy by tightening credit terms to other businesses in the sector or supplying the sector. The result of this may cause multiple further bankruptcies. This process is sometimes called a bankruptcy cascade or alternately the term "chain reaction bankruptcies" may be used.

Bare (Bones) Patent License: a patent license that consists of only patent(s) with no associated technology, trade secrets, or other benefits. A bare license in the trademark context is a synonym for a naked license [q.v.].

Barriers to Entry: the presence or lack of presence of significant barriers to entry is a key criteria considered in competition and antitrust law, particularly in relation to merger review. If barriers to entry are low, competition and antitrust authorities regard it as unlikely that a party with a dominant position could abuse it and in some systems this militates in favor of allowing a merger, **even if** the likely result would be to create a dominant position. Similarly high barriers to entry militates against allowing mergers, even when the result would be simply concentration of the market, without necessarily creating a dominant position on the part of the merging businesses. A wide range of market facts may be considered to be barriers-to-entry, including for example, patents and copyrights, licenses and exclusive distribution arrangements.

Basic Patent: *See* pioneer patent.

BATNA: Best Alternative to a Negotiated Agreement—term used in negotiating strategy to define the threshold of what a theoretical negotiator must be offered before the negotiated offer is better than no deal at all. The term was apparently originally coined at the Harvard Negotiation Project.

Belgian Distributor Rights: Belgian law (under the Act of 27 July 1961) provides that an exclusive or quasi-exclusive distributor must be compensated if terminated without cause. In practice this means that a terminated Belgian distributor who has actual or arguably *de facto* exclusivity for a territorial area within Belgium, will seek and often receive damages, even if that distributor has proved a poor performer or even dishonest. Most companies that have encountered the statute tend to respond by appointing entities based in France, Luxembourg, or the Netherlands as distributors for a territory including parts of Belgium, and unfortunately, this may be the wisest course of action. *See* Distributor, Agency Directive.

Benrishi: a Japanese Patent Agent.

Berne Convention: refers to the Berne Convention [Treaty] for the Protection of Literary and Artistic Works of September 9, 1886, which has been repeatedly revised, most recently in 1979. It is the primary international agreement protecting copyright around the world and sets a common basis for protection and also provides that a work of authorship in any subscribing state immediately creates "copyright" in all other subscribing states. Most major economies are now members of the Berne Convention. Significant subsidiary agreements to Berne are found in the WIPO Copyright Treaty.

Best Mode: Several patent laws, most notably that of the U.S., provide that the disclosure in a patent application must describe the best way of practicing the invention known to the inventor at the time of application. In effect, what this means is full disclosure; keeping the identity of a secret ingredient back or failing to tell about a detail that gets better results can invalidate the patent. The best mode is sometimes referred to as the preferred embodiment of the invention, though this may also refer to one of several embodiments recited in the patent, one of which must be the best mode. No best mode requirement exists under U.K. or EU patent law and failure to recognize this issue is a major pitfall for European patent agents when dealing with the United States. *See* Enablement.

Beta Testing: testing a new product under actual anticipated usage conditions as opposed to an alpha test, which is in-house or laboratory testing under more ideal conditions.

Bid Rigging: an agreement between bidders as to the terms of their bid. Bid rigging in most jurisdictions is at least a violation of Competition Law. However, it is often also a serious criminal offence, especially when it involves public or municipal contracts. A quite large range of discussions between competing bidders could be regarded as bid rigging and it is therefore good practice to curtail and control the contacts of employees involved in a bid with corresponding employees of other bidders, as well as carefully minuting communications, so as to be able to prove their innocent nature. Also known as collusive tendering.

Bifurcate: refers to the division of a legal process, for example a trial, into two phases, typically dealing first with liability, for example, and then with damages, or resolving claims first, then counterclaims. Bifurcation is most commonly used when different facts will be at issue in the different phases of the process, and the second phase may be unnecessary depending on the outcome of the first (e.g., if there is no liability there is no need to consider damages).

Big-Book Application: a patent application strategy used by startup technology companies who have an array of useful technology of potentially broad application, but are uncertain which direction the business will take and are consequently uncertain as to where to focus their patenting efforts. It consists of filing a single massive omnibus disclosure with a patent office and then using it to provide the basis for multiple divisional applications as the commercial direction of the business and commercial value of the inventions in the "big book" becomes clear.

Bigot List: term used to describe a list of company employees who know key trade secrets, know-how, or business secrets, typically maintained by the human resources department in conjunction with the legal department. The origin of the term was World War II when, in 1943-4 as the Normandy invasion was being planned, those Allied officers who knew the secrets of location and time were codenamed "bigots," an unusual and odd, but not totally unnatural word to use in conversation.

Bill of Materials: *See* BOM.

BIS: acronym for the Bureau of Industry and Security [q.v.] of the U.S. Department of Commerce.

Black List: *See* Block Exemption.

Blame God Strategy: negotiating strategy based on one party referring issues out to an absent senior figure (i.e., God), for example a CEO, legal counsel, government minister, director, the board, autocratic boss, or manager, who though not present at the negotiation, has veto powers over his/her side's positions and concessions. It is usually implemented using a phrase such as "sorry, I put it to him but he or she would not agree and told me to go back and get more." This tactic is often used to sell the same horse twice [q.v.] and salami slice [q.v.] the counterparty. The best solution is, if possible, to insist that the senior figure directly participate in the negotiation and be present in person.

Blame-Storming: pun on brainstorming that describes the tendency of some organizations, when problems arise, to focus on fixing blame first, rather than solving the problems. The approach is often seriously counterproductive as members of the organization limit their communication to avoid self-incrimination and because it may target and distract the individuals most necessary to solve the problem, because their closeness to and potential responsibility for it reflects their better knowledge of its nature, causes and cures.

Block-booking: former practice of major movie and production studios of requiring movie theatres and TV broadcasting companies to buy and show a set of movies or programming as a whole, rather than being able to pick and choose which movies or programs they wanted to show and buy them separately. Block booking was ruled to be illegal "tying" [q.v.] in a series of United States Supreme Court Decisions between the 1940s and 1960s. These legal decisions ultimately undermined the Hollywood studio system, which dominated movie production from the 1920s to the late '60s.

Block Exemption: under European Law (specifically Article 81 of the Treaties of Rome and Amsterdam) there is a sweeping prohibition of all agreements that might lessen commercial competition. However, Article 81(3) provides that the European Commission can "exempt" from the prohibition, activities, which, in various ways are economically beneficial and especially those that benefit consumers. Faced with the task of exempting tens of thousands of agreements the European Commission resorted to enacting bulk exemptions of generic classes of agreements provided they met certain criteria and also set size limits below which activities would normally be too small to bother about, i.e., *de minimis*. The bulk exemptions are created by regulations known as "block exemptions." Two important block exemptions for intellectual property law are the Technology Transfer Block Exemption (Regulation 772/2004) and the R&D Agreements Block Exemption (Regulation 2659/2000). A block exemption usually contains three lists, a white list of broadly legal clauses, provisions and classes of companies that can benefit from the exemption; a black list of clauses and provisions absolutely excluded from the exemption, which in addition, are almost always illegal; and a grey list of clauses and provisions and excluded classes of companies that may, under certain circumstances be exempted, usually on a case-by-case basis.

Blocking Patent: a patent held by a third party that blocks commercial exploitation of a first patent, i.e., an essential patent [q.v.] vis-à-vis the invention in the first patent. The usual solution is for both patent-holders to agree to a cross license, often royalty-free. Frequently, when a company is faced with the risk that a competitor will secure a pioneer patent (because it has, for instance, seen the published application) it will seek to obtain blocking patents on essential improvements.

Blue Sky law: a term used to refer to U.S. State laws designed to protect the public against securities fraud by regulating the sales of securities to various persons protected under those states' laws. The provisions can be complicated for foreign startups to deal with, as it is easy to inadvertently find that an investor with relatively insubstantial connections with the U.S. or a particular state is still covered by such laws. The term originated with a judge's ironic comment that a particular stock had as much value as a "patch of blue sky." Blue sky laws supplement U.S. Federal Securities Law [q.v.] and it should be understood that one may avoid a violation of the Federal Law and still be caught under the State Blue Sky law.

Board of Appeal(s), European Patent Office: the EPO has a system of boards of appeal to which decisions of the EPO can be appealed. There are several boards of appeal including the enlarged board of appeals; the Legal Board of Appeals (points of law); Technical Boards of Appeal (mixed issues of technology and law); and the Disciplinary Board of Appeal. The Enlarged Board of Appeals is in effect an appellate board from the Legal, Technical, and Disciplinary boards.

Board Rights: agreeing that an investor shall be entitled to a board seat in exchange for the investment.

Boat Anchor: sarcastic term usually applied to obsolete (and typically relatively heavy) equipment, which reflect the suggestion that the best use of the equipment would be to anchor a boat, i.e., tie a rope around it and drop it in the water. Permanent mooring anchors are typically made of heavy pieces of scrap metal and concrete.

BodyShop, BodyShopping: term for a company whose primary business is marketing the skills of its employees or team of contractors. BodyShopping can be the sole activity of such a company, but the term may also encompass larger companies allowing another company to retain services of skilled in-house teams or departments on a fee or cost-plus basis.

Boiler Plate: standard language found with little variation in many contracts of a given type. The origin of the term is the story, perhaps apocryphal, that when large documents such as prospectuses were produced, the printers, rather than repeatedly typesetting this language, already had it made up and etched on hard steel boilerplate, so that the type section could be reused indefinitely. Simply copying boiler plate into an agreement can be dangerous, since it can vary based on context and sometimes certain boilerplate clauses are ill-suited to a particular contractual situation, for example, blanket no-waiver clauses [q.v.] in development agreements. Such a clause would for example provide that one or both never waive rights to claim breaches of the agreement, and are often combined with a clause requiring a very difficult process for amending the agreement; the difficulty with development agreements is that the details of the agreement are often and repeatedly informally changed, including time lines, prices and specifications. If such a clause is present, it can mean that parties are rapidly in breach from the outset of the agreement. Boilerplate serves two useful purposes: (a) it cuts drafting cost and effort; (b) it serves as a sort of "checklist" for clauses that should be in an agreement. However, it should not be used slavishly and without careful review of the boilerplate's meaning and effect.

BOM: abbreviation for Bill of Materials, a complete list of the components required to make a finished product. A complete BOM will normally include part numbers, quantities, and descriptions. An indented BOM also includes descriptions of sub-assemblies and their relationships to the finished product. A BOM is an essential part of the logistics management process and project planning. BOM is also used as a synonym for the cost of manufacture of a product, in which case it may include labor, shipping to the distribution head, other inputs, spares and warranty replacement costs, etc.

Bomb, Software: colloquial term for an embedded joke or alternately a lockout device [q.v.] that disables software if fees are not paid. *See* Easter Bunny.

Bond, Post a: the deposit of a sum of money or an insurance policy to protect a third party. In intellectual property litigation when interim relief (i.e., a preliminary, temporary or interlocutory injunction, i.e., a court order usually made against a defendant before the case is complete) is granted, the party obtaining the preliminary relief may be required to "post" a bond to ensure that if the case ultimately goes in favor of the other enjoined party, funds will be present to compensate that other party for any damages that the interim relief caused. Bonds can be large sums of money and therefore can make obtaining interim relief economically prohibitive and impossible as a practical rule for small plaintiffs. *See* Equitable Remedy.

***Bone-Fide* Purchaser for Value**: (literally translated as "good faith") where property (including intellectual property) is subject to a recording of title system, either voluntary or involuntary, one legal consequence is that a purchaser of the property, who has properly examined the title records and found no evidence of a third party's claim, rights, or interest in the property, can gain title without being subject to that third party's prior rights, provided the purchaser has paid something of value for the property. This rule usually only applies to those rights that can be recorded, but not to rights that could not be recorded and may be subject to the purchaser also having conducted reasonable due diligence.

Bonus, Inventor's or Patent: *See* Inventor's Bonus.

Bootlegging: term for making illicit copies, typically of packaged software.

Bootstrapping: methods used by early stage business to find resources without paying out the cash raised from investors or banks for them, for example obtaining loans of facilities, equipment, or services in exchange for equity.

Box Rights: the right to place a logo or other mark on a third party's product or the box it is shipped in, or the right to put a third party's logo on one's own product, for example "Intel Inside" on a PC, or "American Dental Association Approved" on toothpaste. *See* Right-of-Endorsement, Right-to-Endorsement.

Boycott: a refusal to deal or use the products or services of a particular person or company. Charles C. Boycott (1832–1897) was, in 1880, the land agent of the Earl of Erne in County Mayo, Ireland, responsible for collecting rents and evicting tenants. The Earl was unpopular because he was an absentee landowner who lived in England, off rents derived from his Irish estates. The leading Irish nationalist politician Charles Stewart Parnell, at that time an advocate of land reform, proposed a policy under which landlords who raised rents to unreasonable levels and then refused to lower them, or any tenant who took over the farm of a tenant evicted because he could not afford them, would be given the complete "cold shoulder" by all other local residents (who for the most part were also tenants), while businesses that did business with such persons would similarly be shunned. Lord Erne refused to allow Boycott to lower rents and he continued to evict tenants. Parnell's Irish Land League then orchestrated the shunning of Boycott and his family, who soon found themselves without servants, farmhands, mail, or shops that would serve them. Boycott's situation then became somewhat of a *cause celebre* in England, with troops being sent to bring in his harvest. This provoked the Land League to use him as an example. Ultimately defeated, Boycott left Ireland, but due to the widespread publicity surrounding his case, the name of Boycott was rapidly adopted in numerous languages as meaning an orchestrated refusal to deal with a person or business. Many historians today regard Boycott as a somewhat unfortunate and tragic figure. Group Boycotts are potentially illegal under competition law and should be carefully considered. Some limited exceptions do exist to the prohibition of collective blacklisting, for example insurance companies have generally succeeded in defending collective black lists of property owners whose buildings have repeatedly burned down in unexplained circumstances.

Brand: term for an identifying source for goods or services, i.e., a trademark. More broadly, a brand is regarded as encompassing a business' image, what it stands for in the eyes of consumers.

Brand Equity: the value of goodwill associated with a brand, i.e., the degree to which a brand enjoys customer loyalty, name awareness, perceived quality, and product associations.

Brand Extension: the process of using a known brand to launch and support the sales of new or modified products.

Brand Image: the perception the public has of a brand and the things it associates with it.

Brand Loyalty: the tendency of established customers to continue buying a specific brand.

Brand (Equity) Mining: the process of using the brand equity to sell larger volumes of goods, particularly brand extensions or goods of lesser quality but higher margins. The term mining is used to indicate that such an approach will, like mining, slowly exhaust the reserves of brand equity.

Break Fee, Break-Up Fee: mergers and acquisition term. It refers to an agreed amount that a putative-target in an agreed but incomplete transaction must pay the putative-acquirer in the event that the target calls off the merger (usually with the exception of deal-cancellation because of a material adverse change [q.v.]), for example because of a more attractive offer from another company. Break-fees are usually only permissible to the extent that they maximize the value of the potential transaction to the target's shareholders. However, too high a break fee may be regarded as contrary to shareholder interests; under Delaware law in particular, too high a break fee may violate the target management's *Revlon* duties [q.v.].

Brevet d'invention, Brevet de perfectionnement: a *brevet d'invention* is a French patent granted on a new invention; a *brevet de perfectionnement* is a patent granted to a person other than the holder of a *brevet d'invention* for an improvement to (i.e., the perfecting of) the invention, e.g. an Incremental Patent [q.v.].

Browse-Wrap License: a license used on the Internet where the materials can be accessed without viewing the license. Instead the license is available by clicking on a hyperlink which may be entitled "license terms" but equally might be the words, "terms of use," "use restrictions," "legal" or copyright "notice." Since no affirmative act of consent to the license terms is necessary before accessing the materials, the enforceability of browse-wrap licenses is debatable; they are generally regarded as at least less legally enforceable than clickwrap [q.v.] or click licenses or shrink wrap licenses [q.v.].

Brussels Convention: two common meanings:

> **(1)** the Convention of 27 September 1968 on Jurisdiction and the Enforcement of Judgements in Civil and Commercial Matters—the key convention between EU Member States on jurisdiction in matters raised before more than one country's courts and the

recognition and enforcement of judgments rendered in each other's courts. The Brussels Convention was modified and amended in all EU member states (except Denmark) by Council Regulation (EC) No 44/2001 on Jurisdiction and the Recognition and Enforcement of Judgments in Civil and Commercial disputes, known as the Brussels Regulation. There is a similar convention, called the Lugano Convention, which applies between EU member states and Switzerland, Iceland, and Norway.

(2) the Brussels Convention Relating to the Distribution of Programme-Carrying Signals Transmitted by Satellite, which relates to constraining the footprint (or accessibility) of satellite broadcasts of copyrighted materials to areas where the programmer has the right to broadcast such materials.

The term Brussels Convention also arises in the family/matrimonial law context, referring to Council Regulation (EC) No 1347/2000 of 29 May 2000 on jurisdiction and the recognition and enforcement of judgments in matrimonial matters and in matters of parental responsibility for the children of both spouses, known as "Brussels II."

BSE: Blame Someone Else. Originally BSE referred to Bovine Spongiform Encephalopathy or mad cow disease, a fatal disease affecting cattle that has been transmitted to humans as new variant Creutzfeldt Jacob Disease or vCJD (nvCJD). However, in Brussels in the 1990s the tactics pursued by the then British Government before the European Commission, after BSE appeared to originate in the U.K. because of local animal feed manufacturing techniques, led to the sarcastic joke that BSE stood for "Blame Someone Else." Since then BSE has often been used to describe this approach to problems in certain quarters, and is occasionally heard for example in Japan. There in particular, a failure to accept responsibility, even for a subordinate's mistake, or something only partly in one's control, is considered a major failing that will undermine the respect that the person or business blame-shifting is held in; conversely, accepting responsibility, especially when the fault is obviously primarily that of a third party may serve to increase respect and long-term trust.

Budapest Treaty: Budapest Treaty on International Recognition of the Deposit of Microorganisms for the Purposes of Patent Procedure. *See* Deposit Requirement.

Bug: refers to a hardware or software fault in a computer. The common use of the term bug goes back to World War II, although its use in the context of electrical devices has been traced back to at least the 1890s.

Build: a build of a software project is a completion of source code such that, when compiled, it will display certain basic functionality—the "first build" is often used as a criterion for a stage payment. In complex software development projects, to avoid large numbers of serious bugs building up in code or major digressions from design criteria, a condition is often inserted in the contracts requiring the software programs under development to be compiled and tested periodically (e.g., weekly, biweekly or monthly) and for subsequent development work to be carried out with respect to the latest build. A build usually has all of the basic components of the final software package, and each component is then further elaborated upon. Usually this is linked to a level of acceptable bugs in a build, excluding any Class A Bugs.

Bundesinstitut für Arzneimittel und Medizinprodukte (BfArM): the German regulatory agency responsible for the approval of drugs (human and veterinary) and medical devices for sale in Germany.

Bundeskartellamt: German entity charged with the enforcement of competition law in Germany.

Bundespatentgericht: German Federal Patent Court, the German court with exclusive jurisdiction over challenges to the validity of German patents, known as nullity actions. Appeal from the Bundespatentgericht is to the German Supreme Court or Bundesgerichthof. In a peculiarity of German procedure, the question of infringement of a German patent is held in special branches of the Landesgericht or Federal State Courts, with appeal to the Oberlandesgericht and then to the Bundesgerichthof so that patent procedure is effectively divided into two separate but related cases.

Bundle of Rights: the legal theory of copyright is that it consists of a collection or "bundle" of divisible rights, indeed it might better be described as copyrights. Thus a copyright owner normally receives the rights to control: reproduction; preparation of derivative works; distribution of copies; public performances; and public display. If owner is also author, he/she may also receive "moral rights" [q.v.]. Copyright owners have generally gone further, subdividing the bundle into a host of other rights, for example, paperback and hardback rights, rights to publish translations, cinematographic rights, merchandising rights, rights to make games, etc.

Bundling Rights: a frequently lucrative form of OEM arrangement similar to box rights. For example when a computer manufacturer bundles licenses to ISP services, such as America Online® (AOL®), the manufacturer may typically receive a fee for each bundle, plus a yield-based fee for every customer who pays to use the service (a common arrangement with bundled services with PCs). Alternately when tied to consumables (and sometimes a recommendation for continued use), for example detergent (with a washing machine), car tires (on a vehicle), branded batteries (packaged with a device), or film (in a new camera), the bundled product will be at least free or heavily discounted or indeed a fee may be paid, because of the likelihood that the customer will replace and renew worn out items and used consumables with products from the same brand. Linking warranty protection to continued use of bundled consumables used to be common (i.e., your warranty depends on using only x-brand of consumable), but this practice has generally been held to violate competition law or consumer protection laws, absent a sound technical basis for the link. Some bundling rights are more valuable than others, but also may also be more controversial, for example maternity hospitals effectively bundling the newborn infant with baby products such as infant formula and diapers. *See* Right-of-Endorsement, Right-to-Endorsement.

Burden of Proof: *See* Presumption.

Bureau of Industry and Security (BIS), United States Department of Commerce: U.S. export control agency with responsibility for controlling the export of dual use goods and certain other categories of goods and (technical information), such as police (crime control) equipment, tools for espionage and encryption and items perceived to be potentially useful to terrorists. BIS administers the Export Administration Regulation (EAR). Until 2002 BIS was known as the Bureau of Export Administration or BXA, and the acronym is still commonly used to refer to it. Trade in weapons and military goods is managed by a different agency, the State Department's Directorate of Defense Trade Controls under the International Traffic in Arms Regulations (ITAR).

Burn Rate: the rate at which a startup company is exhausting net cash available in developing its business. A key measure of how much time the company has to either become cash flow positive, (i.e., start making money rather than losing it) or raise more money.

Business Case: in principle, a decision tool used to make a decision on a given business course of action, such as a project, acquisition, equipment purchase, contract, etc. The idea of the business case is to set forth clear criteria for a "go/no-go" decision on the course of action. A typical business case should include:

- An identification of the key justification for the course-of-action, e.g., the
    - problem it will resolve,
    - need it will fulfill,
    - threat it will neutralize, or
    - risk it will ameliorate;
- a description of how the course of action is a solution for the above, expressed in language all the decision makers who should approve the course of action can understand;
- a discussion of any identified alternative solutions and why they are less desirable than the proposed course of action;
- a total cost (internal and external) of the course of action, including life-cycle costs where appropriate, opportunity costs and premature termination or cancellation costs;
- a return-on-investment analysis (ROI);
- a risk analysis, including technical, financial, and organizational risks, which should discuss factors that may raise or lower such risks, as well as non-cost consequences of a premature termination or cancellation;

- time-lines and delivery schedules;
- a list of any assumptions used to develop the business case, including justification of those assumptions.

The main advantage of developing a business case is better decision making. Thus, for example, when considering a merger, acquisition, or contract, a business case can be used to make a final decision as to whether to close a deal, or walk away from a proposal that cannot be justified in terms of cost, risk and benefit. However, business cases work best if the *a priori* gating factors are not overly "massaged" to change outcomes as facts develop or are determined.

Business Model: a frequently misused business jargon term. A business model is, in principle, complete, and consists of a description of how a business will deliver something of value (or perceived value) to a relevant market, and in return generate profits, e.g., financial revenues that exceed the cost of what was delivered to the customer. Thus a business model will identify ***at least*** the following eight elements:

- The products or services to be offered and delivered;
- The method of or means for producing the goods or services;
- The cost of producing the goods or services;
- A target market for the products or services;
- Methods and means for delivering the goods or services to the target market;
- The value of the goods or services to potential customers in the target market;
- How revenue will be generated as a result of delivering such value;
- Whether the revenue will in principle exceed the costs incurred by the business and by how much (i.e., rate of return).

In addition, a good business model will seek to identify some commercial advantage(s) the business will have, e.g., a unique selling proposition or USP [q.v.]. Commonly, what are described or presented as "business models" are incomplete, in that they contain only some of the elements of such a model.

Business Model/Method Patent: a patent that purports to create exclusive rights to a business model. Such patents are highly controversial and in principle only presently really available in the United States under the Federal Circuit court precedent *State Street Bank & Trust Co. v. Signature Financial Group, Inc.*, 47 USPQ2d 1596, 1604 (Fed. Cir. 1998).

Business Names: in principle a property right separate and different from trademarks. Most jurisdictions allow companies to register or reserve names for their specific business, i.e., the "James Joyce" for an Irish pub, Hilton for a hotel. However, this registration is typically on a local basis, thus in Japan it is canton-by-canton, in the United States, state-by-state or city-by-city. If not used, the right to the reserved name expires after a certain period of time, which varies from place to place.

Business Secrets: commercially useful secret information (such as price or customer lists). The secrecy in business secrets can be in the collective nature of the information. For example, discounts given to customers are known to the supplier and the individual customer, but the pattern of discounts given to all customers, or the discretion sales departments have to discount would-be business secrets, notwithstanding the fact that it is composed of a collection of information items that are not individually confidential. *See* Know-How, Trade Secrets.

Business Week, Curse of, -Slide: legend has it that not sooner does a company (or emergent business sector) have a prominent article about it in the magazine *Business Week* (especially business or CEO of-the-year articles), and especially no sooner is a CEO featured on the cover, than the company and executive's fortunes start a precipitous decline. A similar observation is frequently made about companies lauded in business books, for example IN SEARCH OF EXCELLENCE by Tom Peters. There may be some substance to the theory, especially as extended to other business magazine such as *Fortune*, etc. One suggestion is that managers in promoting such articles are in fact seeking to raise their profile as part of a search for a new job, which may in turn reflect long-term problems at the company.

BXA: *See* Bureau of Industry and Security (BIS).

C

Call Option: the right to buy an asset at a fixed-maximum price at a given time regardless of whether the current market price is higher than that maximum price, known as the "strike price."

Cancellation for Lack of Use: trademarks can be maintained for an indefinite period, i.e., they can be immortal. However, if a trademark owner does not use the mark in a jurisdiction for which it is granted, the trademark can be cancelled for lack of use, usually after a period ranging from three to seven years. Thus an applicant for a trademark in a country that it wishes to expand into should use the mark before this time period expires.

Can't-do-Call: term used for the phone call made to a client by intellectual property counsel who, after assessing a patent with a view to drafting a Non-Liability Opinion, has concluded that such an opinion would be difficult or impossible for counsel to provide, because the counsel has concluded the client does, in fact, infringe. Since privilege may be waived in opinions, a written opinion stating that the client infringes is worse than useless (and indeed may be wrong). Clients are usually charged for the work resulting in the "can't-do-call," but the cost is usually considerably less than drafting a non-infringement opinion and it is tacitly understood that when a non-infringement analysis is requested such a call may result.

Capital Call: when venture capital providers commit funds to a business, the money is often not in the immediate possession of the VC. Instead the VC has commitments from its investors to provide a certain amount of money as capital, which the VC draws down as needed by means of capital calls.

Carlsberg Notice: notice published in the Official Journal (OJ) [q.v.] of the European Commission inviting third party comments on a competition case seeking clearance under Article 81 or under the Merger regulation. Dubbed a Carlsberg notice after such a publication in a joint venture approval matter, *Carlsberg-Tetley* 1992 OJ C 97/21, under Article 4(3) of the

Merger Regulation. The notice usually contains a short summary of the case and the names of the parties and is published with the parties' consent.

Carnet: a customs clearance document permitting temporary import of goods into a country for display, demonstration, or other purposes without paying import duties or posting bonds. Often used to show prototypes to potential purchasers or at trade shows and usually available to commercial travelers for: commercial samples; tools of the trade; advertising material; and cinematographic, audiovisual, medical, scientific, or other professional equipment. Carnets are generally valid for twelve months.

Cartel: an arrangement between competitors to limit the terms on which they compete with one another. Cartels often are based on price fixing, but they can operate in other ways, by for example, non-aggression pacts, i.e., agreements not to enter another market (known as market-partitioning), customer allocation, bid rigging, agreements not to make costly improvements to products and group boycotts [q.v.], etc. All such practices are usually prohibited under Competition Law [q.v.] or Antitrust law [q.v.].

Cartwright Act: *See* Little Sherman Act.

Case or Controversy Requirement: Under Article III Section 2 of the United States Constitution the jurisdiction of the Federal Courts extends to "cases" and "controversies." This has been interpreted to mean that the Federal Courts do not have the power to resolve legal questions that do not arise out of an actual dispute between real parties. One effect is that legal actions cannot be brought or continued after the matter at issue is "moot," i.e., the dispute has been resolved, leaving no live dispute for the court. More significantly from an IP perspective, a suit cannot be brought if it is not "ripe," i.e., before the challenged law, government action, or right has produced a direct threat to the party suing. From this "case or controversy" requirement comes the need for a clear threat of suit from a right holder against a party, (e.g., an accusation of patent infringement and threat to sue) before a declaratory judgment [q.v.] action can be brought. The requirement is also expressed as a prohibition on advisory opinions, i.e., the court cannot consider "what-if" cases, only actual facts.

Cash Call, Cash Round: many companies, especially startup companies, can ask their shareholders to commit more money in order to keep the business solvent. Shareholders who do not meet the cash call or cash round may find their shareholdings diluted. Partnerships, for example law firms, may also levy their equity partners for additional capital using cash calls.

Cease-and-Desist Letter: a warning letter sent to an infringer directing them to "cease and desist" from infringing intellectual property rights. Typical in trademark matters, it should be sent with caution in patent matters since it can provide the basis for bringing a declaratory judgment case. Moreover, in a number of countries, sending a warning letter without a proper legal basis may expose the sender to a legal claim for damages by the recipient or the person accused of infringement. Sometimes known as a letter of protest.

CEN: Comité Européen de Normalisation, the European Committee for Standardization, establishes CE standards for EU and EFTA countries.

CENELEC: Comité Européen de Normalisation Eurotechnique, the European Committee for Electrotechnical Standardisation, establishes electrical safety standards that then fall under the CE marking scheme.

Certainty/Uncertainty Trade Off: refers to the licensing concept that a financial sum certain is worth more and costs more than an uncertain sum. In many licensing situations there are two potential sums that the licensee may pay the licensor: a fixed up-front fee (that could be a paid-up license component); and a running royalty based on the licensee's sales of the licensed products. As a practical matter, usually the larger the fixed fee component, the lower the running royalty. However, for the licensor the fixed fee component is a sum certain, a running royalty a sum uncertain, but potentially much higher than the fixed fee; thus a licensor in effect trades certainty for uncertainty at some potential loss of "upside." For a licensee, a fixed up-front fee involves paying for something of uncertain value, while a running royalty means paying when the value of the license is established, and therefore a licensee will usually be less willing to pay a substantial amount as an up-front fee than a similar or even greater amount in the form of a running royalty. Similarly, for an author, a large advance may come at the cost of lower royalties on actual sales. The concept is also sometimes referred to as "risk premium."

Certificate of Acceptance: a document whereby a recipient of goods or services acknowledges that what has been delivered or completed, is acceptable, and has been manufactured or constructed according to the specification. Such a certificate is often a pre-requisite to payment and is frequently combined with an escrow arrangement.

Certificate of Analysis/Inspection: where certain goods, for example food and medicine, must meet legal quality standards for sale in a given country, the importer or the customs of the importing country may require such certificates as evidence of the requisite quality or conformity. If such a certificate is likely to be required it is important to include its provision as an obligation in relevant supply contracts.

Certificate of Origin: in many instances the origin of goods may affect the customs tariffs applicable to them, or in the event of sanctions, their importability. In such cases customs may seek a certificate of origin. If such a certificate is likely to be required, it is important to include its provision as an obligation in relevant supply contracts.

Certification Mark: a mark that is placed on a product to indicate that it has a certain status, e.g., that it complies with a geographic designation of origin (GDO) [q.v.], is made by a certain process, complies with a standard [q.v.] or industry code of conduct, or is made with unionized labor. It is essentially akin to a trademark and is usually legally treated in the same way.

***Certoirari*, Writ of, Petition for a writ of, Cert' Petition**: a writ of *certiorari* was originally the practical method by which an appellate court "seized itself" of jurisdiction, i.e., control over a legal matter. The writ was an order to a lower court or administrative agency, to certify the matter to the higher court, i.e., turn over (certify) to the higher court the record (or an authentic copy of the record) in the case. In practice, it has come to describe the process whereby an appellate or reviewing court, where appeal is not as-of-right (i.e., automatic) decides it wants to hear the case. In particular, in the United States, a petition to the United States Supreme Court is necessary to obtain most normal appeals. Such petitions must be then supported in conference by four of the Supreme Court's nine justices. About 2 percent of such petitions are granted in most appeals; the most common ground being a split between the legal rulings of different courts of appeal. Since there is only one court of appeal for U.S. patent cases, the United States Court of Appeal for the Federal Circuit, the Supreme Court rarely hears patent appeals.

CFIUS: Interagency Committee on Foreign Investment in the United States. *See* Exxon-Florio.

CFR: acronym for Code of Federal Regulations, a codification of the regulations enacted by the United States Federal Government as opposed to laws and codes, which are enacted by Congress and signed by the president. Generally such regulations implement powers conferred on a federal agency or the federal government by a federal law or statute. Such regulations when first enacted are published in the Federal Register or Fed. Reg. When considering a regulation in the CFR, the latest edition of a particular title (the number before the letters) should be used, and subsequent editions of the Fed. Reg. should then be checked for any amendments. Finally the regulation should always be reviewed for consistency with the underlying federal law or statutory authority.

Chain Reaction Bankruptcy: *See* Bankruptcy Cascade.

Channel Conflict: disagreements and practical difficulties that arise between sales channels when a manufacturer uses multiple channels to deliver its goods and services to market. For example, where a manufacturer uses both VARs [q.v.] and distributors [q.v.], the VARs may engage in straight distribution, using their deeper discounts (higher margins) to compete with the distributors on price.

Chicago School: Refers generally to sub-branch of the "law and economics" [q.v.] movement in legal analysis that strongly favors free market policies, many of whose most prominent members or supporters are or were based at the University of Chicago business and law schools including Nobel Prize winners Milton Friedman, George Stigler and Ronald Coase, as well as U.S. federal appellate judges Richard Posner and Frank Easterbrook. In Europe "Chicago School" is often inaccurately used to refer to all legal theorists who support "law and economics" analysis as opposed to just the strongly free market wing of the movement.

Chinese Wall: a term used to describe the partitioning of a business organization, usually by conduct rules and potentially physical separation, to limit the flow of information between various employees or sections of the organization, done to avoid conflicts of interest or other legal problems that might result from a party having access to specific information or influence on advice, opinions or decisions. The origin of the term is unknown, but it initially came into widespread use after the 1929 stock market crash when the U.S. government sought to separate investment bankers and brokerage firms in order to avoid the conflict of interest between the brokers' advice to their share-purchasing customers and the bankers' desire to place sufficient shares to make their stock offerings successful. The resulting regulations became known as the "Chinese Wall" because they were meant to create a barrier as effective as the Great Wall of China between the two types of business operation co-existing in the same institutions. The term has since come into widespread use.

Chisum: Professor Donald S. Chisum wrote *Patent Law*, an encyclopedic multi-volume "loose-leaf" treatise on U.S. patent law. It is usually referred to by his surname.

Chutzpah: term of Yiddish origin often used by lawyers, particularly in the United States, to refer to a "cheeky" argument. An often-cited example of chutzpah is described as: "a man who, having murdered his parents, seeks the court's mercy on grounds that he is an orphan." Another legal joke about chutzpah is:

> A man goes to a lawyer and asks: "How much do you charge for legal advice?"
> "A thousand dollars for three questions."
> "Yikes! Isn't that kind of expensive?"
> "Very—and your third question is?"

CIF: Incoterm meaning the seller has to pay the cost of delivering the goods to the *port* of delivery including insurance to the port and loading/unloading. Subsequently, risk of loss, transport, and storage (e.g., demurrage) is the liability of the buyer. The term should only be used for sea and inland waterways—but is often also misused in reference to airports.

CIP: Incoterm meaning "Carriage and Insurance Paid to," i.e., the seller has to pay for delivery of the goods to the named destination and insurance while in transit to the buyer and to clear the goods for export.

CIP Application: a U.S. Continuation-In-Part patent application, which consists of new material added to the disclosure of an existing patent application by the same inventor. This can arise when in the course of development the inventor finds a way to further improve the invention. The CIP would potentially result in a second patent. A CIP application has two priority dates, that of the original application for the original disclosure and that of the new material for the new disclosure. Although CIP applications are technically not available in most other patent systems, as a practical matter, provided there has been no publication, an applicant can file a second application containing further developments of the invention as a *quasi*-CIP. It is good practice to revisit pending patent applications periodically to determine whether further improvements or evolutions of the invention have arisen, which might support a CIP.

CISG: acronym for the United Nations Convention on Contracts for the International Sale of Goods, a convention that applies standardized legal terms to international contracts for the sale of goods between countries that are parties to it. The CISG can be opted out of by a choice of law clause, (and where it would not otherwise apply can also often be opted into). The CISG applies to contracts between contracting parties located in the following 63 countries who have entered into the convention: Argentina; Australia; Austria; Belarus; Belgium; Bosnia & Herzegovina; Bulgaria; Burundi; Canada; Chile; China; Colombia; Croatia; Cuba; Czech Republic; Denmark; Ecuador; Egypt; Estonia; Finland; France; Georgia; Germany; Greece; Guinea; Honduras; Hungary; Iceland; Iraq; Israel; Italy; Kyrgyzstan; Latvia; Lesotho; Lithuania; Luxembourg; Mauritania; Mexico; Moldova; Mongolia; Netherlands; New Zealand; Norway; Peru; Poland; Republic of Korea; Romania; Russian Federation; Saint Vincent and the Grenadines; Serbia and Montenegro; Singapore; Slovakia; Slovenia; Spain; Sweden;

Switzerland; Syrian Arab Republic; Uganda; Ukraine; Uruguay; USA; Uzbekistan; and Zambia.

Citations: references to scholarly articles or to patents. Thus the front page of a U.S. patent usually contains a list of citations, i.e., prior art considered in the course of the application (which typically are mostly other patents). A superscript star (*) is usually placed next to art specifically reviewed and discussed by the examiner. It is extremely difficult to overturn the validity of a patent by reliance on prior art found in the list of citations, because it is presumed (not necessarily accurately) that the patent office properly reviewed such art.

Civil Search Orders: new term under English Civil Procedure Rules for an Anton Piller Order.

Claim: defines the scope of the exclusive rights given to the owner of a patent, i.e., they set forth the things that the holder of the patent can prohibit others from doing. A patent usually contains several claims set forth as numbered paragraphs. Claims are written in terms of "limitations," that is to say a claim might give someone the exclusive right to manufacture vehicles [a limitation because it only covers vehicles and not, for instance, buildings], self-propelled [a second limitation] by an electric motor [third limitation], having three wheels [fourth limitation]. Claims fall into two categories, independent claims, and dependent claims. A dependent claim with reference to the claim above would recite that claim number, i.e., "the invention as set forth in Claim 1" but adding the limitation that the wheels should have rubber treads. Claim limitations are sometimes also called "elements of the claim." Claims can be multiply dependent, that is to say a claim can be written so that it is dependent on another dependent claim, which is in turn ultimately dependent on an independent claim. The word "element" is sometimes used interchangeably with "limitations." Claims can be written in three primary ways, as apparatus claims [q.v.], method claims [q.v.], or composition of matter claims. A subcategory of claims also exists that is in some respects a hybrid of both of first type and either of the two latter types, the product-by-process claim [q.v.].

Claim Chart: a usually tabular representation of a particular patent claim compared against an alleged infringing product. The left-hand column usually has each claim limitation or element, the right hand column describes what feature of the accused product meets or fails to meet that limitation and how. Sometimes an extra discussion column is added to the table. Claim charts are also drafted in other formats. *See* Claim.

Claim Tree, Claim Map: both a graphic and a conceptual way of showing the relationship between patent claims. Because a single independent claim can have many dependent and multiply dependent claims, the collection of claims are sometimes drawn as a tree, with the independent claim as the trunk and dependent claims forming boughs and branches. In analyzing a patent, the tree is looked at in different ways: infringement is determined by first looking at independent claims—if a product does not infringe an independent claim, it cannot infringe the dependent claims that by definition are more limited in scope; invalidity on prior art grounds requires each dependent claim to be addressed, since the more limited scope of a dependent claim means that it might be valid even when the independent claim is not. *See* Claim.

Claims Arising Policy: *See* Occurrence Policy.

Claims-Made Policy: Insurance policies come in two basic types with respect to claim/liability timing, "claims-made," and "occurrence" (also known as "claims arising") policies. A claims-made policy will indemnify the insured, within the policy limits, for claims made against the insured during the policy period. Claims made after the policy has expired are not covered, even if the events or actions giving rise to the insured's liability occurred during the policy period. A claims-made policy has the benefit to the insurer of limiting its liability for the future. *See* Occurrence Policy.

Class A Bug (Fault), Class B Bug, Class C Bug: software bugs, (i.e. faults) are often classified in software or product development contracts according to the degree of severity. These classifications may be used to establish when stage payments [q.v.] are due, for example, (e.g., "when no Class A Bugs, no more then X Class B Bugs, and no more than Y Class C Bugs are observable"). Usually a Class A Bug is a "showstopper," i.e., a fault that prevents the software under development from running at all; a Class B Bug is often defined as a fault that the software can run with, but that significantly impairs its basic functionality; a Class C bug is often defined as a bug that impairs the functionality or appearance of the software, but does not impair basic functionality. However, in complex systems more bug categories can be used—with Class A almost always remaining a showstopper, but the latter categories subdivided and more closely defined.

Class Action: a type of litigation where a group of plaintiffs who, in principle, have been injured in similar ways by a defendant(s) action (i.e., they are "similarly situated") bring suit for damages collectively in a single case. Different jurisdictions require that class actions be either "opt-in" or "opt-out." In an opt-in jurisdiction, plaintiffs must be affirmatively found who agree to be parties to the case. In an opt-out jurisdiction, name plaintiffs or class representatives bring suit on behalf of themselves and "all other similarly situated" and other potential plaintiffs must then "opt-out," i.e., state that they do not want to be parties, usually before any final disposition of the case. Much of the world, including the United States, operates an opt-in system. Once such a suit is brought in the United States, there is a second step called class certification, where a judge must be persuaded that the members of the proposed plaintiff class have sufficient in common to justify such a suit. At the conclusion of a class action, either by settlement or final judgment, those plaintiffs who do not "opt-out" may no longer bring a suit, but share in the outcome. Class actions are prevalent in securities, antitrust, environmental, and products liability litigation and derivative suits.

Considerable controversy surrounds the United States class action system, which is largely supported by the legal community and consumer advocates, but opposed by the U.S. Chamber of Commerce and "big" business (as opposed to small). There are advantages and disadvantages to the class action system. One major advantage is that where individual plaintiffs' damages are too small to justify the legal cost to pursue when attorneys' fees are unavailable (which could mean less than $50-100,000, i.e., a lot of money to an individual or small company), a class action can aggregate the claims to make them worth pursuing. In the area of antitrust, individual consumers' damages from a cartel may be small, perhaps a few dollars or cents, but the gain to the cartel could still easily be billions of dollars, and the overall cost of such cartels to an economy huge. In such a situation, a class action makes a case viable, while without class actions scofflaws can persist. For defendant companies there is also the advantage of an opportunity to resolve in a single case a matter, which otherwise could drag on for years.

The disadvantages of class actions are: the pressure to settle what may be dubious cases, because of the aggregate risk; the alleged frequency with which settlements are of little value to victims (e.g., discount vouchers only redeemable on goods or services from the defendant, perhaps only applicable to the full-list price), but the legal fees paid are substantial. It is also argued by large U.S. companies that class actions are damaging to business. Against this argument it should be noted that when efforts were made in the 1990s to rein in class actions in securities suits, at least anecdotally there was a subsequent epidemic of companies engaging in securities fraud, e.g., WorldCom, Enron, etc. In addition, many commentators attribute high prices in Europe (especially the U.K.) to the difficulty in bringing class actions for price fixing. Firms which specialize in securities class actions in the United States sometimes maintain what are known as "professional plaintiffs," i.e., individuals who own tiny blocks of stock in many companies, so as to be situated to be a lead plaintiff if an actionable claim arises (whose lawyer may thus have a better chance of becoming lead counsel and thus get the lion's share of the legal fees); recent legal changes have restricted this practice by limiting the number of actions such a person can be a party to over a period of time.

Class, Trademark: trademarks are divided into classes of goods or services—thus trademark applicants must state what category of products, e.g., cosmetics, they wish the trademark to be granted for. Any subsequent application for the same mark in the same class would presumptively give rise to a risk of confusion and would normally be denied. Trademarks can be applied for in multiple classes, for example both goods and services. The international classification system for trademarks is established and maintained by WIPO, the World Intellectual Property Organization.

Clayton Act: 15 U.S.C. §§12-27, antitrust law enacted in 1914 to clarify and supplement the Sherman Antitrust Act of 1890. It prohibits under various circumstances exclusive sales contracts, local price cutting to freeze out competitors (i.e., predatory pricing), rebates, interlocking directorates in corporations capitalized at $1 million or more in the same field of business, and inter-corporate stock holdings.

Clean Room: usually means developing technology in a room (or development team) from which all trade secrets and know-how obtained from a competitor under license, or all copyrighted materials, have been excluded, thus ensuring the technology is independently developed and therefore not subject to the license and any restrictions in the license or royalty obligations. Clean room development is notoriously difficult to do since it involves careful selection of all materials provided to the clean room developers to ensure the absence of any proprietary information, as well as the location of talented individuals who, oddly enough, during their careers lacked the curiosity to consider details of major technology influencing their industry, e.g., Java programmers who never looked at how Sun's Java Virtual Machine (JVM) works, or semiconductor developers who were devoid of interest in Intel's X86 instruction set or the ARM architecture (*See* Click License, Shrink-Wrap License and Tar-Baby License). One well-known case arose when Advanced Micro Devices, Inc. sought to develop its own processors compatible with the X86 instruction set used by Intel using a clean room, i.e., a room from which all Intel intellectual property had been excluded, trumpeting its achievement with an "Independence Day" promotion. However, in reality, the hygiene of AMD's clean room was not complete and its developers had used Intel's IP. As a result, AMD found itself with two legal problems—a lawsuit with and liability to Intel, and an SEC action resulting from the inaccurate representation of the room's cleanliness, which AMD ultimately settled.

"Clean room" may also be used to refer to a laboratory or manufacturing facility from which contaminants have been excluded, which are usually subject to a classification system, depending on how rigorous the air cleaning controls are. Clean room standards range from the basic class 1,000,000 and class 100,000 clean rooms to class 100 and class 1 at the highest level of cleanliness. To elaborate, at class 100,000 up to 3.5 million particles (of less than $1/2$ mm) are permissible in each one m^3 of air, while at class 100 only 3,500 would be allowed. The classification system also relates to how often air in the room is sampled for contaminants, at 100,000 twice a week is acceptable, at higher levels sampling is more or less continuous. The level of clean room used is a function of the quality control requirements for the product—semiconductors for example have high-level clean rooms—and products for use in such facilities usually have to be made in similar environments.

Clean Search Report: a patent prior art search report that contains no X-References or Y-References [both q.v.]. When a patent application receives a clean search report, the subsequent grant of a patent or patents can be regarded as extremely likely, particularly if the search reports comes from a patent office known for its rigor, e.g., Germany, Japan, the EU, or U.K.

Click Fraud: form of fraud where Internet users are recruited to deliberately click on links on a Web site, causing the site to be directed to an online merchant Web site that pays a commission for such clicks under an affiliate program. This may be done by the Web site owner itself, or by a competitor with a view to undermining the merchant's affiliate program. Some major search engines use "pay-per-click" arrangements, where the merchant must pay the search engine, whether the directed person buys or not; click fraud can be a particularly acute problem in such an arrangement. Rumor suggests that automated software engines have also been used for click fraud purposes.

Click License: a license usually used in Internet downloads or software installation, where users click on a screen-box to indicate their agreement with the terms of or conditions of the license. In-house lawyers are often wary of employees "clicking" on such licenses and it is frequently prohibited without the permission of the IT or legal department. The reason is that the licenses are often not read by the person doing the download or installation and may indeed contain onerous terms and conditions or even be a Tar-Baby License [q.v.]. Such a license is often an End User License Agreement or EULA [q.v.]. *See* Shrink-Wrap License, Browse Wrap License.

Closed Claim: a patent claim, which recites a list of elements in such a way that the addition of any other elements would render a product or process non-infringing. Closed claims are rare and are usually only found in metallurgy or in the patenting of chemical entities. *See* Claims; Consisting of.

Closeout Insurance: *See* Runoff Insurance.

Clowns, Code of the: early form of trade dress [q.v.] or trademark [q.v.] under which clowns maintained a register of the designs of face paint they used and that other clowns, at the risk of boycott, should not use. The code eventually extended to cover stage-name (moniker), costume, and "gags" and "bits" (i.e., personally distinctive aspects of performance).

Clustering, Patent: a term that refers to the focusing of a company or inventor's patenting efforts so as to establish patent thickets. It is usually advisable to supplement a pioneer patent with a number of CIPs [q.v.] on evolutions and incremental inventions so as to ensure the inventor or company's work cannot be easily designed around. One advantage of clustering patents is that it increases the likelihood that a company will obtain blocking patents, which from a defensive perspective, may result in cross licenses [q.v.] or sleeping dog licenses [q.v.].

Cluster Theory: theory of economic and industry development most notably described by Professor Michael Porter in his book *The Competitive Advantage of Nations*. Clusters are geographic concentrations of interconnected companies in a country or region including competitors, suppliers, service vendors, university departments or research groups, and other institutions in a specialized business or technology space. Clusters develop because of the advantages in terms of recruitment, financing from knowledgeable investors, equipment, services, etc. in the region, which increase the ability of all companies in the sector to operate effectively, but also because companies tend to compete more rigorously with local rivals, improving each other's effectiveness. The advantages of a cluster often can substantially outweigh cost savings derived from locating elsewhere. The best-known cluster is Silicon Valley. Clusters also exist in many other fields, e.g., printing presses (Germany and Switzerland), banking and finance (New York and London), consumer electronics (Japan's Kanto-plain), pharmaceuticals (France and Francophone Switzerland), contract software development (Bangalore), aircraft leasing (Ireland), software for mobile devices (southeast England), eyeglass-frames (Belluno Italy, Sabae-City Japan) etc. Building clusters is a major objective of industrial development agencies.

Cockroach Problem: term used to describe companies or groups that announce bad news repeatedly or in such a way as to indicate that might be more bad news to come, i.e., problems that are bigger and more prolific and widespread than they first appear. Derived from the idea that if one spots a single cockroach, there are always many more that one cannot see.

Code Comparison: the process of comparing two software programs, whether versions of the same program or from two different sources, to look for similar or identical code in each. A computer program, both in source code and in object code can be regarded as a series of alpha-numerical strings. If there are large areas of coincidence between one program's code and another (i.e., identical strings are found in each) this coincidence is considered strong evidence that some of one program was copied from another, a potential copyright violation. However, not all coincidences mean that part of a program was copied. Software techniques often use similar algorithms loaded from public libraries, or they may contain utilities intended to interact with the same feature of an operating system of a CPU on which programs are run, resulting in some code commonality.

Code-napping: pun on kidnapping with two common meanings:

(1) Refers to a software developer copying third party source code into his work, thereby infringing third-party copyright. In poorly run software-development houses, this can be a significant problem. The code may often come from a previous job or project or indeed be obtained from a friend or off the Internet; or

(2) Refers to employees or contractors withholding developed code until paid-in-full or paid additional money for their work.

Coercive Licensing: licensing, usually of patents, driven by the threat of litigation by the patent holder.

Coexistence Agreement: an agreement between two users of a mark to the effect that both have limited rights to use the mark, subject to certain rules. Coexistence agreements are most common in the international context, a well-known example being a 1939 agreement between Budjovicky Budvar, národní podnik (i.e., the original Czech Budweiser company) and Anheuser Busch Inc. (US Budweiser) to divide the world so that the Czech company had Europe as a territory and the U.S. North America—an agreement which ended in well known and ongoing worldwide litigation. Coexistence agreements can be a short-to-medium term solution to a trademark problem, though, as the Budweiser case demonstrates, where the balance of commercial strength of the parties changes over time they can become increasingly problematic. Coexistence agreements in a national or single territory context present much more substantial legal difficulties, since it can be very difficult to arrange for concurrent ownership of a single trademark registration.

Coffee-Pot Effect: organizations that are small and located on a single or small number of sites are said to benefit from what is variously called "the coffee-pot effect," "tea-room conferences," "the water cooler channel," "toilet talks," and "elevator encounters," that is to say informal channels for communication where individuals from different groups or senior and junior employees meet and communicate ideas and issues while using common facilities; this may lead to substantial improvements in corporate performance through better problem identification and solving, internal communication and take-up of ideas. When companies are divided on multiple sites this effect may be lost.

Coined Terms/Words: *See* Invented Words.

Collar Agreement: clause in a stock-for-stock company sale or transaction (e.g., a "full form merger" [q.v.]), which provides for adjustment on the closing date of the amount of the stock of the acquirer to be exchanged per share of the target if the acquirer's share price fluctuates between the date of the sale agreement and the closing.

Collateral Estoppel: legal doctrine under which a court can refuse to re-open an issue of fact if it has previously been litigated in another forum. Usually for a court to apply collateral estoppel, it must find that:

(1) the instant issue is identical to the one decided in the first action;

(2) that the instant issue must have been actually litigated, (i.e., argued) in the first action;

(3) a finding on the instant issue was required as part of the final judgment in the first action; and

(4) the party against whom estoppel would apply had a full and fair opportunity to litigate the issue in the first action.

Collateral estoppel is similar to issue preclusion [q.v.] except that usually the former is at the discretion of the judge while issue preclusion is mandatory, i.e., the issue cannot be reopened. However, it is a different legal concept from equitable estoppel [q.v.].

Collecting Societies: *See* Performing Rights Society.

Collective Mark: a trademark applied for by an association of individuals or a club. For example, the right to place initials or an acronym after one's name to indicate membership of a society, or to use the trademark of the society or club, as well as club ties, crests, union names, etc.

Collective Work: a work created by multiple authors. To the extent that the contribution of an author is segregable, for example an article in a magazine, the author enjoys a separate copyright in that contribution, and the owner of the collective work a license limited to use of the author's contribution in the collective work. If the contributions are not segregable, the work is considered as one of joint authorship and ownership of the work usually depends on the agreement between the authors or with their employer.

College ter Beoordeling van Geneesmiddelen (CBG): Netherlands agency responsible for regulating medicines.

Collusive Tendering: *See* Bid Rigging.

Comfort Letter: term common in competition law that usually meant the letter sent by the European Commission in response to most notifications made to it prior to May 2004 on a Form A/B (when new procedures came into force) advising the notifying parties that the Commission saw no grounds for action against an agreement or commercial arrangement *as notified* under Article 81 of the Treaty of Rome, because it did not restrict competition or affect trade between member states of the EU (a negative clearance) or that the agreement fulfills the conditions for granting an exemption under Article 81(3) of the Treaty (usually referencing an existing block exemption). Although such letters were and (to the extent that they were issued with respect to an agreement still in force) are not, in principle, legally binding, it would be remarkably difficult for any party to argue that an agreement is illegal under EU law, or that the parties should be civilly liable or fined, if a comfort letter has been issued, unless the complaining party was able to show that significant aspects of the agreement or commercial arrangement had not been disclosed in the notification or had subsequently changed. The term is also sometimes used to describe reassuring letters sent by other regulatory agencies or authorities in response to a query as to whether an agreement or practice violates applicable laws or regulations. Comfort letters have been replaced under the new European Union competition law procedures with so-called informal guidance letters.

Commitment Fee: a term used in many contexts, the most common being by banks and other sources of lending for a charge made to a potential creditor for reserving funds for a pre-approved loan. In essence if, for example, a bank agrees in principle to lend a large sum of money to a potential borrower if certain conditions are met, to be drawn down at the borrower's demand over a period of time, the bank must set aside funds to meet that lending obligation, usually at a relatively low rate of interest. The commitment fee compensates the bank for the lost profit that results from reserving these funds. Commitment fees may also be charged in other areas, for example, in professional services and consulting, or contract manufacturing, where a party agrees to hold a limited resource available for another party. Commitment fees are usually non-refundable.

Commercial Agents Directive: *See* Agency Directive.

Commercially Essential/Vital Improvement/Patent: *See* Economically Vital Improvement/Patent.

Commodity Business: a business whose products are largely fungible (i.e., interchangeable) commodities. Such businesses are characterized by the sales being price driven, i.e., that customers are primarily concerned and effected by price and not by other differentiating factors, e.g., quality, reputation, etc. In other words, the business lacks any USP [q.v.].

Common Law Trademark: an unregistered trademark in a "common law country," i.e., a country sharing its legal traditions with England. Common law trademarks are protected under the tort of passing-off or "unfair competition." Common law marks are created when a vendor sells goods or services under the vendor's name or a brand for an extensive period of time, which it has not registered as a trademark. If a third party seeks to sell products under that mark or brand without permission of the original vendor they may be liable to the original vendor for damages, notwithstanding the lack of a formal trademark registration. It exists because in most countries, formal trademark laws evolved after the tort of "passing off" already existed and it was not subsequently abolished. One risk in distribution systems is that when a supplier had failed to register the trademark locally, their local distributor may come to have "common law" rights to the mark, which can prove problematic if the distributor is terminated.

Community Design: refers to a European Union Registered Design [q.v.] filed at OHIM [q.v.].

Community of Interest when Bordering Insolvency: under company law in the United States and a large number of other legal systems, the board of directors of a company's only fiduciary obligation [q.v.] is, under normal circumstances, to represent and protect the interest of the company's shareholders; this restricts their fiduciary liability for their decisions. However, cases, particularly in the United States have held that when a company is bordering on insolvency, creditors gain an equitable interest in the business and directors acquire an obligation to also protect creditor interests. In such a situation, directors can be held to have violated this duty if they, for example, allow the company to transfer significant amounts of capital to shareholders in such a way as to ensure that little remains to pay its creditors. *See* Trading While Insolvent.

Community Patent: a proposed single patent covering the entire European Union. Such a patent has been under discussion since the Community Patent Convention was adopted in 1973. The most recent version of this proposal is usually available from the Web site of the European Patent Office. Despite recent progress toward legislation enacting a Community Patent, at the time of writing the project is again stalled for a number of reasons, including the objections of vocal groups in the free software movement, anti-globalization activists, and assorted conspiracy theorists (including some members of the forgoing groups). The existing proposal has also been criticized for different reasons by intellectual property professionals, primarily as creating a system likely to highly expensive, for example:

- Applications would have to exist in English, French and German, and fees will have to cover translation costs;
- Claims would have to be translated into all community languages (at least 20);
- 50 percent of the renewal fees [q.v.] will be paid to National patent offices (since EPO fees are already high, this is regarded as very discouraging).

Moreover, it is intended that national patents would continue to exist as alternatives to the community patent, creating in the EU a highly complex patchwork of IP protection. Whether the community patent will in fact take the form currently proposed is hard to predict, but three previous proposals in 1975, 1985, and 1989 have faded away.

Community Patent Court: the proposed single EU court system to deal with cases involving the Community Patent [q.v.]. As with the Community Patent, the proposal is heavily criticized by many intellectual property professionals as having many failings. In particular, it is proposed that cases be held in the country of the defendant, using the defendant's language, which may present considerable difficulties where the defendant is for example a subsidiary of a larger corporation located in a small member state with a language that is not widely spoken internationally. Moreover, since the court would only have jurisdiction over infringement cases involving "community patents" it would be a long time before it had a substantial amount of work.

Community Trademark: a trademark granted by the European Union for all of its territory; the European trademark office goes by the complex title of Office for Harmonisation in the Internal Market or OHIM and is based in Alicante.

Compensation, Inventor's: *See* Inventor's Bonus.

Competition Commission: U.K. entity that inquires into mergers, markets, and the regulation of the major regulated industries. The Competition Commission has no authority to initiate an inquiry on its own; rather the matter must be referred to it by another agency, e.g., the Office of Fair Trading.

Competition Law: laws enacted in most modern economies to protect competition in their marketplace from cartels, abuse of a dominant position, anticompetitive mergers, and other detrimental practices. In the United States it is known as "antitrust law."

Complementary Merger: a merger justified on the basis that the combining companies' business lines compliment each other and will enable growth either through combined offerings or cost savings. Sometimes also called a synergistic merger. Contrast with consolidating merger, conglomerate merger, expansive mergers, and diversifying merger.

Complementary Technologies: technologies that typically will or need to be used in combination. The term is commonly used in the legal analysis of the legality of package licenses and patent pools. Combining complementary technologies in a single package license usually does not raise competition or antitrust law issues of potentially illegal tying.

Compliance Program: internal programs and training by businesses to ensure that their employees know, understand, and comply with applicable law. The existence of compliance programs is a key factor in determining a business' liability under competition and securities law. Although "off the shelf" compliance programs are available, the program should usually be tailored to the particular circumstances of the business, and may need special tailoring when a business is subject to the laws of more than one jurisdiction, e.g., international companies traded on European and U.S. stock exchanges. Proof that employees have undergone compliance training and regular refresher courses should be retained by the business. Although delivered and built by legal departments, human resources departments usually control the administration of compliance programs.

Compliance Testing: also known as conformance testing, means the testing of a product to determine whether it complies (or conforms) with a standard. There are two types of such standards, industry technical standards and mandatory safety standards. The latter include the CE electrical and EMC/RFI safety standards for the EU, the FCC electromagnetic interference standards, and more. It is usually not legal to sell products that do not comply with the mandatory standards applicable in a given jurisdiction. A good summary of the EU approach to standards is available from www.newapproach.org.

Composite Currency: *See* Synthetic Currency.

Comprising: a term used in patent claim language, which means that to infringe, the accused product or process must include at least those elements or their equivalents, but may include additional elements, e.g., if the claim says comprising a+b+c, something containing a+b+c+d could likely infringe, but a product with a+b+d would usually not (unless d was the equivalent of c). Such a claim is also usually described as an Open Claim. *See* Claims, Closed Claim, Consisting of, Open Claim.

Compulsory License: the patent and other intellectual property laws of several jurisdictions, as well as the TRIPS, provide that countries may, in limited circumstances, compel the grant of a license. Usually such provisions apply to pharmaceuticals not otherwise available in that jurisdiction, although other goods may be subject to a compulsory license on similar grounds. The TRIPS Agreement provides strict conditions under which compulsory licensing may be required by states, and requires fair compensation, based on the value of the product. In addition, compulsory licensing is sometimes used as a remedy in competition and antitrust cases, or as a remedy in otherwise potentially anti-competitive mergers and acquisitions, particularly with respect to "essential facilities" [q.v.]. *See* Magill.

Computer Implemented Invention: term used by the European Commission and European Parliament in draft legislation and discussion to describe inventions that must be implemented using a computer including, potentially, what may be described as a software patent.

Concentration, Concentrative: Competition Law term for an agreement (e.g., a merger or joint venture) that reduces the number of competitors or potential competitors in a given economic space. EU competition law generally uses the term to describe either a merger between competitors or the formation of a full function joint venture [q.v.] by competitors (a so-called concentrative joint venture). It may also be used to describe placing key competive assets under joint control. If a concentration rises above the Turnover Thresholds (*See* Merger Regulation, European) it must be notified [q.v.].

Concertation Procedure: *See* Euro Foreign Exchange Reference Rates.

Concerted Practice: refers to two or more parties "acting in concert," i.e., coordinating their activities, with or without a formal agreement. Where concerted practices are anticompetitive they can be regarded as a cartel.

Concerted Refusal to Deal: *See* Group Boycott.

Condition, Contractual: something that must be fulfilled for obligations under a contract to be effective. Conditions can be written as conditions precedent (preconditions) in which case the obligation is not triggered until the condition is fulfilled; or as conditions subsequent, in which case the obligation may be terminated or suspended if the condition is not fulfilled or if it ceases to be fulfilled. In English common law, as well as the laws of Ireland, Australia, New Zealand, and other countries following the English legal tradition, a contractual condition is something different from a warranty: (a) a condition goes fundamentally to the purpose and intent of the agreement, i.e., the ability of the delivering party to actually deliver the goods or services promised and breach of a condition gives rights to both damages and to the legal remedy known as rescission; (b) a warranty is an agreement with reference to the goods or services, which are the subject of the contract of sale, but collateral to the main purpose of such contract and breach of a warranty gives rise to a claim for damages, but not a right to rescission.

Condition of Good Title, Right to Sell: English law (and the laws of countries following the English legal tradition) holds that an implied condition to any contract for the sale of goods or services is that the selling party has <u>at the time of sale</u> either: (a) good title to the goods; or (b) the right to supply the goods or services. It is unclear whether the conditions are in fact one condition described in different ways or two different conditions. Case-law, (e.g., *Niblett Ltd v Confectioners' Materials Co Ltd*, [1921] 3 KB 387) has held that agreeing to sell goods that violate another's intellectual property rights (in the leading case a trademark) extant at the time of delivery, is a violation of the condition of right to sell. However, sale of goods, which later become subject to the intellectual property rights and claims of a third party, is a breach of the warranty of quiet enjoyment but not of the condition of right to sell (*Microbeads AC and Another v. Vinhurst Road Markings Ltd.* [1975] 1 All E.R. 529). That the vendor was not aware that it lacked the right to sell has been held not to nullify the right of the buyer to claim under the condition (*Rowland v Divall* [1923] 2 KB 500).

Confidences, Law of: term used in English law for the law applicable to Trade Secrets [q.v.], Business Secrets [q.v.], and Know How [q.v.].

Conflict of Law (Rules): refers to a situation where the laws of more than one jurisdiction may apply to the same transaction, action, or event, especially where there is a difference between the laws of each. Conflict of law rules can be highly complex and may indeed be different in each jurisdiction. Moreover, the choice of law rules for each jurisdiction may produce different results. Indeed, it is fair to suggest that when a conflict of law problem arises, a large legal bill will be the most reliably predictable outcome. For this reason, and to avoid uncertainty, many international contracts specify the law applying to the contract, in what is known as a choice of law clause, that usually contains some form of the phrase "subject to the laws of _____, *without regard to its conflict of law rules.*"

Conformance (Conformity) Testing: (also known as Compliance Testing) the process of testing a product to determine that it meets key requirements of a standard [q.v.], for example for interoperability.

Confusion, risk of, likelihood of: a key factor in showing that a non-identical brand name, logo, or other item infringes a trademark. If the trademark owner can show that consumers might be confused into believing that the trademark owner was the source of the infringing product, an injunction may be secured. Risk or likelihood of confusion is usually shown with market surveys, which can be expensive to carry out; once brought to court, the methodology of such surveys will be closely considered by the judge, who may, if unhappy with the fairness and reliability of the survey, rule it inadmissible.

Conglomerate Merger: an essentially diversifying merger, designed to assemble businesses in different sectors together in a single group, aspiring to use their different business cycles to offset one another. Conglomerate mergers were fashionable in the 1960s and 1970s, but most proved unsuccessful and the conglomerates were subsequently broken up. *See also*, consolidative merger, complementary merger, and expansive merger.

Consent Decree: a type of settlement of an enforcement action, particularly prevalent in the United States, where the defendant concedes that certain of its actions were illegal, pleading guilty, (with or without an immediate fine or legal sanctions, recompense to victims, or efforts to repair harm) and undertakes not to act in that manner again. The key feature of a consent decree is that if the defendant is subsequently proven to have violated the decree, by acting in a manner it had promised not to, there is no defense of legality, rather the case goes straight to the penalty phase. However, penalties are not always specified in consent decrees and such decrees can be poorly worded, so that the existence of a violation of the decree is not clear and ends up being litigated. Nonetheless, a consent decree is a powerful weapon in a regulator's arsenal, and its existence can prove useful evidence in a subsequent or parallel civil action brought by victims. Consent decrees are frequently used in consumer cases, environmental enforcement actions, and in antitrust, competition and securities law.

Consisting of: term of art which, when used in U.S. patent claim language, is generally accepted as meaning that only the listed elements may be present to infringe. It is thus a "closed claim." These types of claim are rarely used, typically only in metallurgy or chemical claims, and even then usually have long lists of potential substitutes for each element. "Consisting Essentially of" is a not completely closed claim, i.e., it allows the possibility of some additional items if not "essential" to the invention. *See* Claims, Comprising, Closed Claim.

Consolidative (Consolidation) Merger: a merger occurring in an industry with a large number of competitors and relatively static revenue growth. Because of the effect of competition law, absent special treatment by the authorities, a consolidative merger is unlikely to create any value other than benefits-of-scale (i.e., better bargaining power for inputs and elimination of some management duplication). Contrast with diversifying merger, complementary merger, expansive merger, and conglomerate merger.

Consolidation Threshold: International Accounting Standards (IAS) and U.S. GAAP require that a public company's financial reporting incorporate the activities in its group accounts of associates, i.e., affiliates and subsidiaries. The definition of an associate is variously defined, but typically is any entity in which the "parent" is in a position to exercise significant influence over. This is typically presumed when the parent has a 20 percent or greater shareholding, or participation in the financial and operating policies of the subsidiary-entity or has representation on that entity's board. For this reason many companies investing venture capital in other companies try to keep their investment at 19 percent, i.e., below the consolidation threshold.

Conscious Parallelism: a market situation where competitors offer closely comparable prices and terms. Conscious parallelism may not be automatically illegal, but it is regarded as highly suspicious by competition authorities and many competition and antitrust law systems prohibit or penalize exchanges of information between competitors or business practices that are useful to supporting such parallelism, regarding them as cartel-like practices. The existence of such parallelism is also regarded as a strong indictor of the existence of a formal cartel [q.v.] and may spur authorities to investigate.

Construction, Claim: has the same root as the word construe and means the process of working out what the claims of a patent mean. *See* Claim, Claim Chart, Markman Hearing.

Constructive Dismissal: where the terms or conditions of an employee's position are unilaterally varied by the employer, by for example lowering pay or substantially reducing benefits or by a demotion or effective demotion (e.g., the reduction of responsibilities), this action can in many common law countries (except most of the United States) be considered tantamount to firing the employee and may give the employee the right to claim damages. *See* At Will Employee, At Will Employment.

Continuation Application: a patent application filed when a parent application is still alive, which continues to seek patent claims not granted in the parent application. For example, if a patent application is filed with twenty claims and the patent office agrees to issue a patent with ten of those claims, a continuation application could be filed prosecuting the remaining ten un-allowed claims. *See* Divisional Application, CIP Application, Submarine Application, Claim.

Continuation-In-Part: *See* CIP Application.

Contractor IP: an exception to shop right in most jurisdictions is the presumption, absent contractual provisions to the contrary, that a client only has an implied license to IP created by a contractor or consultant while the contractor or consultant retains full ownership and rights to use, license, etc. If there is no written agreement with the contractor or consultant, this interpretation will typically always apply. *See* Marriage Contract First.

Contracts (Rights of Third Parties) Act 1999: U.K. legislation that provides that, in principle, third parties will normally be able to claim under and enforce contracts subject to English law if that third party can argue to have been a beneficiary of the contract, *unless* it is clear that the parties to the contract did not intend to create such a right. For this reason, it is usual to insert into contracts touching on the United Kingdom (and not just contracts with English/Scottish/Northern Ireland Law) a sentence specifically excluding any third party rights arising under the Act.

Contributory Infringement: the concept, especially in U.S. law, that someone who supplied a key thing to allow actual infringement to take place is liable for the infringement. For example, if a patent covers a+b+c, someone who supplied c might be liable for infringement. This is limited by the requirement that c be adapted solely or primarily for the infringing purpose, which means that infringement must be the only significant use of c. If c has a substantial non-infringing use, it is deemed a "staple article of commerce" and cannot form the basis of a claim of contributory infringement. *See* Infringement, Inducement of Infringement.

Controlled Composition: a term referring to a copyrighted musical work recorded **and** performed by the songwriter, i.e., a singer/songwriter. Normally, a songwriter is entitled to "mechanical royalties" for each recording sold. Usually record companies treat or try to treat a singer/songwriter differently, since the singer also receives a fee for the performance.

Convoyed Sales: term used with reference to damages, particularly in patent cases and more recently in copyright. It refers to sales made in conjunction with the goods covered by the intellectual property right. Thus in a patent case a plaintiff might seek additional damages for sales of non-infringing accessories sold with or for the infringing goods as well as damages for the loss of the plaintiff's own convoyed sales. The term is also used in licensing to describe the extension of the royalty base beyond the licensed products to accessories, consumables, and other associated goods. *See* Damages.

Copyleft, Copy-Left: a term used to designate dedication to the public used in the context of Copyright, normally associated with open source licensing, shareware, and the Free Software Foundation.

Copyright: refers to the right of the author of a work to control the creation and distribution of copies of the work once it has been recorded in a tangible medium, i.e., film, paper, tape, CD, picture, photograph, etc. A dichotomy in copyright exists between abstract ideas, which are not protected, and the recorded expression of those ideas, which is. To qualify for copyright, a work has to be original and have a modicum of creativity, which is why the copyright of, for example, simple mechanical lists such as telephone directories is frequently disputed. Copyright is often described as a bundle of rights. An author should usually indicate that it asserts copyright when the work is published, typically by use of the copyright symbol, i.e., ©, followed by the date or dates of publication/creation and the claimant's name.

Copyright Term: as a result of the TRIPS minimum, copyright terms are now uniform around the world. Nonetheless the calculation of copyright terms is complex. Typical terms for the EU and U.S. are set forth as follows:

EUROPEAN UNION	
Type of Work	**Term**
Work of a Single Author	Life of the Author + 70 Years
Work of Joint Authorship (Multiple Authors)	Life of the Longest Lived Author + 70 Years
Pseudonymous work where real identity of the author is known or identifiable	Life of the Author + 70 Years
Pseudonymous work where author is genuinely anonymous	70 years after first publication
Collective Works—where contributors are not identified in published version	70 years after first publication
Joint works vested in a legal person (e.g., a company) where contributors are not identified in published version.	70 years after first publication
Segregable elements of a collective work	Life of each Author + 70 Years
Work published in episodes, installments, volumes or parts	Separate terms in accordance with the above rules, i.e., each installment, volume, or part is treated as distinct work for copyright purposes.
Unpublished works with term not calculated according to life of an author or authors	70 years from date of creation
Cinematographic or Audiovisual Works	Life of the last living of: (a) principle director; (b) author of the screenplay; (c) author of the dialogue; or (d) author of musical score
Performers	50 years after first performance—except that if it is first performed for the public during this period, 50 years from such public performance
Phonograms, sound recordings	50 years after first recording—except that if it is published during this period, 50 years from such publication
Films (producer rights)	50 years after fixing of the film; except that if it is published during this period, 50 years from such publication
Broadcasts	50 years from first public transmission

| Scientific Publications | Member states may protect such works that have entered the public domain for 30 years |
| Computer Generated Works | 50 years from date of first compilation (Europe) |

All European Terms are calculated from the January 1 date following the event that otherwise triggers the start of the term, e.g., if an author dies in June 2006, the copyright term is 70 years from January 1, 2007.

UNITED STATES	
TYPE OF WORK	**TERM**
Unpublished works—Single Author	Life of the Author + 70 Years
Unpublished works—Multiple Authors	Life of the Longest Lived Author + 70 Years
Unpublished anonymous and pseudonymous works, and works made for hire (corporate authorship)—except where author is identified to copyright office	120 Years from Date of Creation
Unpublished works when the death date of the author is not known	120 Years from Date of Creation
Published Works of a Single Author	Life of the Author + 70 Years
Published Works of Multiple Authors	Life of the Longest Lived Author + 70 Years
Original Designs	10 years from publication or first availability to the public

U.S. terms expire on December 31st of the year in which they are calculated to expire, e.g., if an author dies in January 2006, the copyright will expire on December 31st 2076.

Copyright Term Extensions: the TRIPS standardized copyright terms in all WTO member states to life plus seventy years, with other terms for collective works, etc. This presented a number of problems in those countries, which hitherto fore had provided for shorter terms, typically life plus fifty years but sometimes much less (Beatles recordings in Japan dating from the 1960s, for example, had by the 1990s started to fall into the public domain), in particular:

- How to deal with works that would still be subject to copyright under the new term, but which had entered the public domain due to the expiry of the old copyright term?

- Where copyright had been transferred in whole or in part to third parties, who were entitled to own the term extension, the original performer(s), artist(s), composer or author, or the transferee?

Most jurisdictions provided for copyright to be restored (in most cases it would be a short term) and for the original artist, composer, or author (or more usually their estate) to own that term extension.

Copyright Trap: fictitious features included in maps or reference works such as encyclopedias, designed to catch infringers who assert that the origin of, for example the map, is their own work.

Copyright Tribunal: a unit within the U.K.'s copyright office whose main function of the Tribunal is to set, when parties cannot agree, terms and conditions of licenses offered by performing rights societies with respect to copyright and neighboring rights. Its decisions can only be appealed to the English High Court and Scottish Court of Session on points of law. Anyone who has unreasonably been refused a license by a performing rights or collecting society or considers the terms on offer to be unreasonable may refer the issue to the Tribunal. The Tribunal also has the power to decide some matters referred to it by the Secretary of State, for example, disputes over the royalties payable by publishers of television program listings to broadcasting companies.

Core License: software license that is technically tied to a processor core, for example on a server, PC, or other computer. There are occasionally problems with such licenses when multi-core processors are used and the increasing presence of such devices in powerful computers and servers has required changes to the license model.

Cost-Plus, Cost-Plus-Contract: refers to a contract for the supply of goods or services where a supplier is paid the cost of the goods or services plus an amount of overhead and profit. Cost-plus contracts are simple in principle and reduce supplier risk substantially, but they also reduce the benefit to the supplier of keeping costs down. A bonus mechanism for delivery on or below cost is therefore usually wise, which should be arranged in such a way that delivery at or below projected cost (on time and to quality standards) is more profitable than a cost overrun. Cost-plus-contracts are frequently used by governments and are highly criticized in this context.

Costs-Follow-the-Event: *See* Indemnity Principle.

Costs, Legal: in most of the world, legal costs means all the costs associated with taking a course of action, so that in most countries an award of legal costs at the end of litigation means all expenses *plus* legal fees. In the United States legal costs (or "taxable costs") means a limited list of expenses associated with a case, such as filing fees, discovery expenses and other items. U.S. legal costs vary, but are typically between 5 percent and 15 percent of the cost of a case, i.e., a non-trivial sum, but not full recompense either. *See* Attorneys' Fees, Indemnity Principle, English Rule.

Counterclaim: a claim by a defendant for damages against a plaintiff, for example, where a defendant in a patent suit counterclaims that the plaintiff is also infringing the defendant's patents.

Counterfeit: used to refer to infringing products bearing an exact copy of a trademark and sold as if they come from the manufacturer, i.e., an infringing product, good or service that uses the trademark. By contrast, a product can use a logo that is confusingly similar, but not a copy: consider the difference between $25 watches sold in Itewan, Korea bearing the logo "LOLEX" or bearing the logo "ROLEX®," the first may infringe Rolex's mark on grounds of confusing similarity, the second is an infringing counterfeit. In many jurisdictions, sale and supply of counterfeits is a criminal offence.

Countervailing Duties: duties imposed by a country on imports to offset subsidies on such products in their country of origin.

Covenant, Contractual: a promise in a contract to do something or to refrain from doing something.

Cow/Calf Analogy: *"Le gach bain a bainin, le gach leabhar a leabhrán,"* (Gaelic, translation: *"to every cow its calf, to every book its copy,"* also reported as *"le gach bó a gamhain (a boithre) agus le gach leabhar a mhacasamhail."*) Refers to what is sometimes described as the first copyright case. In the 6th century, the monk who was to become Saint Columcille (pronounced Kuhlum-kill) was an enthusiastic copyist, transcribing every book he had access to—which was significant, since many such books were regarded as providing great mystic power that was also present in their copies. He was so notorious that the Abbott of one monastery dug a hole in his orchard in which to hide his books when Columcille visited. One night Columcille stole into the monastery of his former master, Finnian and copied a rare book of psalms. The incensed Finnian brought suit under the Brehon laws to the High King of Ireland, Diarmuid Mac Cearbhaill, who, analogizing from the legal rules applicable to livestock, ruled against Columcille with the phrase. Columcille refused to accept the judgment and later reclaimed the book in a battle in 561 at Cúl Dreimne (Drumcliffe) in Sligo, but not before an asserted 3,000 lost their lives in the fighting. Two years later he would leave Ireland for good, banished by the church Synod and consumed with guilt for the deaths his pride had caused. The book he created, known as the "Cathach," was said to grant the possessor victory in battle if carried thrice around the battlefield. As penance for his sins, Columcille was required to convert 3,000 pagans, and thus rose to sainthood by converting the Picts and Saxons and, in self-imposed exile establishing a monastery on the island of Iona.

CPT: Incoterm meaning "carriage paid to [named destination]" i.e., the seller delivers the goods to the carrier named by the seller and the cost of delivery to the named destination. Risk of loss passes to the buyer once the goods are delivered to the carrier.

Cram Down: the massive dilution of the shareholdings of investors who participated in the early capital rounds of a company as a result of a rights issue, which they chose not to participate in, down round, or because of uplift provisions negotiated by later venture capital investors.

Crandall('s) Call: Bob Crandall, the CEO of American Airlines placed a telephone call to Robert Putnam the CEO of Braniff Airlines on February 1, 1982. Unfortunately for Crandall, Putnam recorded the call, which was memorably laced throughout, on Crandall's part, with remarkably profane and indeed blasphemous language. Stripped of most of the foul language, the core statement in the call was: "Raise your [expletive deleted] fares 20 percent. I'll raise mine the next morning. You'll make more money, and I will too."

Putnam subsequently turned over the tape to the United States Justice Department, who sued American Airlines under Section 2 of the Sherman Act. The suit was dismissed on grounds that, though Crandall might have "solicited" Putnam to raise prices, this did not constitute an "attempt" to raise prices under Section 2 of the Sherman Act; the United States Court of Appeals for the Fifth Circuit vacated the lower court's dismissal (743 F.2d 1114 (1984)), but on appeal to the Supreme Court the case against American was dismissed without comment (474 U.S. 1001 (1985)). It is reasonable to suggest that Mr. Crandall was lucky indeed not to have been convicted. However, Crandall's very colorful call has lived on in antitrust compliance programs around the world as an example of what not to say to a competitor, especially in a CEO-to-CEO conversation. The tape also would also constantly "come up" in competition and antitrust matters involving American Airlines, and so came to haunt Crandall.

Cross License: an agreement between two intellectual property holders, typically of patents, to license one another to use their IP. Frequently cross licenses contain a "balancing fee" where the holder of the stronger IP receives a net royalty. Cross Licenses are frequently negotiated to resolve problems related to blocking patents as well as parallel patents obtained by different entities in the United States, and the rest of the world because one was the first-to-invent [q.v.] and the other the first-to-file [q.v.]. *See* Patent Pool.

Cross-Licensing Campaign: cross licenses tend to be agreed in cycles of about three to six years, often after the dominant player in the cross-licensing deals (typically a holder of a large patent portfolio) has won or brought a major piece of litigation, typically against industry players in a particular region or sector, e.g., Europe or Asia. As a result, the sector falls into a cyclical pattern of cross-licensing campaigns. Sometimes, in certain industries, the balance of innovation shifts heavily between one campaign cycle and the next, with the result that a strong player in an early campaign may live to regret the emphatic arguments made earlier about patent value, when they are subsequently directed back at that player.

Cumulative Royalties: a term that denotes the net effect of adding and subtracting the royalties owed to each other by cross-licensees, usually resulting in a balancing fee [q.v.].

Currency Peg: in international trade, a currency peg usually means a decision by a country to tie the value of its currency to that of a major country such as the U.S. dollar (a single currency peg) or to a basket of currencies (a composite currency peg). In contracts, it is a clause that sets a fixed exchange rate. Currency pegs are often used where contracts are priced in a currency different from the currency in which one of the parties to an agreement conducts most, or a substantial part of its business. They are especially useful where one party in fulfilling its obligations may be incurring substantial liabilities in a currency other than the currency of the contract, but in long-term agreements they can cause substantial risks. A rolling currency peg may also be used, where the exchange rate is determined periodically (or the average over a period is taken) and fixed until the next measurement—such provisions are useful for planning purposes but may still be risky when exchange rates are volatile.

CVQ, CV [writer] Quotient: a key measure of whether employees are still "drinking the Kool-Aid®," i.e., whether they still believe in management or in the business plan, or their future employment prospects in the company, is the number or proportion of employees who can be observed to be working on their *curriculum vitæ* (résumé) and the relative brazenness of this activity (i.e., do they bother to switch screens when more senior employees pass by). Also known as RWA, i.e., "résumé writing activity."

D

Damages: financial compensation awarded to a complaining party for a breach by the defendant of its legal obligations to the complainant. Where an intellectual property right has been infringed, the holder of that right or in certain circumstances its licensees are entitled to pecuniary damages. Damages may be calculated in various ways, usually described as "heads" of damages, some of which are cumulative (i.e., the damages for various heads can be added together) and some of which are exclusive or in the alternative (i.e., receiving damages under one head excludes the possibility of receiving damages under another specific head, or perhaps under all other heads). In the case of heads of damages that are exclusive, some procedural systems may require a plaintiff to opt for a form of damages at the outset of the case or before trial, rather than seeking heads of damages in the alternative.

In the general case, damages are designed to place the intellectual property owner (or perhaps the licensee) in the position that it would have enjoyed, had the infringement not taken place. Under such an analysis, that the infringing activity was not profitable, or that it was not as profitable as the IP owner's use of the IP, does not reduce the infringer's liability (e.g., the infringer could be a double loser, both commercially and in damages). One common basis for damages is that they should be not less than a reasonable royalty, i.e., the royalty the infringer would have had to pay in order to obtain a license. However, where damages can be shown to exceed a reasonable royalty, the higher sum would usually be paid.

In addition, in some jurisdictions, particularly with respect to trademarks and copyrights, profit disgorgement by the infringer may be required (in the event that profits exceeded other measures of damages) on the basis that a wrongdoer should never be allowed to profit from its wrong. Substantial heads for damages may include: lost sales; price erosion (which may result in massive damages if it is shown to be permanent); convoyed sales; and assorted market damages. Many systems provide for statutory damages [q.v.], which may substantially exceed the actual damages traceable to each act of infringement. Other jurisdictions also allow enhanced damages [q.v.], or exemplary damages [q.v.], though not typically the U.K. *See Georgia-Pacific Factors.*

Dark Fiber, Dark Swap: during the late 1990s telecom boom, very large amounts of optical fiber were laid in Europe, Asia, and the U.S. However, at the same time new multiplexing techniques increased the amount of data that could be passed through optical fiber at least 20-fold. As a result, a large amount of the optical fiber laid was never used, i.e., it never illuminated by lasers and remained "dark fiber." A "dark swap" was an accounting fraud carried out by telecom companies that had large quantities of such dark fiber, which worked by selling rights to use such dark fiber to another telecom company, and then in a back-to-back transaction, buying similar rights to use the other telecom's dark fiber; neither telecom usually needed the dark fiber capacity. Instead, they could book the sale as revenue and the purchase as capital investment (CapEx), thus flattering the balance sheet and avoiding a "write-down" of the asset value of the dark fiber. The term "dark swap" has come to describe as a generic class of accounting frauds where companies sell similar non-performing assets to one another in back-to-back transactions, booking the deal as revenue and capital investment, regardless of whether they involve optical fiber or telecom assets.

Database Rights: a new *sui generis* (i.e., unique) form of IP. In 1996 the EU adopted a Database Directive (European Data Directive 96/9/EC of the European Parliament and of the Council of March 11, 1996, 1996 OJ L77/20). This provides that database creators and owners have intellectual property rights in their databases, which endures for 15 years, but can be refreshed by substantially updating the database. Usually authors hold copyright in the contents of a database to the extent that such contents can be owned, while the database makers (i.e., those who created or compiled the database) own the Database. The Database Right is the right to prevent the "extraction" or "reutilization" of substantial parts of the database. Other major economies, in particular the United States, have not yet created such a right, but it is uncertain when and how many will do so. One important provision of the Database Directive is that it applies only to companies based in the European Union and EU citizens. For protection to extend to non-EU parties, their government must conclude an agreement with the EU that in principle would likely require that the government enact equivalent legislation providing corresponding and reciprocal protection for EU citizens. The Database Directive has been implemented by means of legislation in each EU member state.

Data Mining: the process of analyzing accumulated data, particularly data accumulated by a business for commercially useful or valuable information.

Data Protection: the European Union, through the medium of the Data Protection Directive (Directive 95/46/EC of the European Parliament and of the Council of 24 October 1995 on the protection of individuals with regard to the processing of personal data and on the free movement of such data, 1995 OJ L 281/31), has enacted strong legal protection for individuals with respect to their personal data as gathered by third parties such as companies; other countries have followed suit, although not the United States. Companies gathering data on individuals based in countries with such data protection laws typically must implement various measures to protect against misuse of the data. In addition, export of personal data to countries without such protection, absent the consent of the individual to whom the data relates, is usually prohibited. Other countries around the world are enacting similar data protection laws and companies that store substantial amounts of data on individuals should be careful to track such developments. The EU has approved a set of standard contractual clauses, which, if used in transfers of data to non-EU countries, should protect the transferor. *See variously,* Commission Decision 2001/497/EC of June 15, 2001 on standard contractual clauses for the transfer of personal data to third countries under Directive 95/46/EC, 2001 OJ L 181/19; Commission Decision 2004/915/EC of 27 December 2004 amending Decision 2001/497/EC as regards the introduction of an alternative set of standard contractual clauses for the transfer of personal data to third countries, 2004 OJ L 385/74. There are "Safe Harbor Privacy Principles" issued by the United States Department of Commerce under an arrangement with the EU, which allows data exchanges with U.S. entities who agree to abide by them.

Dawn Raid: slang for a surprise onsite inspection by European Competition authorities. Such inspections are usually conducted as part of an investigation and are often coordinated at several sites and companies, typically occurring at the open of business (hence dawn raid) with a view to locating incriminating evidence.

DDP, DDU: Incoterms meaning "delivered duty paid [to named destination]" and "delivered duty unpaid [to named destination]." In each case the seller is responsible for freight and risk of loss only transfers at the point of delivery.

Deal-*itis*: coined word use to describe the effect of negotiators becoming overly psychologically (or politically) committed to the transaction they are negotiating, such that they lose perspective and the ability to stop pursuing what on its face looks likely to be a bad deal for the party they represent. Establishing a clear business case [q.v.] before entering negotiations may help to resist this problem.

Death by PowerPoint®: business school term for presentations that are short on facts and substantive detail, but are made in a glossy fashion using a large number of Microsoft PowerPoint slides, and drone on and on, through slide after slide. PowerPoint's overuse in organizations is frequently criticized, in part because PowerPoint is, in principle, a selling tool that allows users to gloss over key facts and is often alleged to be overly persuasive. Its overuse was, for example, held to have been part of the internal NASA procedural failures that resulted in the loss of the Space Shuttle Columbia. *See, Columbia Accident Investigation Board: Final Report*, 2003, Vol. 1 at pages 182 and 191. *See also, PowerPoint is Evil: Power Corrupts. PowerPoint Corrupts Absolutely*, Wired Magazine, September 11, 2003.

Declaration: literally, a formal legal statement of a fact or facts. In many patent systems inventors are required to make declarations attesting to key facts about their inventorship.

Declaratory Judgment (DJ Action): a case taken in which the plaintiff is seeking from the court a declaration that the plaintiff is not liable to the defendant. A DJ action is best described as "a lawsuit in reverse," where the putative defendant sues the putative plaintiff rather than waiting, in uncertainty, for a case to be filed. Usually to bring a declaratory judgment case the plaintiff has to show reasonable grounds to believe that the defendant may make a claim against the plaintiff. This is usually achieved by showing that warning letters have been sent to the plaintiff or the plaintiff's customers, or that other threats of litigation have been made.

Declaratory judgment cases are common in patent infringement litigation, where they can convey considerable advantages on the purported infringer. Indeed, some statistical studies have shown that, in the United States all things being equal, an alleged infringer may be twice as likely to win a declaratory judgment as an ordinary infringement case. Among the advantages a DJ gives the accused infringer is the ability to choose the court in which the case is filed, because the *lis pendens* rule [q.v.] will usually preclude the same issues being heard by a second court. Because perceived jury bias and local or anti-foreigner chauvinism in the United States varies on a court-by-court basis, as does time to trial, and because of procedural differences in different European court systems, this choice may result in a considerable advantage. Moreover, bringing a DJ case presents an image of forthright confidence and innocence on the part of the alleged infringer, which presents a more positive image to a jury or judge, than that of a reluctant defendant, haled as an alleged miscreant into court. Declaratory Judgment in the United States is generally only available in patent cases because of the so-called "case or controversy" requirement in the U.S. constitution limiting the courts to hearing actual as opposed to hypothetical disputes. *See* Warning Letter, Italian Torpedo, Forum Shopping.

Decompiling: the process of converting object code into a high level programming language similar to the original source code, so that the manner in which the software works and its API's and data transfer protocols can be determined. Although some major software houses have sought to make decompiling [q.v.] a violation of license terms or a form of copyright infringement, their efforts have been largely unsuccessful. As a technical legal matter, decompiling involves making a derivative work of the object code, which is, in principle, a copy—this is referred to as "intermediate copying." The legality of decompiling in Europe is protected in narrow and specific circumstances under Article 6 of the European Software Directive, which provides:

(a)   **Article 6 Decompilation**

1. The authorization of the rightholder shall not be required where reproduction of the code and translation of its form within the meaning of Article 4 (a) and (b) are indispensable to obtain the information necessary to achieve the interoperability of an independently created computer program with other programs, provided that the following conditions are met:

> (a) these acts are performed by the licensee or by another person having a right to use a copy of a program, or on their behalf by a person authorized to do so;
> (b) the information necessary to achieve interoperability has not previously been readily available to the persons referred to in subparagraph (a); and
> (c) these acts are confined to the parts of the original program, which are necessary to achieve interoperability.

2. The provisions of paragraph 1 shall not permit the information obtained through its application:

> (a) to be used for goals other than to achieve the interoperability of the independently created computer program;
> (b) to be given to others, except when necessary for the interoperability of the independently created computer program; or
> (c) to be used for the development, production, or marketing of a computer program substantially similar in its expression, or for any other act that infringes copyright.

3. In accordance with the provisions of the Berne Convention for the protection of Literary and Artistic Works, the provisions of this Article may not be interpreted in such a way as to allow its application to be used in a manner that unreasonably prejudices the right holder's legitimate interests or conflicts with a normal exploitation of the computer program.

Decompiling has also been the subject of a decision of the United States Court of Appeals for the Ninth Circuit, which applied the fair use doctrine to further expand the ability of computer software developers to legally make intermediate copies of computer software for the purpose of developing non-infringing products. However, the fair use doctrine might not apply to breach of contract claims where a licensee "covenants" not to decompile.

Trade secret law [q.v.] might also be used to challenge decompiling in certain circumstance. However, a claim of trade secrets in publicly sold software (i.e., off the shelf) has been held to be "completely frivolous" in the U.S., although such a claim has been upheld in software sold or licensed privately.

Dedication to the Public: refers to the process by which the party that would otherwise own an intellectual property right makes it freely available to the public to use without charging a royalty or other fee. Usually refers to copyrighted items on which rights arise automatically on creation and not to patented products. (If you were going to give it away, why spend the money on patenting?)

Deep Pockets: term that refers to a defendant with funds sufficient to pay a large judgment. Being recognized as having deep pockets may attract litigation.

Default Judgment: case won by a plaintiff when the defendant failed to mount a defense or ceased to defend. Default judgments entered in the complete absence of the defendant can be difficult to enforce unless the defendant had proper notice of the case and was properly served with process, in a manner satisfactory to the jurisdiction where enforcement is sought. *See* Hague Convention.

De-featuring: removing product features to lower cost or complexity.

Defensive Publication: in instances where a company has decided not to file a patent on technology it has developed, but intends to use, it may choose to publish a description of that technology in order to make it prior art to any subsequent patent applications made by third parties. Thus it is protected against the risk that such a party might obtain a patent covering its products.

Delaware General Corporation Law: Originally enacted in 1898, the DGCL is one of the world's most significant company law statutes. This is because its management-friendly provisions make Delaware by far the most popular state in the U.S. for incorporating a company; indeed more companies in the Fortune 500 are incorporated in the State of Delaware than in any other U.S. state. The DGCL is considered in particular to afford incumbent management more substantial protections against their easy removal by corporate raiders than the law of other states. The provisions and application of the DGCL is frequently at the center of hostile takeovers and other corporate controversies in the United States and worldwide. In recent years, and particularly since the highly publicized corporate scandals involving Enron and other U.S.-based corporations, many politicians and commentators have increasingly called for a federal corporation law, but such efforts have been so far been effectively rebuffed. Most cases involving the DGCL are initially heard before the Delaware Court of Chancery. *See Revlon* Duties.

Delphion: a subscription patent database widely used by intellectual property lawyers.

***De Minimis* Notice**: a notice published by the European Commission (Commission Notice on agreements of minor importance which do not appreciably restrict competition under Article 81(1) of the Treaty establishing the European Community (de minimis), 2001 OJ C 368/13) that establishes a cut-off below which it will usually regard competition issues as not having a large enough effect on intra-community trade to justify an investigation or enforcement action by the European Commission. The notice states that in general, the Commission will not regard otherwise anticompetitive agreements between actual competitors as restricting competition if the combined market share of the competitors is less than 10 percent of the relevant market. The notice should therefore be seen as a semi-formalized statement of the first part of the "Appreciability Test." [q.v.] The limited legal effect of the *de minimis* notice should be carefully understood:

- it only applies to violations of Article 81 (formerly Article 85), but not Article 82 (formerly Article 86, i.e., abuse of a dominant position);

- it is, in principle, not legally binding on the Commission (though it has a substantial evidentiary effect);
- it does not suspend the operation of national competition law;
- it does not limit the private (or civil) law rights of parties, who can still argue in litigation that a provision is illegal and void under Article 81;
- its interpretation is highly dependent on definitions of the relevant market; and
- it has an exception for situations where the cumulative effect of parallel agreements between market participants renders the market uncompetitive.

The origin of the Latin term *de minimis* is the phrase *de minimis non curate rex* i.e., "the king does not care about small (trivial) things."

Demurrer: *See* Motion, to Dismiss, Summary Judgment, Set Aside the Verdict.

Denied Person: Export Controls [q.v.] term. U.S. export control agencies in the Commerce and State Departments publish a list of persons who have violated export control regulations and have been as a result denied export rights from the U.S. or of goods subject to U.S. technology controls. Generally, denied persons are arms dealers or person who have been involved in suspect transactions, though anecdotally, some unfortunate persons have ended up on the denied persons list for relatively unserious offenses. Nonetheless, if a business is involved in an international sale of dual use goods and it is uncertain or suspicious about the receiving party it should at an absolute minimum check the denied persons list, both locally and on the Web site of the United States Department of Commerce Bureau of Industry and Security (export control entities share information). Before doing any further business with a denied person specialist legal advice ***must be sought***. Other similar categories of persons or companies include the Unverified List, the Entity List, the Specially Designated Nationals List, and the Debarred List.

***De Novo* Appeal, Trial, Review**: refers to an appellate review or retrial where all the facts determined by an original court or agency are tried and established again, rather than presumed to be established. *De novo* review usually provides the highest likelihood of reversing a prior ruling. *See* Standard of Review, Appellate.

Dependent Claim: *See* Claims.

Deposition: the process in discovery of taking sworn testimony from a potential witness in a court case, usually recorded in at least a transcript and also frequently on tape. A deposition is considered an extension of the court case and as such, evidence taken at a deposition is usually introducible in court. In the United States, depositions can sometimes be difficult affairs, which has led some wits to describe them as displays of "lawyers behaving badly."

Deposit Requirement: is the requirement that in order to secure certain intellectual property rights, some public deposit of the subject matter of the intellectual property must be made. In the context of copyright, the requirement that copies of works be deposited with copyright libraries (e.g., the National Library, the Library of Congress, etc.) was prevalent before Berne Convention abolished most copyright formalities—many publishers still make such deposits, especially in the United States where they are necessary for Copyright Registration (which increases the remedies available to a copyright holder in infringement cases). Depository requirements also exist with respect to plant patents and where patents are based on the use of micro-organisms, either naturally occurring or man-made, and arise because of the "enablement" requirement in patent laws. The latter deposit requirements are usually fulfilled by placing samples on deposit with an Escrow Agent. Examples of materials subject to such a deposit requirement are antibiotic expressing microbes or cell-lines of hybridomas that express specific antibodies. *See* Budapest Treaty on International Recognition of the Deposit of Microorganisms for the Purposes of Patent Procedure.

De-Proliferate, Brands, a Brand: a term used in two different ways. First, where a company has such a large number of brands that its marketing focus is diffuse, it may choose to drop or "de-proliferate" certain brands. Alternately, it may refer to reducing the number of products sold under a brand in an effort to refocus the brand.

Derivative Suit, Shareholders': the company law of most American states provides that shareholders of a company can bring a suit on the company's behalf, in instances where the company chooses not to. Derivative suits are most often brought against management, directors, or powerful shareholders, seeking damages on behalf of the company and its shareholders. The causes of action for such a suit typically range from ordinary contract claims to claims over self-dealing and insider trading.

Derivative Work: a copyrighted work that is based on another work, but which includes additional creative ideas, for example a screenplay based on a book, a musical arrangement, or a translation of a book. A derivative work infringes the underlying work and so cannot be sold without the permission of the original copyright holder, while the original work's copyright term is unexpired. However, the derivative work is in all other respects a work in its own right, with a copyright term calculated from its date of publication or creation.

Derived Subject Matter: another way of saying that a claimed invention was not invented by the inventor in a patent application, i.e., that it is in fact the invention of another person.

Descriptive: a term used in trademark law to describe marks that are "merely descriptive" of the goods they are attached to, rather than distinctive and distinguishing. A trademark will not normally be issued on a "descriptive mark." An exception arises when the mark describes a fanciful feature of the product, e.g., GoldCard for PCMCIA cards colored gold by the manufacturer. Trademarks can also be granted for descriptive marks provided evidence of public recognition through long use of their distinctive association with the trademark applicant's products or services, known as a secondary meaning [q.v.] or acquired distinctiveness, can be presented.

Design-Around: an approach to dealing with a third party patent by designing the product or process so that it does not infringe. Design-arounds typically look for prosecution history estoppels [q.v.] or approaches that the patent teaches away from [q.v.]. Usually a company that develops a design-around will seek a non-liability opinion from counsel. A patent that cannot be designed around is usually described as an essential patent [q.v.].

Typically, pioneer patents [q.v.] have broad claims and are more difficult to design around while incremental patents [q.v.] have narrower claims and are easier to design around. Many fundamental technological breakthroughs have resulted from efforts to design around, a well-known example being SONY's Trinitron CRT television tube.

Design Directive: the European Design Directive, [1998] O.J. L 289/28 was enacted to provide uniform legal protection for industrial designs in the member states of the EU—member states are required thereby to enact conforming legislation into their domestic law. Protection is granted for an initial period of five years, extendable to twenty-five years. Not all aspects of a design are protected, and in principle the aesthetic/functionality distinction applies. *See* Community Design.

Design-In, Design-Win: describes the process of selection by the manufacturer of an assembly of a non-fungible, non-interchangeable component of the assembly. Early in the process of design, manufacturers of technically complex products will typically need to identify those sub-components that have a broad impact on the overall design; moreover, the supplier of those components may need to engage in some customization of the component, or indeed a complete custom-design. In order to ensure the supply of such sub-components when the supplier is a third-party vendor, and to compensate the vendor for any customization or development work, a contract will usually be agreed to with the component vendor. The decision to use such a component is known as a design-in or sometimes a design-win.

Design Patent: along with and registered designs [q.v.] describes a form of IP protection that fall between patents and copyrights. These rights essentially protect the aesthetic aspects of product design rather than the technical aspects. *See* Hague Agreement Concerning the International Deposit of Industrial Designs. *See* Community Design.

Device: in patent terms the opposite of a process or method. A device claim covers something that usually can have a physical tangible existence.

Device License: a software license that is tied to a particular device, e.g., a particular computer.

DG III, DG IV: *Directorate Generals* are the departments of the European Commission. DGs used to be numbered, thus DG III was the old title of the Enterprise and Industries Directorate, DG IV the Competition Directorate. Although the number-titles have been dropped, out of habit, experienced competition lawyers still often refer to the Competition Directorate as DG IV. The European Patent Board(s) of Appeal are organically part of the Enterprise and Industries Directorate, although a pending restructuring is intended to make them independent of the European Commission.

DGCL: *See* Delaware General Corporation Law.

Dicta, Mere: comments made by a court that are not in reference to an issue that is actually before it, i.e., a point of law it needs to resolve in the case it is actually hearing. Dicta is considered in principle to be of limited precedential value, hence the tendency to describe it as "mere dicta." However, in practice dicta may be very influential: for example dicta from the appellate court with jurisdiction over an instant case will prove persuasive with a judge concerned about being reversed. In addition, some judges are or were notable jurists, with the result that their dicta tend to be taken seriously by other judges, e.g., Richard Posner (U.S. Court of Appeals for the Seventh Circuit); Frank Easterbrook (U.S. Court of Appeals for the Seventh Circuit); Benjamin Cardozo (Associate Justice, U.S. Supreme Court); Oliver Wendell Holmes (Associate Justice, U.S. Supreme Court); Lord Justice Denning (U.K.: Master of the Rolls); Justice Richard Goldstone (Constitutional Court of South Africa).

Differentiation, Doctrine of Claim: a doctrine of U.S. patent law that requires that each patent claim have a different meaning and scope. This means that where two claims, including two independent claims, have interpretations that can be read to cover the same exact thing, those interpretations should be taken that render the claims different from one another.

Digital Certificate: a file that includes the name and e-mail address of the certificate holder, its period of validity, an encryption key usable to verify the holder's digital signature, and the name of the issuer. Most commonly used to facilitate the secure socket layer's (SSL) communications with electronic commerce Web sites.

Digital Millennium Copyright Act (DMCA): U.S. statute (Act of 1998, Pub. L. No. 105-304, 112 Stat. 2860 (Oct. 28, 1998)) intended to render illegal the supply of tools and software designed to circumvent copy-protection and other anti-copyright infringement features (17 USC § 1201 *et seq.*) and raised penalties for Internet-based copyright infringement while limiting ISP liability (17 USC § 512), as well as adding to U.S. law legal protection for boat hull-forms (17 USC § 1301). The DMCA has been held not to preclude reverse engineering.

Digital Rights Management: a broad term for a number of methodologies that permit the vendor of rights to intellectual property supplied in digital form (typically copyrighted material) to control and limit access to licensed users. The best-known form of DRM is content scrambling in broadcasts.

Digital Watermark: *See* Watermark, Digital.

Diluted-to-Death, DtD: slang term for what may happen to an investor in a startup company who buys early round shares, e.g., the A-Round, if heavy dilution occurs in later rounds. Such an investor's shares have been so diluted as to be essentially worthless. *See* Anti-Dilution Clause.

Dilution: two meanings: (a) a basis for claiming injury and damages in trademark cases. Dilution refers to the idea that the commercial impact of a trademark, its connection with a particular product source, the values it is supposed to represent, or its reputation for quality will be damaged or has been damaged by the alleged infringement; (b) a reduction in the proportion of the value of a company represented by existing shares through the issuance of new shares or rights. The latter may be addressed or prohibited by an anti-dilution clause [q.v.].

Directed Shares: *See* Friends and Family Shares/Allocation.

Direct Infringement: refers to infringement of a patent by an infringer selling goods or services that, in-of-themselves, infringe the patent. Contrast with Contributory Infringement, Inducement of Infringement.

Direction Générale Médicaments/Directoraat Generaal Geneesmiddelen: Belgian agency responsible for regulation of medicines.

Directive: perhaps the largest category of European Union legislation is the directive, which instructs member states to enact legal instruments to meet certain objectives, purposes, and parameters. The principle rationale for this process is the differing legal systems of the member states—drafting directly applicable EU law that can be used in every country of the EU is inherently very difficult. However, one well-known phenomenon is the so called "gold plating" of directives by national bureaucracies and legislatures, who use the need to pass implementing legislation as an opportunity to enact much larger, more extensive, complex and wide reaching item of domestic legislation, while placing the blame for the whole on Brussels. From a legal perspective, one can generally argue in court if the national implementing legislation "under-implements" the directive; it is very difficult to protest that it went too far.

Discipline Pricing: form of predatory pricing where the strongest player in the market cuts prices to an uneconomic level to impose price discipline by other competitors, punish perceived threats to its position, or encourage the formation of a cartel. If discipline pricing is considered "predatory" it may be illegal under applicable competition law, or if it involves import/export trade may be dumping.

Disclaimer: something that gives up a right or potential right. In the context of intellectual property, means the right-holder giving up rights they otherwise could have asserted, which could be some or all of the rights associated with the intellectual property, or some of the term of the IP.

Disclosure: in the context of patents refers to the disclosure of the invention. Patents are sometimes described as a bargain with the public, under which the inventor discloses his or her invention in return for the time-limited exclusive rights provided under the patent. *See* Enablement, Continuation-in-Part.

Discovery: the process by which information is sought by parties to a litigation from the other side. Discovery can be limited in many countries, but is extensive in the United States, where documents of all types may be searched for and demanded, including e-mail records, third party subpoenas issued, interrogatories issued, and depositions taken, so long as the activity might lead to evidence usable in court. It is not uncommon for U.S. discovery to result in millions of pages of documents being produced and reviewed, at great expense. The level of discovery granted in the U.S. is controversial, while the limited discovery granted in other jurisdictions is similarly criticized.

Discriminatory Pricing: arises when a supplier or distributor supplies different customers on different price or commercial terms under similar circumstances. Discriminatory pricing can be prohibited under unfair competition laws in certain circumstances. In particular, some countries' unfair competition laws seek to protect small shopkeepers and businesses by seeking to limit the scale of the discounts that larger players can obtain—however, most provisions of this type are generally being abolished as unduly inflationary.

Disintermediation: the process of removing layers in the distribution channel—for example, the Internet has caused disintermediation between airlines and passengers by allowing tickets to be purchased more easily directly from the airline rather than through a travel agent. Disintermediation is also a standard aspect of a maturing technology: as consumers become more familiar with the technology and it becomes easier to use, they are less likely to want to buy the technology from consultants and VARs.

Disruptive Technology: technology that changes fundamental aspects of business or industry, changing the methods of doing business in that industry and potentially changing the competitive position of key players.

Distributor: an entity or individual who sells a principal's product on the distributor's own account. A distributor buys products from the supplier at a discount and resells the products with a mark-up or profit margin. The distributor is therefore liable to the supplier for the value of goods received, unless there is a "sale or return" provision in the distribution agreement. By contrast, an agent sells on the supplier's account the goods or services, i.e., the agent never takes title to the goods and contracts of sale are between the supplier and the customer with the agent usually being paid a commission. Although distributors and agents are in principle different legal "animals," in practice, agency and distribution agreements often create hybrid creatures that are difficult to categorize the parties as either. It is usually wise to ensure that such agreements explicitly define which type of relationship exists. Even where the status of the distributor or agent is stated in the contract, courts may consider the facts of the relationship as opposed to the description, applying a duck test [q.v.]. It is also the case that relationships may overtime have evolved from an agency to a distributorship or *vice-versa*. *See* VAR, Agency Directive, Agent, Belgian Distributor Rights, Franchise.

Diversifying, Diversitative Merger: a merger by which the combining companies each add new lines of business. Various justifications are for example the benefits of being in markets with different business cycles. Also described as a conglomerate merger. Contrast with a consolidative merger, complimentary merger and expansive mergers.

Divisional Applications: arise when a patent application discloses two or more distinct inventions. In such a situation, the patent office can require, or the applicant can decide, that the application should be divided into one application per invention. The additional applications are called Divisional Applications or simply Divisionals. *See* Omnibus Disclosure, Provisional Application.

DJ-Action: *See* Declaratory Judgement.

DMCA: abbreviation for Digital Millennium Copyright Act.

Dollar One: entertainment industry jargon that denotes money "taken across the counter," i.e., the money moviegoers pay to see a film or show, the fees paid by a TV broadcaster to show a movie, etc. before the funds have passed through any other companies' hands (each of whom may take a commission). Identifying dollar one as the basis for participation [q.v.] is a key issue in entertainment industry deals, since the amount of money left shrinks with each successive "pass of the cash." *See* Gross Participation, Net Participation.

Domain Name: the full name of a system or Internet domain including its local hostname and its domain name and a top-level domain ("TLD") such as .com, .uk, .org, etc. Domain names have become a valuable IP asset of companies, particularly those bearing certain TLDs such as **.com**.

Dominant Position: a Competition Law term that refers to companies whose market position is so strong that they can essentially dictate the terms of competition to other customers and market participants. Under EU law, abuse of dominant position is prohibited by Article 82 of the Treaty of Rome and a "firm" is in a dominant position if it has the ability to behave independently of its competitors, customers, suppliers, i.e., it can do what it likes and force other market participants to accept its decisions. However, what actually constitutes a dominant position is a subject of intense debate and litigation, since it depends on what is defined as the relevant market [q.v.]. In general, worldwide, dominant positions have not been found where the accused business has a less than 40 percent market share. Businesses can be dominant in one area of activity, but non-dominant in others. Having a dominant position as such is not prohibited, *abuse* of that position is. However, since only a dominant firm can abuse a dominant position, being dominant brings into consideration a host of new legal considerations. A key factor in merger regulation is that mergers will usually not be allowed where they would tend to create or reinforce a dominant position. Control of essential facilities [q.v.] is typically held to confer a dominant position.

Donnelly Act: New York General Business Law § 340[6]. *See* Little Sherman Act.

Don't Buy the Same Horse Twice: negotiating aphorism, which urges a negotiator to ensure that one concession is definitely traded for another, rather than the possibility of another. Certain negotiating cultures are expert at appearing to present concession (a) to trade with a counterparty for concession (b), but obtaining (b) without actually surrendering (a). As a result, concession (a) can then be used again to trade for concessions (c), (d) etc. Alternately, where renegotiation of an agreement is sought, there may be a risk of simply re-buying the "horse." Tactically this is often achieved by salami slicing [q.v.] or deploying the "blame God" strategy [q.v.].

Don't Drink the Kool-Aid: macabre aphorism that admonishes the listener to be careful about believing in nonsensical business plans, "spin," marketing "hype" or internal marketing, particularly that originating from within their own organization or from associates or partners. The phrase refers to the 1978 mass suicide and massacre of members of a cult led by a Rev. Jim Jones in Jonestown, Guyana. The members of the People's Temple committed suicide by allegedly drinking cups of the fruit-flavored beverage Kool-Aid®, that had been laced with cyanide, though it has been suggested (perhaps by public relations for Kool-Aid?) that a competing product, Flav-R-Aid®, was in fact the beverage in question.

Double Patenting: a situation that arises where a patent applicant files two patents whose claims would cover the same invention. This particularly can occur with Continuations-in-Part and in the U.S. is usually resolved by filing a Terminal Disclaimer giving up any excess term the second patent would enjoy over the first. In all other instances, it would usually lead to invalidity of the second patent.

Double Taxation Agreement: *See* Tax Treaty.

Down Round: issue of shares in a company at a lower subscription price per share than earlier rounds. *See* Anti-Dilution Clause, Dilution.

Drive-By VC: slang term for a venture capitalist, who contributes some funds to a startup business, but no advice or other assistance.

DRM: acronym for Digital Rights Management.

Droit de Suite: *See* Artists' Resale Rights.

Droit Moral: French for moral rights [q.v.]. As moral rights are widely considered a concept of French legal origin, there is a widespread tendency to use the French term when referring to them, particularly in the United States.

Drugs Pipeline: refers to the compounds a company has undergoing the human (or veterinary) trials process for licensing for sale as drugs.

DtD, D-to-D: Acronym for Diluted-to-Death. *See* Anti-Dilution Clause, Dilution, Down Round.

Dual Use: Export Control [q.v.] term referring to goods which have both legitimate civil as well as military, security, policing or weapons uses. Trade in dual use goods is regulated by most industrial countries under various international agreements arrangements including the Australia Group [q.v.], the Nuclear Suppliers Group [q.v.], the Wassenaar Arrangement [q.v.], the Chemical Weapons Convention, and the Zangger Committee [q.v.]. Most major industrialized nations publish lists of dual use goods including the EU Dual Use List (Council Regulation (EC) No. 1334/2000, as last amended by Council Regulation (EC) No. 1504/2004) which is incorporated into the export control use lists of EU member states (for example the UK's Strategic Export Control Lists) or the United States Commodity Control List (the "CCL" [q.v.]).

Duck Test: "if it looks like a duck, walks like a duck and quacks like a duck, it most probably is a duck." Frequently applied United States' legal principle, which elevates substance over form, i.e., suggests, in areas such as tax and company law, that what a situation in fact is, rather than what it is described as, should drive the analysis and application of legal rules.

Due Diligence: originally referred to the level of investigation that professional advisors should, if not negligent, perform on behalf of a purchaser into title and other issues surrounding an asset being acquired. It is now generally taken to refer to examining the files, contracts, licenses, intellectual property, deeds, and other papers and property of a business being acquired to determine if there are any undisclosed liabilities, losses, or risks. A certain amount of cynicism exists about the due diligence process, since it is largely carried out by the most junior lawyers and accountants the acquirer's advisors have (usually under instructions to cause little trouble or disruption); given such persons' lack of authority and experience, how likely are they to find something managers and employees at the target are successfully concealing, often from their own superiors, auditors, and advisors? Moreover, even where substantial problems are found during due diligence, if a merger has been publicly announced, management prestige and company politics, as well as the vested interest of some powerful advisors in completing the deal, often means that only massive problems are enough to stop the transaction.

Dumping: in principle dumping is defined as importing (selling) merchandise into a country below the cost of manufacture (or below fair market value) in its source economy. In practice the methods of accounting used in a dumping investigation (i.e., a case) for establishing the cost of manufacture of the goods in their domestic market are usually heavily skewed in favor of finding dumping. Under international trade rules, if dumping is found to be taking place, the country of import can impose a tariff called a "dumping margin" on the goods to increase their imported value to "fair market value."

Dutch Clause: Article 22 of the EU merger regulation (Council Regulation (EC) No 139/2004 of 20 January 2004 on the control of concentrations between undertakings) that allows EU member states, within 15 days of the notification of a concentration [q.v.] to request the Commission to examine it, even if it does not have a "community dimension" but does affect trade between Member States and may significantly affect competition within the territory of the Member State(s). This provision was sought by the Netherlands (hence "Dutch clause") with the intent of protecting the economies of Member States that did not have a genuine national merger control legislation.

Duty: Two legal meanings: (a) an obligation to act in a particular way in specific circumstances—someone subject to a duty is without choice in the matter; (b) a tax on imports imposed by the country. Import duties are generally based on the value of the product being imported (*ad valorem*), on quantity (specific duties), or a combination of value and other factors (compound duties). They are also known as tariffs.

Duty of Candor: Each individual associated with the filing and prosecution of a patent application in the United States Patent Office has, under Rule 56 of the Rules of Practice of the USPTO, a duty of "candor and good faith" in dealing with the Patent Office, which includes a duty to disclose all information known to be material to patentability, including information that might detract from patentability. Failure to do so is at least inequitable conduct, but can rise to the level of "fraud on the patent office." Disclosures should include information and publications that might tend to undermine arguments made by the applicant in favor of patentability as well as art cited by non-U.S. patent offices in related applications.

E

E-Reference: a classification for prior art references established by WIPO in Standard ST. 14 for patent search report. An E reference is an earlier document published on or after the international filing date. *See* A-Reference, Y-Reference, X-Reference, and P-Reference.

EAR: *See* Export Administration Regulations.

Early-Adopters/Adaptors: a term often used to describe those who are prone to using a new technology before it is popularized. Considerable marketing effort is made to identify likely early adopters/adapters for a technology and market a given new product directly to them. The term comes from a classification of five categories of buyers for new technology developed by the American Management Association in the 1980s:

(1) **Innovators**, a very small group, typically adventurous technophiles, often technologists themselves they read journals and magazines in their area of interest and will purchase new products before they are proven or accepted. They are somewhat influential with other buyers in their group, but typically represent only 2 percent or so of the target market;

(2) **Early Adopters/Adaptors**, generally broad opinion leaders and influencers, they will adopt a product, or adapt to a change (product or method), if they believe it works and may enhance their lifestyle or business efficiency and usually represent about 15 percent of the target market;

(3) **Early Majority**, who are pragmatic adopters of technology, who only start to buy once their peers and role models have created a comfort factor by buying first, typically form about 39 percent of a target market;

(4) **Late Majority**, who typically wait until the product is a universally accepted solution and prices have dropped, indeed they may wait until the innovators and early adaptors have moved on to new product generations, price driven and dependent on mass media for an impetus to buy, will usually represent about another 39 percent of the target market;

(5) **Laggards**, who only buy when shunning the technology is no longer a viable option, perhaps because the early solution is no longer available, typically represent about 5 percent of the market.

Earn-Out: term used to describe payment after the sale of a business or other income-generating asset (e.g., an assignment of IP) of a proportion of profits or turnover (gross or net earnings) or a fixed sum to be derived from the post-sale profits or turnover. Usually the vendor retains title or a recorded security interest until the earn-out is complete. From the perspective of a purchaser, the use of an earn-out clause: (a) allows it to avoid paying the full capital sum up-front; (b) encourages the vendor to ensure that the business is transferred in the most optimal way, preserving customer goodwill; and (c) can protect against overvaluation of the business, since part of the price depends on the ability of the business to generate the earn-out. From the perspective of the vendor, an earn-out clause means that payment is not made upfront so there is no clean break and usually at least part of the purchase price is uncertain; however, it can maximize price, and where a business has substantial growth prospects, allows the vendor to retain some of the post-sale upside. The main difficulty with earn-out clauses lies in specifying what specific actions, activities or events, as well as their timing, entitle the seller to the post-sale payments and quantifying the amount of such payments. In addition, in some instances the buyer may find the seller's ongoing assistance unnecessary to realize value and seek to frustrate the seller's efforts to fulfill its obligations under the earn-out provision in an effort to avoid payment.

Easter Bunny: Nasty surprise or joke embedded and hidden in software code. The original was allegedly a rabbit or "bunny," embedded in a game and timed to appear at Easter, performing an obscene act of self-indulgence. Now used as a generic term for embedded software "bombs"— a big risk when dealing with companies with poor employee relations or where the programmer is about to leave, be laid off or is made redundant. A key problem with an Easter Bunny is that it may not appear until the product is already on sale and puzzled children are asking, to their parents' consternation, "Who is the rabbit and *WHAT IS HE DOING?!!!*"

Economically Vital Improvements/Patents: improvements to a product that, although not technically essential for it to work, are almost impossible to sell the product without, i.e., a feature without which the product is not commercially viable because most customers will require it. *See* USP.

Economic Espionage Act of 1996: United States law, 18 U.S.C. §§ 1831-39 that criminalizes trade secret theft. The statute has one particularly controversial feature in that it establishes two offenses, under §1831 theft of trade secrets to benefit a foreign, i.e., non-US entity and under §1832 theft of trade secrets in general. Violations of §1831 can attract a fine of $500,000 and/or imprisonment of up to 15 years for an individual while organizations involved may be fined up to $10,000,000. Violations of §1832 attracts lower penalties, $500,000 and/or a prison sentence of up to 10 years, while organizations can be fined up to $5,000,000. Moreover, §1832 imposes a higher standard for conviction in that the defendant must be shown to have: (1) acted with the intent to convert (i.e., take) the trade secret; (2) so as to economically benefit someone other than the owner of the trade secret; and (3) to have done so with the intent or knowledge that the conversion would injure the owner of the trade secret. Finally, perhaps the strongest sanction of the Act is that it also provides that the facilities used by an entity, to commit or facilitate the violation of the Act, may be seized by the U.S. government. The statute has also been criticized as so vague, that it could easily be employed in license disputes, criminalizing what should be treated as civil matters. Moreover, the statute could have a chilling effect on the ability of employees to change jobs, especially as language in early drafts of the act that made an exception to the information covered by the act of "knowledge, experience, training, or skill that a person lawfully acquires during their work as an employee or independent contractor." One key requirement of the Act is that a company asserting that its trade secrets have been taken must have taken reasonable steps to protect that information's secrecy.

Economy Class Effect: describes the adverse effect of cutting the level of travel or standard of accommodation employees are provided with when on business travel. Companies under strain typically respond by seeking to cut costs and a favorite budget to target is travel; such costs are cut by seeking to reduce the amount of travel and lowering travel's cost by using cheap and very basic hotels and requiring employees to fly long haul in economy class rather than business class. The former cuts can damage business relationships directly. Anecdotally, the latter cuts often tend to be counterproductive, as they deter key employees, relationship managers, and sales executives from traveling to meet customers, with a consequent adverse impact on business relationships—a consequence sometimes described as the economy class effect. The consequences are typically even worse if the changes do not apply to senior executives including the CEO, since morale is usually lowered and cynicism raised.

EDGAR: the United States Securities and Exchange Commission's (SEC) **E**lectronic **D**ata **G**athering, **A**nalysis, and **R**etrieval System, a database of corporate filings made by companies whose securities or ADRs [q.v.] are traded on U.S. exchanges.

Edifice Complex: term coined by the lawyer and historian Professor Cyril Northcote Parkinson in *Parkinson's Law: The Pursuit of Progress*, London (John Murray 1958, Houghton Mifflin, 1962) referring to the tendency of successful organizations to build new headquarters just before they begin to decline. *See* New Headquarters/Office Syndrome, Shiny.

EEA: *See* European Economic Area.

Effective Date: a term used in contracts where the agreement is intended to have legal effect on a date different from the date on which it is signed— usually used to back-date the effectiveness of an agreement.

Effects Doctrine: Antitrust and Competition Law principle that holds that where an anti-competitive agreement or activity outside a jurisdiction (i.e., the United States or EU) has an effect inside the jurisdiction, its authorities can take action against extra-territorial offenders and in some instances injured parties can also bring suit. The effects doctrine was broadly deplored outside the United States, where it originated, especially by politicians in Europe, where many countries enacted blocking statutes to limit its impact. However, Europe embraced the effects doctrine in *Gencor Ltd v Commission*, [1999-2] E.C.R.753. Since then a number of ill-advised U.S. politicians have deplored the EU's unprecedented application of the effects doctrine to U.S. companies, seemingly under the impression that it is a uniquely European legal principle, or indeed of European origin, and echoing the horror with which European politicians in the past complained of the U.S. version. The effects doctrine is, for example, used to enable U.S.

authorities to review the merger of two non-U.S. companies, or the EU to review the merger of two U.S.-based companies, where there is substantial competitive impact in the EU or *vice versa*.

EIPR: the European Intellectual Property Review, a leading international intellectual property journal published monthly by Sweet & Maxwell covering issues from all over the world (i.e., not just Europe). Probably the most widely read IP journal among international practitioners and large corporate IP departments.

Electronic Frontier Foundation: U.S.-based lobbying and pressure group, which opposes legal and commercial measures that it believes may constrain freedom on digital networks, including censorship and certain IP rights.

Element, Claim: one of the distinct parts of the invention as set forth in a patent claim. The term is used interchangeably with claim limitations.

Elevator Encounters: *See* Coffee-Pot Effect.

EMEA: two meanings:

(1) European Medicines Evaluation Agency, a coordinating organization for the European national agencies that evaluate medicinal products for human and veterinary use. It was created by the European Commission in 1993 to administer a centralized approval procedure, which is mandatory for biotechnology and optional for other high-technology and innovative pharmaceutical products, and also to arbitrate disputes under decentralized procedures in order to achieve mutual recognition of EU member state's national approvals of medicines;

(2) in marketing and management terms, an acronym for Europe, Middle East, and Africa or alternately Asia.

Employee Rights in Invention, Intellectual Property: *See* Inventor's Bonus.

Enablement: One of the requirements for the grant of a patent in all jurisdictions is that the disclosure in the patent (usually, the specification) must enable persons of ordinary skill in the art to practice the invention, i.e., make the invented device or successfully practice the disclosed method. Failure to enable is grounds for invalidating a patent. *See* Best Mode, Disclosure.

***En Banc* Appeal**: United States Federal Courts of Appeals have, per circuit, a large number of judges appointed to them, usually between eleven and twenty. Not all judges sit on each appeal. Instead a panel of three judges initially hears the case (in a procedure that is usually as-of-right (*See* Appeal-as-of-Right) or relatively automatic). After they rule, the parties may petition for a hearing by the entire court of appeal (or in some very large courts such as the 9th circuit a selection of eleven judges (one the chief judge)), sitting *en banc*. However, such an *en banc* hearing is not automatic. Rather, under the rules of the appellate court, a number of judges, usually just less than a majority of the total number on that appellate court must review the petition and decide that it justifies such a rehearing. For this reason, unanimous rulings of a panel are unlikely to secure an *en banc* rehearing. *Amicus* briefs are often filed in support of petitions for rehearing *en banc*. Such re-hearings are rare. For example, between September 1999 and 2000 the regional federal appeals courts heard 27,516 appeals of which only seventy-three were decided *en banc*. Although *en banc* re-hearings by the United States Court of Appeals for the Federal Circuit are more common, they are still comparatively rare.

End-of-Life Clause, Notice ("EoL"): a supply contract provision that requires a manufacturer to provide a specified notice period to buyers before it terminates manufacture of a product or component, in order to allow those buyers to make suitable alternative arrangements and place final orders.

End-User: the person who will use a technology product sold through a distribution chain; a key term in Export Control law and in certain license agreements.

End-User License Agreement (EULA): a type of license typically used in consumer and desktop business software sold on media (such as disks) with shrink-wrap licenses, only activated by installation on a suitable computer. Such a license is directly from the software house to the user, but is brokered by the software retailer. For example, one might go into a shop and buy a copy of a Microsoft application in a shrink-wrapped box. In this situation the shop is not licensing the Microsoft application, rather in the box or shown on the install-screen is an End-User License Agreement, between the user and Microsoft, to which the user agrees by either: (a) breaking the wrapping; (b) clicking a dialogue box in the course of installation. The shop is therefore in the business of selling intangible goods, i.e., end-user licenses from Microsoft or another software house associated with physical goods, the media carrying the software.

English Clause: clause in an exclusive supply contract that allows the buyer to purchase goods from other suppliers if they offer better terms (i.e., a lower price), usually provided that the buyer first discloses the more favorable terms to the exclusive supplier and allow it an opportunity to match them. English clauses present some difficulties, in that they may require disclosure of information that a bidder regards as confidential; in addition some competition authorities regard them with suspicion since they allow competitors to know about one another's pricing, creating a possibility of competitive coordination.

English Rule: known in common law countries other than the United States as the "indemnity principle," it is the rule that provides that the loser in litigation usually pays the winner's legal fees. In most jurisdictions the rule is mitigated by a "taxing master" who reviews the bill submitted to the losing party for fairness and by provisions that allow a defendant to record or register a pre-trial offer of settlement (sometimes paying the sum into court), which if the plaintiff fails to exceed at trial, may result in legal costs being shifted the plaintiff as a penalty for wastefully pursuing litigation despite the offer. *See* Costs, Attorneys' Fees.

Enhanced Damages: in the United States infringement of intellectual property rights and antitrust laws may expose the infringer to "enhanced damages" where more substantial damages are paid than normal "actual damages." In the case of patents, courts may, if they find willful infringement (i.e., infringement with knowledge of the patent and no good faith reason on the infringer's part to believe that there was no infringement), grant up to three times actual damages based on various factors (three times is not automatic) as well as attorneys' fees. For copyright infringement where the copyrighted work is registered, the ceiling on [q.v.] amounts are substantially increased from $20,000 to $150,000 (per defendant, per work). In trademark infringement a finding that an infringer used a counterfeit mark can result in treble damages. Enhanced damages are often referred to as punitive damages or exemplary damages, although they are not strictly the same, since they are statutory in origin. Although enhanced damages for patent infringement are *up to* three-times proven damages, studies have shown the average enhancement to be about 1.68 in the *minority* of cases in which damages are enhanced. Thus, automatic treble damages exist for certain antitrust and RICO claims, *but not for patent infringement.* See Non-Liability Opinion.

Enterprise License: a software license, which encompasses an entire company's (or a local branch or division's) use of the licensed software. Typically the enterprise license allows the company to load software on individual machines from an IT department server. Fees to be paid may depend either on enterprise size (assuming that all computers have the software loaded, usual for office software), the number of machines that the software is loaded on, or a number of concurrent users that the software can be enabled for. Usually enterprise licenses are both cheaper and are administratively more convenient for the licensee.

Entire Agreement Clause/Provision: *See* Integration Clause.

EPC: the European Patent Convention is the international agreement establishing the European Patent Convention and the European Patent Office.

Epistolary Incontinence: sarcastic term used to describe the excessive use of e-mail for all sorts of communications. It is a source of concern for legal advisors due to the tendency of sufferers to say or confess unwise and potentially incriminating things, which may also be factually inaccurate. Due to the difficulty of removing all copies of an e-mail from backups, local hard drives, etc., such correspondence appears with amusing frequency (provided it's not you or your client who wrote the e-mail) in court cases.

EPO: The European Patent Office—the agency to which applications for European Patents are made. The European Patent Office is a branch of the European Patent Organization.

Equitable, Equity: refers in common law countries to legal rules that originated in what were ecclesiastical (church run) courts, which evolved into courts of chancery and equity, as opposed to courts of law which applied rules established by the state. Such courts applied legal rules that were largely of Roman origin (hence equity's taste for the use of Latin maxims) and which were predicated on principles of fairness and equity. Equity and law have long been merged in most legal systems, but equity remains a distinct component in common law with different rules and principles of application. The law of equity is administered by judges and not juries, thus equitable aspects of a case will usually be reserved from the jury in common law courts.

Equitable Estoppel: an equitable defense in United States patent cases, which precludes enforcement of a patent against an infringer who was aware of the patent but who relied on the prolonged inaction of the patent-holder to conclude that the patent-holder would not enforce the patent and has detrimentally changed his or her position based on that reliance. Equitable estoppel usually has to be proved by the alleged infringer, but after six years of inaction it becomes presumptive and must be disproved by the patent-holder. Equitable estoppel should be compared with the similar defense of *laches*. Equitable estoppel is in principle a different legal concept from collateral estoppel.

Equitable Remedy: refers to the remedies that are equitable in origin and that a judge may impose. The principle equitable remedy in intellectual property cases is an injunction, which prohibits ongoing sales of infringing goods or other infringing activity. Preliminary, interim or interlocutory injunctions can be provided to an intellectual property holder, provided that it can show that it would likely succeed in its case at trial, that it will suffer irreparable harm without one (i.e., harm that money damages will not repair), and that the balance of the hardships weighs heavily on it. Even so, such a preliminary injunction is frequently subject to the posting of a bond.

Equity Mining: *See* Brand (Equity) Mining.

Equivalence, Doctrine of: a U.S. equitable doctrine developed to prevent someone from circumventing a patent by using substitutes for claim elements that have the same effect as the substituted element. If a substituted element performs the same function, in essentially the same way, with the same effect as the claimed element it may be regarded as an equivalent of the element and the claim may be infringed under the doctrine. Something similar to the doctrine of equivalents is, in some form, applied by most patent systems, but most broadly in the United States and in a more limited way in most other systems (where it will usually be referred to by other names). It is also limited by prosecution history estoppel (also known as file wrapper estoppel). Infringement that does not depend on the doctrine of equivalents is known as literal infringement. *See* §112 Equivalence, Reverse Doctrine of Equivalence.

Escalation Clause, Escalation Path: a provision in an agreement, which provides how disputes must or shall be escalated before any litigation can begin. Usually, the path provides for a reference of the dispute to senior managers, then to senior uninvolved managers of the parties, thence to the CEO's of the parties, before initiating suit.

Escalator Clause: a clause in a contract or license that raises the amount to be paid to one party, if certain conditions are met or come to exist, which make the contract or rights conveyed more valuable to the other. Thus, for example, merchandising rights associated with a book or novel might be set at one royalty rate, which would increase if a movie were made. Escalator clauses are most appropriate where the recipient of payment is, to some degree, in control of the condition that would benefit the maker of the payment; they thus act as an incentive for that recipient to help cause the condition to occur. *De*-escalator clauses can also exist, especially where a contract is for a stream of payments (for example, royalties), if some specified event occurs (or fails to occur within a set period), making the contract less valuable to the paying party. *See* Kicker.

Escrow: a deposit of an item by a first party with a third party known as an "Escrow Agent," who is contractually required to turn over the escrowed item to a second party in certain circumstances. Any sort of item within reason can be escrowed, including money, software, data, title deeds, signed but undated assignments, shares, etc. To give a typical example, a company purchasing software may request that a copy of the software source-code be deposited with an Escrow Agent, who has instructions to turn it over to the buyer if the vendor goes bankrupt or defaults on maintenance obligations. In another arrangement, where parties are seeking to settle a dispute in a manner, that requires the second party to do a series of things, and the first party to then pay funds, the first party might escrow the funds subject to the condition that they be paid to the second party when it has completed its side of the settlement; alternately executed documents may be placed with the Escrow agent, to be released to one party or the other in specified circumstances. Escrow arrangements are often used in the United States, particularly in real estate sales.

Espacenet: a free database of patents maintained by the European Patent Office.

Essential Facilities: a doctrine of competition law that relates to a situation where a powerful competitor in a market can control access to a key asset required to compete in that market, such as an API, aircraft slot, distribution channel, etc., conferring on it a dominant position. When a market participant controls an essential facility, it may be compelled to provide access to other competitors on reasonable and non-discriminatory terms. *See*, Competition Law, Compulsory License, Magill.

Essential Patents: patents to which one must have ownership or a license to practice a particular technology. Most pioneer patents, if the claims are properly drafted, will be essential patents; incremental patents may be essential if they cover technically or economically vital improvements. Where two Essential Patents held by different parties preclude the other from using his invention, they are usually referred to as "blocking patents" [q.v.].

Estoppel: equitable legal doctrine that refers to someone being precluded, i.e., estopped, from taking a position inconsistent with past statements, positions, or behavior, including inaction. There is a civil law equivalent of estoppel, derived from Roman law, as stated in the maxim: *non concedit venire contra factum proprium*, i.e., do not allow someone to go against their own facts (statements).

ETSI: European Telecommunications Standards Institute, establishes standards for Information and Communication Technologies (ICT) within Europe, including telecommunications, broadcasting, and related areas such as intelligent transportation and medical electronics.

EULA: *See* End-User License Agreement.

Euro Foreign Exchange Reference Rates: standard daily exchange rates for the world's major trading currencies against the Euro (base currency) as a result a regular daily "concertation" procedure between central banks within and outside the European System of Central Banks, which normally takes place at 2.15 p.m. Central European Time (CET). The reference exchange rates are published both by electronic market information providers and on the ECB's Web site shortly after the concertation procedure has been completed. There are no rates on weekends. If a transaction falls on a Saturday or Sunday for a rate, the following Monday is usually used. These rates are considered the most reliable and fair way of tracking exchange rates, since the procedure is based on many markets and eliminates anomalous rates based on local conditions—moreover a single rate is provided, which eliminates arguments. As a result, the Euro Foreign Exchange Reference Rate is often specified in contracts that require ongoing payments for which currencies must be converted, for example an *ad valorum* (percentage of sales) royalty bearing license, where some sales are for example in Euro, but the payments due in U.S. Dollars. Since the number of decimals used for a rate may vary, it is usual to round the result of any calculation to the number of decimals of the Reference Rate with the largest number of decimals used in the calculation.

European Economic Area: The European Economic Area consists of the European Union and Iceland, Norway and Liechtenstein. Switzerland was to have become a member, but did not ratify the EEA Agreement. The non-EU members of the EEA have undertaken to comply with many of the economic rules with respect to markets of the EU including many intellectual property provisions and effectively to apply EU competition law. In particular, Articles 53 and 54 of the EEA agreement essentially mirror Article 81 and Article 82 of the Treaty of Rome (Amsterdam). The EEA was formerly referred to as the European Free Trade Association

(EFTA, Switzerland is the sole remaining member) and its status is sometimes referred to as External Association with the EU.

Examination, Preliminary, Substantive: the process by which an application for an intellectual property right such as a patent or trademark is considered by the patent or trademark office. There are usually two stages to the process, the preliminary examination where the application is examined to determine whether it is complete and correct, and the substantive examination, which determines as a legal matter whether the intellectual property right should be granted.

Exclusive Distributor: a distributor [q.v.] who, under its distribution agreement, is protected against the appointment of competing distributors. The scope of the exclusivity may vary. Thus it may be territorial exclusivity (most common); but it may also be market exclusivity, i.e., sale rights to sell the product to a certain class of customers, or a combination of the foregoing.

Exclusive License: a license in which the licensor undertakes to the licensee, that it will grant no license of the same rights to any further licensee. There are a number of points that can be misunderstood about exclusivity: first, there may be pre-existing non-exclusive licenses, the exclusivity simply means there will be no more licenses (although failure to disclose the existence of prior licensees may permit the new licensee to seek rescission of the agreement). Second, depending on the terms of the license and applicable contractual law, exclusivity may be limited to the field-of-use of the license or may preclude any further licenses of the intellectual property rights in any field-of-use. To avoid these complications, exclusivity provisions should be carefully drafted and explicit. Usually a well-drafted exclusive license will condition continued exclusivity on minimum sales/royalties as well as activity in each exclusive market. *See* Field-of-Use, Minimum Sales Requirement.

Executory Contract: a contract under which at least one party has obligations that remain to be fulfilled. For example, a license agreement usually provides for the payment of royalties on an ongoing basis, in arrears and is thus an executory contract. Similarly development agreements, until completed, are executory contracts. That a contract is executory has two major implications: (a) revenue recognition under GAAP and IFRS accounting rules is effectively deferred, in whole or in part (depending on the nature of the unfulfilled obligations and the agreement) until the contract conditions are fulfilled; and (b) most bankruptcy systems allow the trustee, receiver, administrator or liquidator of the bankrupt to avoid (i.e., terminate) executory contracts existing as of the time of the bankruptcy. However, most legal systems prohibit the exercise of this right with respect to licensing where the bankrupt is a licensor.

Exemplary Damages: a term for punitive damages. Exemplary damages exceed actual damages and are intended to make an example of the defendant, as a warning to others. Enhanced Damages are in some respects intended to serve the same purpose but are normally provided as part of a statutory scheme. While some legal systems will award exemplary damages, many legal systems have a strong policy bias against them, especially in contract law.

Exemption: under European Law (specifically Article 81 of the Treaties of Rome and Amsterdam [q.v.]) there was a sweeping prohibition of all agreements that might lessen commercial competition. However, Article 81(3) provides that the European Commission can "exempt" from the prohibition, activities which in various ways are economically beneficial and especially those that benefit consumers. *See* Block Exemption.

Exhaustion of Rights: refers to the concept that an intellectual property owner "exhausts" his or her rights with respect to the intellectual property right on first sale. That is to say that once the goods covered by the trademark, patent, or copyright have been sold for the first time with the authority of the right(s) holder, it has no right to seek an additional royalty or further control the use of the goods. There are limitations to the doctrine, which can arise in grey-market imports, if the right holder has limited sales by the first vendor to a particular territory, although such limitations are usually not viable or indeed legal within a single economy, for example the European Union.

Exim Bank: usually refers to the Export Import Bank of the United States, a Federal Government agency that extends loans and export guarantees for sales of U.S. goods and services. Analogous institutions exist in other countries, some also known as Exim Bank, for example the Export Import Banks of India, Malaysia, Thailand, Hungary, Turkey, China, Jamaica, and Korea. The Japanese Equivalent, JExIm has been reorganized and renamed the Japan Bank for International Cooperation (JBIC).

Exit Strategy: venture capital term describing the strategy by which investors will convert their stake in a startup company into a liquid asset, for example, by an IPO [q.v.], or a trade sale [q.v.] for cash or marketable securities.

Expansive Merger: merger justified on the basis that the acquirer can extract more value out of the existing and acquired lines of business under its management and in combination with the merged assets, e.g. by better leveraging combined sales channels. Contrast with diversifying merger, conglomerate merger, complimentary merger, and consolidating merger.

Ex Parte: Latin term widely used by lawyers to denote a legal procedure or proceeding, at which one of the parties to the case is absent. In general, in most legal systems, *ex parte* proceedings in litigation are regarded as anathema and they are only allowed under certain specific circumstances. It is usually required that all *ex parte* communications with a judge, magistrate, or arbitrator be recorded and the recording or transcript made available to the party not present at the earliest opportunity. Contrast with *Inter Partes*.

***Ex Parte* Re-examination**: refers to a patent office proceeding to re-examine the grant of a patent, usually in light of prior art not before the patent office in the original examination. In the particular case of an *ex parte* re-examination, only the patent holder appears and makes arguments to the patent office, which obviously confers considerable advantages. All U.S. re-examinations used to be conducted on an *ex parte* basis, but recent legal changes provide for *inter partes* re-examinations where third parties, for example competitors, are allowed to be present and argue against the re-grant of the patent or for more limited claims. *See Inter Partes* Re-Examination.

Export Administration Regulations: U.S. export control [q.v.] governing the export of dual use goods and certain other categories of goods and (technical information), such as police (crime control) equipment, tools for espionage and encryption and items perceived to be potentially useful to terrorists. The EAR is administered by the United States Department of Commerce, Bureau of Industry and Security (BIS). Among the classes of goods falling under the EAR are nuclear materials, facilities and equipment, certain chemicals, microorganisms and toxins, certain equipment for materials processing, various electronic items, very fast or powerful computers (though this category is problematic as infrequent adjustment of power levels has resulted in the regulation applying over time to fairly ordinary machines), telecommunications and information security (i.e., encryption and anti-eavesdropping), sensors and lasers, navigation equipment and avionics, certain marine equipment, propulsion systems, and space vehicles, and satellite technology. The goods and information covered by the EAR are set forth in the Commerce Control List ("CCL") which identifies controlled goods with an Export Control Classification Number ("ECCN"). Weaponry and military equipment is governed by a different set of regulation known as ITAR (International Traffic in Arms Regulations) administered by the United States Department of State (the "State Department.")

Export Controls: refers to laws designed to control exports of sensitive technologies such as weapons systems, espionage equipment (and equipment useful to prevent espionage) and dual use [q.v.] goods, i.e., goods that have peaceful and weapons manufacturing purposes. Dual use goods are regarded as particularly sensitive when they can be used to make nuclear, biological, and chemical weapons, or missiles. Many high technology exports, licenses of technology, and transfers of technical information are subject to export controls and for this reason, clauses frequently must be included in license agreements to control dissemination of the technology. U.S. export control law continues to apply to technology of U.S. origin, even after it has been exported to a third country under an export control license. Countries that apply export controls issue various types of export licenses, but there are certain differences: for example, as a technical matter all U.S. goods are, in theory subject to export licensing, but most benefit from a "General License" that means that an export license in unnecessary unless the goods are going to an embargoed country (e.g., North Korea, Cuba, etc.). In other regimes, the term General License or Open License usually applies to dual use goods being exported to a country which is a member of one of the international multilateral export regimes, e.g., the Australia Group [q.v.], the Nuclear Suppliers Group [q.v.], the Wassenaar Arrangement [q.v.], the Chemical Weapons Convention, and the Zangger Committee [q.v.]. General or Open Licenses do not need to be applied for each shipment of goods or delivery of services. By contrast "Individual Licenses" or "Special Licenses" are usually required for weapons, military equipment, and very-sensitive dual use goods. Export controls are rigorously enforced and usually backed up by criminal sanctions for violators (and their managements) as well as heavy fines. Depending on the nature of high technology a business manufactures, it should familiarize itself with applicable export control laws and the controls applying to its goods and services.

Export Credit Insurance: insurance usually available from government funded export credit agencies or banks, which will usually cover the majority of accounts receivable owed by specified foreign customers. Typically, such insurance is available to cover up to 85 percent of the accounts receivable for a relatively low premium (this ceiling has been set by international trade agreements). Some international agencies such as the World Bank's Multilateral Investment Guarantee Agency (MIGA) also offer such insurance, especially for political risk, but have a poor reputation for paying claims. Export insurance tends to be used by large corporations in connection with big-ticket transactions, e.g., airliners, power generating plants, etc. However, arguably it is small- and medium-sized enterprises (SMEs) and startup companies who are most vulnerable to a default and most likely to need such insurance (but paradoxically are least likely to obtain it).

Export License: *See* Export Controls.

Export Trade Zone: *See* Foreign Trade Zone.

Export Trading Company: a business that purchases one company's products and assumes thereafter responsibility for marketing and selling the products outside that company's domestic market.

Expression: copyright protects the "expression" of ideas, but not the ideas themselves. Thus, for example, without permission, to copy this glossary and republish it on another Web site would infringe the author's copyright, but to use the descriptions as instructive in drafting one's own definitions would not.

Extinction Pricing: *See* Predatory Pricing.

Exxon-Florio: the Exxon-Florio Amendment to the 1988 Omnibus Trade and Competitiveness Act, 50 U.S.C. § 2170, permits the President of the United States to halt or reverse the acquisition of a U.S. business by a foreign firm if he believes it would harm national security in a manner not adequately addressed by other federal laws. The White House, in turn, has delegated to the Interagency Committee on Foreign Investment in the United States (CFIUS), the authority to determine when a proposed transaction warrants review, to conduct investigations, and to submit recommendations to approve, limit, or halt transactions. Facts likely to cause a transaction to be subject to Exxon-Florio review would be a target company's contracts with the U.S. military or intelligence agencies, any manufacture of components of weapon systems, the supply of secure communications facilities to the United States or allies or ownership of the acquirer by a foreign government. Once CFIUS has received a complete notification, either from the parties or U.S. government agencies, it reviews the transaction. An investigation, if necessary, must begin no later than thirty days after receipt of a notice and is required to end within forty-five days. The CFIUS process is widely regarded as highly politicized, with intense lobbying of Congress and the White House common in transactions exposed to the process.

EXW: Incoterm meaning Ex Works, i.e., the seller delivers by placing the goods at the buyer's disposal at the seller's premises (e.g., warehouse, factory, works) not cleared for export and not loaded onto shipping vehicle.

F

Fad Surfing: term coined by Eileen C. Shapiro in a Harvard Business Review Article, *Fad Surfing in the Board Room* (HBR Jan/Feb 1993) (and described later in more detail in a book by the same name published by Addison-Wesley, New York, 1996) to describe the regular embrace by management and consultants of business fads and buzzwords, usually touted by the latest corporate guru (or Tom Peters), such as total quality management (TQM), reengineering the corporation, "boundaryless" organizations, employee empowerment, etc. etc.

Fair Dealing: term used to describe a free speech-based defense similar to fair use. It allows the limited use of copyrighted materials or a trademark for purposes of research, private study, reporting current events, and criticism and review. It, in the copyright context, can be a difficult defense to assert and will usually not be interpreted so as to allow more than use of a minority of a copyrighted work. It also may depend on a showing that the user had no other way to obtain the work for the purpose concerned. The defense can also be undermined if the dealing results, or was intended to result, in a profit primarily derived from the taken work (profit is broadly defined as any revenue resulting from the dealing) or if the "taking" is substantial or total (i.e., the whole of a copyrighted work rather than small parts is used). A number of legal systems have no clear recognition of the concept of fair dealing, e.g., Germany, France, the Netherlands, Spain, Sweden, and Switzerland, and in those countries where it exists in the scope of the defense is highly variable. *See also* Fair Use, Incidental Copying.

Fairness Opinion: an assessment, typically in the form of a letter, prepared by experienced appraisers, analysts, or investment bankers (often independent of the transactions,) addressed to a company's board of directors or a special committee of the board of directors, which addresses the fairness of a proposed course of action or transaction from a financial point of view. Usually no further assessment or statements are made in a fairness opinion and it will not contain a specific recommendation as to how directors should act in connection with the matter (or *inter alia* how shareholders should vote), nor in a full form merger does it usually offer an opinion as to the investment quality of the securities (shares) at issue. Although fairness opinions will often appear in mergers or other transactions, they are in reality of limited real merit for two reasons: first, management is unlikely to solicit a fairness opinion from anyone who would provide a negative response, i.e., they will only formally ask for the opinion once they know that answer will be that management's proposal is fair (indeed it often suggested that advisors on transaction typically recommend as providers of the opinion other advisors for whom they regularly serve in the same role, creating somewhat of a *quid-quo-pro*); second, for a transaction to be "fair," it only needs to fall in the range of vaguely defined fair market values (which in a merger usually is somewhere in the normal trading range for companies over a time interval, the length of which can be varied as necessary), which may mean that the price that a seller may receive may not be the highest price possible, or the price the buyer pays may reflect an inflated value over present market value. The main apparent advantage of fairness opinions is that they provide legal "cover" for boards of directors or management in accepting or recommending transactions.

Fair Trade Law: usually a synonym for Unfair Competition Law.

Fair Use: a defense to copyright and trademark infringement. Fair use finds its origins in free speech rights and allows the limited use of copyrighted materials or a trademark for purposes of comment and satire. It is a difficult defense to assert, and can be undermined (though not necessarily fatally) if the purpose of the use is profit rather than comment or humor or if the "taking" is substantial or total (i.e., the whole work rather than small parts is used); however, members of the public often perceive the scope of the defense as much more extensive than it actually is. A number of legal systems have no clear recognition of the concept of fair use, e.g., Germany, France, the Netherlands, Spain, Sweden, and Switzerland, and in those countries where it exists, the scope of the defense is highly variable. *See also*, Fair Dealing, Incidental Copying.

Family Brand: a brand name that is used on a wide array of diverse products and usually acts primarily as a quality mark [q.v.].

Famous Mark: certain trademarks can be designated as "famous marks," which may entitle them to special protection, for example under United States Federal Trademark Dilution Act. Internationally famous marks (described as "well-known marks" in the TRIPS [q.v.]) are also treated differently in the context of additional national trademark registrations, in that the owner of such marks is regarded as having priority in trademark offices, even if someone has attempted to file before the international user.

Fanciful Terms: *See* Invented Words.

Fast Track (Approval): because the normal new drug application or IND process can be protracted, there has been considerable controversy about the resulting delay in providing potentially new drugs to victims of chronic degenerative or terminal diseases, i.e., by the time the drug is approved they may be dead or unlikely to benefit. In response drug regulatory agencies, in particular the United States FDA, have developed faster approval processes for such drugs. The U.S. version, known as Fast Track, is intended for the combination of a product (usually a drug) and a claim that the product addresses an unmet medical need. The benefits of Fast Track include scheduled meetings to seek FDA input into development plans, the option of submitting a New Drug Application in sections rather than all components simultaneously, and the option of requesting evaluation of studies using surrogate endpoints, (i.e., information that can be used to make an educated guess at the endpoint of actual trials were they to be conducted in the long term, which is then substituted for by information derived from long-term monitoring of the drug after market approval). A surrogate endpoint is described as:

> "a laboratory or physical sign that is used in therapeutic trials as a substitute for a clinically meaningful endpoint that is a direct measure of how a patient feels, functions, or survives and that is expected to predict the effect of the therapy."

However, while surrogate endpoints have always been used where there is a direct and established causal relationship between a condition and a result, e.g., high blood pressure and stroke, the fast track rule allows reliance on more tenuous predictors for an endpoint, by defining allowing in Fast Track use of a:

"surrogate endpoint that, while 'reasonably likely' to predict clinical benefit, is not so well-established as the surrogates ordinarily used as bases of approval in the past"
(Fed. Reg. 58942 at 58944 (December 11, 1992)).

Fast track was established under the Food and Drug Administration Modernization Act of 1997, 21 U.S.C. §21. Obtaining Fast Track approval is regarded as a major event for a pharmaceutical company by financial markets and may cause rapid share price appreciation. The downside is that there is at least anecdotal evidence that drugs approved under Fast Track have a higher rate of complications leading to withdrawal from the market, creating a higher post-marketing level of risk.

FCA: Incoterm meaning free carrier, i.e., that the seller deliver the goods to the carrier nominated by the buyer at the named place. If delivery occurs at the seller's premises, the seller is responsible for loading. If the delivery is anywhere else, the seller is not responsible for unloading.

FCC: United States Federal Communications Commission, established in 1934 to regulate interstate and international telecommunications originating in the United States.

FCN Agreement: Freedom, Commerce, and Navigation Agreement, the basic type of trade agreement under which countries establish, usually bilaterally the commercial and economic rights of each other citizens in each.

FCPA: *See* Foreign Corrupt Practices Act.

Federal Circuit: The United States Court of Appeals for the Federal Circuit is an appeals court established in the United States to hear all appeals of patent cases, appeals of USPTO decisions, and appeals from the United States Court of Claims (the Claims Court, established to hear civil claims against the Federal Government). Decisions of the Federal Circuit are published on various Web sites including the court's own site as well as in searchable form on various university Web sites such as that of Emory University (to 1995) and the Georgetown University Law Center (to 1995).

Fiduciary: someone who owes a duty of loyalty, good faith and scrupulously honest dealing to another (i.e., a fiduciary duty). Usually a fiduciary must act always in the best interests of the party that it owes a duty to, usually at a higher priority to the fiduciary's own interest. Among those who typically owe a fiduciary duty are directors and officers of a company, lenders to borrowers, lawyers to clients, agents to principals and sometimes promoters to investors. A fiduciary should also generally avoid or disclose any conflict of interest it may have to the party to which it owes the fiduciary duty, or otherwise make sure that the party is aware of the conflict.

Field of Search: the technical area that is searched for prior art with respect to a pending patent application. Technology is subdivided into a taxonomy by patent offices so that they can more effectively search for prior art. The field of search is noted with respect to any patent to render subsequent searches for prior art more efficient.

Field of Use: owners of intellectual property can grant licenses limiting the use that the licensee can make of the IP to particular purposes or fields of use, for example, licensing an antibiotic for use in veterinary purposes, but not for humans. The term is most commonly used in patent licensing, although it can arise in trademarks. Technically licenses of rights in a copyright license, that are not among the statutorily enumerated rights in the bundle of rights, are always field of use licenses and should usually be drafted as such, for example separating the paperback rights from hardback rights (both of which are technically carve-outs from the broad right of reproduction).

Figure: refers to the use of an image, drawing, or symbol as a trademark.

File Wrapper: colloquial phrase used to refer to the prosecution history of a patent, i.e., the application, amendments, IDS, office actions, etc. The phrase file wrapper is used because the United States Patent and Trademark Office used to use a paper file wrapper to bind such documents on which an index of all the documents therein was inscribed.

File Wrapper Estoppel: *See* Prosecution History Estoppel.

Firmware: two common meanings. It can be used to describe software stored on a read only memory or ROM that initializes a CPU when first switched on, e.g., a BIOS (Basic Input/Output System). However, the term has also come to describe product specific software usually shipped by the manufacturer with a hardware component or product, especially one included or integrated into more complex systems that serves to make that specific item of hardware operate and interact with the larger system. In this usage, (device) driver (software) is firmware.

First Dollar, First Money: another term for "dollar one," i.e., the money moviegoers pay to see a film or show, the fees paid by a TV broadcaster to show a movie, etc. before the funds have passed through any other companies' hands (each of whom may take a commission or share). *See* Gross Participation, Net Participation.

First Mover Advantage: term used to describe the advantages that can accrue to the first player to enter a competitive space, e.g., establishing early customer relationships, etc. However, in contrast some commentators point to the existence in some circumstances of "last or late mover advantage," which typically includes lower cost for equipment, greater ease in locating and hiring skilled employees, and learning from first mover mistakes. Late mover advantage as compared to first-mover advantage has been significant in Internet business, as early in the development of the Internet, hardware and software was expensive, relatively few potential customers had good Internet connections or were familiar with the Internet, while individuals with the ability to create Web-pages were hard to find and consequently highly paid; all of these costs were significantly lower after a short period of time which meant that the capital costs of later movers (and hence debts) were much lower. Patents usually form a key element of a first mover's strategy for defeating late mover advantage.

First Sale: Used for at least four different purposes: (a) as a term in license agreements, usually defined as the first sale to an unrelated party, to provide a basis for calculating royalty rates; (b) exhaustion-on-first sale refers to exhaustion of rights [q.v.], which typically occurs on the first sale by the holder of an intellectual property right or a licensee; (c) first sale of a newly invented product or product made by an invented method (or indeed the first offer for sale) can preclude applying for a patent, a rule known as the on-sale-bar [q.v.]; or (d) demonstrating first use or first sale may be important in disputes over entitlement to a trademark in some jurisdictions such as the United States.

First-to-File: refers to the system of priority for patent applications used in most of the world. Under the first-to-file system the first person to file a patent application for a given invention is entitled to any patent that issues on that invention. *See* Priority Date, First-to-Invent.

First-to-Invent: refers to the system of priority for patent applications used in the United States and the Philippines. Under the first-to-invent system, the first person to reduce an invention to practice is entitled to any patent on the invention. The first-to-invent system leads to a type of administrative patent litigation in the USPTO known as an interference. First-to-invent is usually defended in the United States as protecting the small inventor, who may not be sophisticated enough to file a patent quickly; however, it should be noted that it gives rise to the patent interference process, which can prove prohibitively expensive to a small inventor. *See* Priority Date, First-to-File.

Fixed: Copyright arises when a creative work or expression is first fixed (recorded) in a tangible medium, i.e., written on a page, recorded on a disk or tape, film, etc.

Flipping a Company: venture capital term for an exit strategy based on selling the startup business to a larger company rather than taking it to an initial public offering.

Flipping Shares: term for the rapid resale of shares obtained through an allocation in an initial public offering, profiting from the usual post-IPO bounce.

Floating License: a software license, usually for a network, which allows one copy of the software to be running at any given time on a single computer on the network. A floating license can also provide for a fixed number of copies to be run simultaneously, in which instance the number of floating users is typically referred to as "seats."

FOB: Incoterm abbreviation for Free On Board meaning the seller has to pay the cost of delivering the goods onto the *ship (or vessel)* at the specified port. Once the cargo crosses the ship or vessel's rail, risk of loss, transport, and storage (e.g., demurrage) is the liability of the buyer (or the shipper depending on the buyer's contract with the shipper). The term should only be used for sea and inland waterways, but is often also (mis)used in reference to airports. It is also often misunderstood as meaning that once the cargo has been delivered to the shipping company, risk of loss shifts—it **does not shift until the goods are across the rail of the shipping vessel.**

FOLDOC: the Free Online Dictionary of Computing, a useful and thorough dictionary of computer terms, maintained by Department of Computing of Imperial College, London.

Foreign Access Zone: Japanese term for a foreign trade zone [q.v.].

Foreign Corrupt Practices Act (FCPA): U.S. federal statute rendering it an offense for U.S. citizens, companies, and direct foreign subsidiaries of U.S. companies to offer, promise, or pay anything of value to any foreign government official in order to obtain or retain business i.e., an anti-bribery statute.

Foreign Sales Corporation: a U.S. program, which allowed United States-based corporations to set up offshore shell companies to carry out export sales that provided substantial tax breaks. For various reasons the vast majority of such FSC's were established in the Virgin Islands with the result that so many were established that it was estimated that there was one for every 28 members of the population. The FSC program and its successor the Extraterritorial Income Act were held to be illegal subsidies by the WTO repeatedly, which authorized the EU in 2004 to impose tariffs of up to $4 billion on U.S. exports. The EU began in March 2004 to impose tariffs of 5 percent on various U.S. products, targeting goods manufactured in key electoral districts and provided that the rate would increase by one percentage point per month up to 17 percent; by October 1, 2004 the tariff rate was 12 percent. The American Jobs Creation Act of 2004, abolishing the illegal programs was enacted rapidly by the U.S. Congress (House passage October 7, 2004, Senate October 11) and signed by President

George W. Bush on October 22, just in time for the November 2004 Presidential and Congressional election.

Foreign Trade Zone: a zone within the physical territory of a country that for tax and customs purposes is legally designated as being outside the country. FTZs are useful for the manufacture of products that may incorporate high value components or where high value inventories must be maintained. Their key benefit is that goods kept in an FTZ are not formally imported and so are not subject to VAT or customs duties. While such taxes are typically reclaimable from most governments when manufactured goods are exported, paying the duties and taxes for the period between import and export is a substantial cash flow burden and also imposes substantial administrative costs. FTZs are usually located near ports, border-crossings, or airports.

Form A/B, Form CO (long-form, short-form), Form RS, Form C: EU competition law terms for a series of forms for submitting agreements, mergers or complaints to the European Commission's Competition Directorate. The use of the various forms is or was as follows:

> **Form A/B**: until May 2004, when new procedures were introduced this questionnaires for the notification of agreements or arrangements that raised issues under European competition law was filed with the European Commission seeking an individual exemption or approval of the agreement or arrangement under Article 81 of the Treaty of Rome (Amsterdam). Although the notification procedure was abolished under Regulation 1/2003 (and all pending notifications lapsed in May 2004) the new regulation contained a "savings clause" effectively preserving the benefit of decisions and procedural action taken under the old regulation. Since under that old regulation, patent pools and various were exempted from illegality under Article 81(1) (or the subject of comfort letters), provided the notified information was full and correct, the contents of the Form A/Bs filed pre-2004 remain of some relevance.

> **Form C** is used to make a complaint to the European Commission regarding a violation of European Competition Law and in

particular Articles 81 and 82 of the Treaty of Rome (Amsterdam) [q.v.].

Form CO is a detailed questionnaire that is required to be filed on concentrations, typically mergers, that fall within the EU turnover threshold (*See* Merger Regulation, European). There are two versions of Form CO, the long form and the short form. The long form is filed on agreements that are considered to raise competitive concerns in that they involve a joint venture with a turnover of more than €100 million, a merger where the parties combined market share in relevant EU markets is more than 15 percent. In effect, the long form is required for most mergers and joint ventures between entities that are substantial competitors. The short form CO may be used for mergers which are eligible for treatment under the EU's simplified procedure [q.v.] because the merging companies are not substantial competitors (e.g., their combined market shares is under 15 percent, the concentrative joint venture they are establishing will have a turnover of less than €100 million, etc.)

Form RS is used to make a "Reasoned Submission," under Article 4(4) of the EU merger regulation, to the effect that the competitive impact(s) of a proposed merger effects the market within a single member state and as such, the merger or at least a specific competitive issue with respect to the merger should be reviewed by the competition authority(ies) of the state(s) specified in the Form RS. Effectively a form RS is a request to the Commission to transfer the review of an issue from the Commission and EU law to a member state and its domestic competition law. *See* German Clause.

Formalities, Copyright: Refers to requirements for copyright protection, such a depository requirements or applying for a copyright. Copyright formalities are prohibited by the Berne Convention [q.v.] for those rights guaranteed under the convention, so that copyright subsists from the moment expression is fixed. Nonetheless, in the United States carrying out certain formalities, known as copyright registration, can confer rights in litigation over and beyond those guaranteed by the Berne Convention, such as statutory damages and attorneys' fees.

Forum Shopping: Refers to choosing a forum in which to bring litigation that favors the plaintiff, either because of local chauvinism, variations in rules of procedure or of substantive law, or convenience. Since forum shopping is frequently deplored by judges (who often piously maintain that there is no advantage to be gained and all courts are equally fair), it has negative connotations and is thus an activity many, if not most lawyers publicly deny engaging in, but most reasonably competent litigators indeed do, and most plaintiffs faced with a choice of forums would be very foolish not to. *See*, Italian Torpedo, Declaratory Judgment.

Forward References: refers to citations of a patent or patent application as prior art to subsequent patent applications; they usually start to appear within a few months of the patent being issued or the application being published. The number and rate of forward references for a patent is one way of assessing its value and importance. Forward references are normally done with a single type of patent, usually U.S. patents, which explicitly state prior art considered in their examination on their cover page. Another use of forward references is to look for potential infringers of technology, since the potential infringer's own patent applications would be likely to cite the patent. Most patent information databases offer the ability to do a forward reference check. When used in licensing negotiations, it is important to make sure that the forward citation analysis excludes or separately counts self-references, i.e., references in which the owner of a patent cites that patent (or its own publications, e.g., white papers) as prior art in its own subsequent applications. This is for three reasons: (a) holders of patents tend to cite them because failure to do so would give rise to claims of inequitable conduct; (b) holders of patents tend to know their portfolio and previous work well; and (c) citing a patent allows a holder to raise the profile of its own intellectual property. It should also be noted that the USPTO appears to cite as references patents filed by U.S. entities much more frequently than those of foreign entities, especially when the original language of the foreign parent patent application was not English.

Founders' Rights/Shares: the founders of a company may insert provisions into its corporate governance to protect their interests, usually attached to special shares. These rights may take many forms including veto powers or alternately extra voting weights, e.g., ten times the votes of each ordinary share. Founder's shares are often heavily criticized, though to be fair, some very successful companies use founder's shares. Anecdotally, problems typically arise with founder's shares in the second and later generations of a business, when it is no longer controlled by its founders.

Framework License, Framework Agreement: where two companies expect to be regularly licensing different items of IP for similar purposes and for similar terms, it is common to agree a broad generic license, which does not identify the licensed IP and then license the items using *addendum* agreements or schedules, which set forth the *sui generis* [q.v.] terms applying to each item, e.g., price, field of use, etc.

Franchise Disclosure Document: the law of several U.S. states including New York and California as well as Canadian law require franchisors to provide potential franchisees with a disclosure document that includes an array of specified information about the business opportunity on offer. Misrepresentations in the franchise disclosure document will usually give rise to a cause of action on the part of the franchisee. A similar document called the Uniform Franchising Offering Circular is required in a number of other U.S. states as well as under the United States Federal Trade Commission Franchise Disclosure Rule.

Franchising: the selling of a license by a franchisor to a third party (the franchisee) permitting the use of a particular business format. In most instances the business format will involve a common brand (and a trademark license) as well as a marketing format and usually joint marketing program. Franchising is most common in the services sector, particularly food service, McDonalds, for example.

Fraud on the Patent Office: involves the deliberate deception of a patent office, especially the United States Patent and Trademark Office, in order to obtain a patent. This can result in at least unenforceability and potentially invalidity, legal, and even criminal penalties and the risk of counterclaims. Fraud on the patent office is sometimes referred to as inequitable conduct, although strictly speaking inequitable conduct has a lower level of proof and does not require the same degree of bad faith and/or deliberate-falsehood (indeed it can be based on silence as to relevant information) as fraud. *See* Unenforceability, Inequitable Conduct.

Free Rider: term, regarded as deprecatory, for someone who uses the economic contributions of others to the broader economy without paying for it through some corresponding contribution, e.g., taxes, fees, donated information. In essence, some intellectual property commentators say the reason for its existence is to stop "free riders" from taking advantage of an inventor or author's contribution to the world for the free rider's own sole benefit. In reality, the existence of a genuinely "free rider, i.e., someone who takes but contributed nothing to the general welfare is highly unlikely; although such a person could contribute little to the general welfare. The bigger issue is that an author or inventor might not contribute to the general welfare if much of the benefit would accrue to free riders and little or none to the author or inventor.

Free Software Foundation: A group opposed to proprietary rights in software, i.e., intellectual property rights in software. The free software foundation has developed the GNU public license.

Freezing Injunction: new term under the English Civil Procedure Rules and Practice Directions for a *Mareva* Injunction [q.v.].

Friends and Family Shares/Allocation: in an IPO (initial public offering) the management may choose to either distribute shares to "friends and family" or cause some of the IPO allocation to be directed to such persons. In many respects, this is designed to minimize founder's tax liabilities by providing that person who might subsequently benefit from their largess, e.g., children, obtain the benefits of the IPO directly and thereby pay tax once rather than twice.

FTC: United States Federal Trade Commission, entity that administers a large number of Federal commercial regulations including fair trade law and antitrust law under the Lanham Act, laws against deceptive advertising and consumer protection statutes.

FTZ: *See* Foreign Trade Zone.

Full Form Merger: a merger or acquisition in which the acquiring company pays for the target company with shares of the acquirer's stock.

Full Function Joint Venture: EU Competition Law [q.v.] term that refers to a separate, distinct, and fully functional business entity that is jointly controlled by at least two parents that are not part of the same corporate group. To be fully functioning, the JV must operate in the market performing the operations usually carried out by other autonomous entities in the market (e.g., sales, marketing, purchasing, etc.). To do this it will typically have to possess management dedicated to its day-to-day operation and access to those resources such as staff, finance and tangible and intangible assets, necessary for it to conduct business agreed in the joint-venture agreement on a lasting basis. Where a joint venture does not have access to the markets, for example an R&D joint venture it is not usually regarded as Full Function. The key Competition Law aspect of a Full Function Joint Venture is that it is regarded as concentrative [q.v.]under EU Competition law and so needs to be notified to the European Commission in the same way as a merger, if the joint venturers exceed the Turnover Threshold [q.v.] (*See* Merger Regulation, European).

Full Line Forcing: a form of tying where a supplier requires a retailer to offer a complete range of products or none at all. Its legality can be less questionable than ordinary tying, especially where explicit numbers of cross-tied items are not required (i.e., "to get so many of A you must take this much of B," rather than "you can have A, but you must also stock some B").

Full Ratchet, Weighted Full Ratchet: *See* Anti-Dilution Clause.

Fully Packaged Product: software sold in retail packages, usually including media carrying the software, as well as manuals, product information, etc.

Functionality, Functional: design patents, registered designs, and architectural rights cannot usually protect functional aspects of the design, i.e., features of the design whose main or primary role is to fulfill the purpose or function of the design. *See*, Aesthetic.

Fundamental Patent: *See* Pioneer Patent.

Fungible: a product or service that is available from several sources, each of whose goods or services are largely interchangeable and substitutable without deleterious consequences—sometimes called a commodity. *See* Commodity Business.

G

Gartner Group (report): a well known research and analysis company in the broad technology sector, Gartner provides detailed reports on a wide array of business sectors including government, semiconductors, pharmaceuticals, etc., in part based on wide industry surveys. It will also perform, for a fee, targeted research. Its reports are widely read and it should be assumed that any reasonably competent executive negotiating major agreements, at least in part, has been briefed using materials derived from Gartner.

Geek Gap: rude term used to describe a shortage of technical personnel as compared to a competitor. Typically used by non-technologist senior managers. Alternately, it is used to denote the comprehension gap between non-technologist managers and executives who commission or sell technology projects and the technologists who implement and develop them.

Genericization (Genericide): refers to the loss of trademark rights because the mark comes to be used as a generic name for the class of goods and loses distinctiveness. The best-known example was Aspirin, originally registered as a trademark by Bayer for the sodium salt of acetyl salicylic acid. As the term came to be used for the drug in general, regardless of supplier, Bayer lost exclusive rights to the mark in most countries. Trademarks often used as examples of being close to genericization are Hoover®, Xerox® (who promoted the generic term photocopy) and Walkman®.

Geographic Designation of Origin (GDO): form of mark that designates that a product comes from a geographically defined area and usually also requires that it meet certain quality standards and be manufactured in a particular way: the best known example are the French system of *appellations contrôlées* for wines, but it is also applied in various countries to cheese (e.g., *reggianno parmagiano*), shellfish (Whitby Oysters), spirits (Bourbon Whisky), etc. GDOs are heavily supported by European countries, but are frequently opposed by the major international food companies who wish to market products, e.g., powdered parmesan-style cheese, that are not made in the geographic area or in the specified way. The United States agreed to recognize GDOs under the TRIPS agreement. The control of most GDOs has been devolved from government to associations of producers, who set standards and requirements. New GDOs are occasionally granted, but it is an under-exploited form of intellectual property. Perversely, some economists oppose GDOs while endorsing trademarks, somehow contriving to rationalize an economic distinction between the two: of course they could be influenced by major international food companies, who value their trademarks much more than they hate GDOs. *See* Lisbon Agreement for the Protection of Appellations of Origin and their International Registration.

Georgia-Pacific Factors: one of the bases for an award of damages in most jurisdictions is at least a "reasonable royalty," i.e., not less than the royalty the infringer would have paid for a license of the patent at issue. In the U.S. case *Georgia-Pacific v. U.S. Plywood Corp.*, 318 F. Supp. 1116, 1120 (S.D.N.Y. 1970) the court listed a series of factors that could be used to determine a reasonable royalty and the case and its factors have come to be widely cited in patent litigation, although it is frequently criticized for looking at the issue as if products required only one patent and ignored the royalty rate stacking present in many complex high technology products. The *Georgia Pacific* factors are:

> "1. The royalties received by the patentee for the licensing of the patent in suit, proving or tending to prove an established royalty.
> 2. The rates paid by the licensee for the use of other patents comparable to the patent in suit.
> 3. The nature and scope of the license, as exclusive or non-exclusive; or as restricted or non-restricted in terms of territory or with respect to whom the manufactured product may be sold.
> 4. The licensor's established policy and marketing program to maintain his patent monopoly by not licensing others to use the invention or by granting licenses under special conditions designed to preserve that monopoly.

5. The commercial relationship between the licensor and licensee, such as, whether they are competitors in the same territory in the same line of business; or whether they are inventor and promoter.

6. The effect of selling the patented specialty in promoting sales of other products of the licensee; the existing value of the invention to the licensor as a generator of sales of his non-patented items; and the extent of such derivative or convoyed sales.

7. The duration of the patent and the term of the license.

8. The established profitability of the product made under the patent; its commercial success; and its current popularity.

9. The utility and advantages of the patent property over the old modes or devices, if any, that had been used for working out similar results.

10. The nature of the patented invention; the character of the commercial embodiment of it as owned and produced by the licensor; and the benefits to those who have used the invention.

11. The extent to which the infringer has made use of the invention; and any evidence probative of the value of that use.

12. The portion of the profit or of the selling price that may be customary in the particular business or in comparable businesses to allow for the use of the invention or analogous inventions.

13. The portion of the realizable profit that should be credited to the invention as distinguished from non-patented elements, the manufacturing process, business risks, or significant features or improvements added by the infringer.

14. The opinion testimony of qualified experts.

15. The amount that a licensor (such as the patentee) and a licensee (such as the infringer) would have agreed upon (at the time the infringement began) if both had been reasonably and voluntarily trying to reach an agreement; that is, the amount that a prudent licensee—who desired, as a business proposition, to obtain a license to manufacture and sell a particular article embodying the patented invention—would have been willing to pay as a royalty and yet be able to make a reasonable profit and which amount would have been acceptable by a prudent patentee who was willing to grant a license."

German Clause: Article 9 of the EU merger regulation (Council Regulation (EC) No 139/2004 of 20 January 2004 on the control of concentrations between undertakings) that allows EU member states, within 15 days of the notification of a concentration to request the Commission to refer a merger for review by member state authorities under applicable national legislation, even if it does have a "community dimension." This provision was sought by Germany (hence "German Clause.") Such a request can be made if the market concerned: (a) is a "distinct market" within the member state that does not form a substantial part of the Common Market (i.e., the EU or EEA economy as a whole); or (b) if the transaction at issue threatens to affect such a distinct market. If the Commission concludes that (a) is the case, it must refer the distinct market aspects of the merger to the national authorities of the requesting government for review (which could be some or all); if it concludes (b) is the case, it may refer the matter to the member state authorities. Finally, the parties to the notified transaction may make a "Reasoned Submission" on Form RS seeking a referral to member state authorities. Although the Commission has in principle broad authority to decide whether it should refer a transaction under the German clause, if it were to bar a deal, a refusal to refer might be one basis for appeal, while opposing parties might also appeal.

Get them Pregnant Strategy: crude, rude, and sexist term used to describe a selling strategy for technology of securing design-ins [q.v.] by over-selling a product or service, based on the theory that the purchaser, once committed, will be forced to stay with its choice, because switching costs would be too-high. The strategy is regarded as unethical and the term is usually used to describe the tactics of a party other than the person using it, such as a competitor or supplier to the user. The phrase should be used with caution as many persons would reasonably regard it as offensive. "Overselling to achieve buyer lock-in" is a close, non-offensive alternative that is better descriptively, but lacks the shock impact.

Getting to No, Getting to Yes: the latter is a book by Roger Fisher and William Ury, *Getting to Yes: Negotiating Agreement Without Giving In*, published in 1983, which promoted a theory of four principles for effective negotiation: (1) separate the people from the problem; (2) focus on interests rather than positions; (3) generate a variety of options before settling on an agreement; and (4) insist that the agreement be based on objective criteria. "Getting to No" is a pun on the title of the book and refers to the assessment that deals rarely close until one party starts to refuse further concessions, thus convincing the other party that the deal on the table is as good as it is going to get, e.g., it has reached the other party's BATNA [q.v.].

Ghost Brand: product brand that though still in use, is almost forgotten, but can be revived for a new generation of consumers. Many ghost brands often have strong cultural significance, which can aid in their restoration, for example the hair cream brand Brylcream® was widely used in reference to Second World War British airmen, as in "Brylcream Boys." Occasionally, a ghost brand can be something that the company had used in the past and seeks to revive, e.g., Daimler Benz's revival of the Maybach brand for luxury cars.

Gist (of the Invention): what is the heart of the invention, the fundamental ideas that make it different from the prior art.

GNU General Public License (GNU GPL): an open public license promoted by the Free Software Foundation. The original GNU Public License was criticized because its vague wording led to a threat that use or incorporation of software under the GNU Public license could give rise to infectious public licensing. In response the Free Software Foundation has developed what is known as the GNU II license, but is officially called the GNU Lesser General Public License, which does not go as far in opening up all ownership of software provided pursuant to it.

Goodwill: in principle, means the positive reputation and warm "fuzzy" feelings the world, and in particular customers and clients, has toward a business, brand, or person. In accounting terms, it has come to be used as a valuation "slop-bucket" when businesses are purchased for the price paid for the business over and above the value of the fixed assets. Formerly all intellectual property used to be "slopped" into this bucket, but recent accounting changes means that IP needs to be identified and valued on the post merger balance sheet. Historically courts, lawyers, accountants, and especially taxmen have struggled to define goodwill. One of the best definitions was set forth by the United States Supreme Court in 1893 (albeit quoting a former Supreme Court Justice):

> the advantage or benefit which is acquired by an establishment, beyond the mere value of the capital, stock, funds, or property employed therein, in consequence of the general public patronage and encouragement which it receives from constant or habitual customers on account of its local position, or common celebrity, or reputation for skill or affluence or punctuality, or from other accidental circumstances or necessity, or even from ancient partialities or prejudices

> *Metropolitan Nat. Bank v. St. Louis Dispatch Co.*, 149 U.S. 436, 446 (1893) *citing* J. Story, PARTNERSHIPS § 99 (1841)

Google Bomb: inserting features in a Web site so as to influence its rankings in the results of a search using an Internet search engine, in particular Google®. Techniques for doing so involve gaming the search engine algorithm by for instance inserting a large number of links to the Web site on other Web pages.

Grace Period: refers in general to a period during which the application of a strict time limit may be softened, provided a party cures its time default during the grace period. For example, although in principle a publication or sale of an invention before filing a patent application may preclude patenting, many patent systems provide a limited "grace period" after such an error during which an inventor can cure its error by filing an application. Such periods vary between six months and one year. Similarly, a failure to pay fees to patent or trademark offices when due can in many instances be cured by payment of the fees during a grace period, frequently with a late payment penalty. The problem with grace periods is that they do not exist universally and are not consistent; they can vary in length and in the nature of the exceptions they make. Thus there is a risk that an inventor or patent agent from a jurisdiction that provides for a grace period will assume that it applies in jurisdictions where none exists or alternately, that it is of the same length, or "graces" the same acts (for example); vice versa, one should not assume that because the possibility of securing a patent has been precluded by, say, publication in a home jurisdiction, it has expired in several important jurisdictions that do apply grace periods. About thirty-eight countries do provide for grace periods with respect to patents including the United States, Japan, and Canada. There is no grace period in Europe, though introduction of one is under discussion.

Grandfathering, Grandfather Clause: colloquial term describing the principle that already vested rights usually cannot be taken away by changes in law or regulation (and sometimes contracts). Thus a classic example of a grandfather clause arose in the United States when states raised their legal age for the purchase and consumption of alcohol from 18 years to 21; the new laws generally provided that those who were over the age of 18 as of the date that the new drinking age came into force, could continue to buy and consume alcohol. While grandfathering usually applies to reduction in or removal of vested rights, it does not normally apply to the expansion of rights. Thus copyright term extensions were often granted under the TRIPS, even to copyright authors whose rights were already lapsed when the TRIPS extended the copyright term in a relevant jurisdiction.

Grant-Back Clause: provision in a license agreement, which requires a licensee to license any improvements it develops back to the licensor, usually with rights to sublicense. Grant-back clauses are common where the licensor wishes to preserve a standard. Grant-back clauses can raise problems under Competition Law, especially if they require the licensee to grant the licensor an exclusive license to the improvement.

Graphical Element: refers to a drawing or figure component in a trademark.

Gratuitous Transfer: a gift, a transfer of goods or assets of value for no consideration (i.e., payment). Gratuitous transfers can give rise to a tax liability and may also be avoidable (cancelable) transactions under bankruptcy laws. In addition, the term "gratuitous transfer from the public to authors" was used by Justice John Paul Stevens to describe term extensions to intellectual property rights arising *ex post facto*, i.e., after the original copyright had expired, due to U.S. legislation extending copyright terms in his dissent to the decision in the United States Supreme Court Case *Eldred v Ashcroft*.

Greenmail: the repurchase of stock from a potential acquirer at a substantial premium over the market price. Pun on the word "blackmail" and "greenbacks," a slang term for dollars.

Grey/Gray Market Imports: colloquial term for Parallel Imports.

Gripe Site: internet Web site set up by disgruntled consumers to complain about company's behavior or products, *see* http://www.untied.com for a particularly painful example (in this case the target sued and lost on free speech grounds). To avoid the risk of such sites many companies register likely gripe site domain names such as www.ford-sucks.com by the Ford motor company.

Gross Participation (the Gross): movie and entertainment industry jargon for a form of participation in which the amount a recipient gets is a "share of the gross" or a "piece of the gross" i.e., a percentage of the gross receipts or total revenue a production generates before expenses are deducted (some minor expenses are usually still deducted, these are typically limited to taxes and the cost of collecting the revenue). A share of the gross, calculated from "dollar one" is the most desirable position to be in with respect to a production. Contrast with "the Net." *See also* Adjusted Gross Participation.

Gross Receipts: movie and entertainment industry jargon for the total revenue that a production generates, from ticket sales, sales for broadcast, DVDs and Videos, etc.

Group Boycott: an agreement between companies or businesses not to deal with a third party which may violate competition and antitrust laws especially if it tends to raise prices, eliminate a potential competitor, or restrict customer/consumer choice. Sometimes referred to by the technical term concerted refusal to deal.

GSA Schedule: the United States General Services Administration uses a system of contracts with commercial firms to provide supplies and services to the Federal Government at stated prices for given periods of time. There are two major types of schedule: Multiple Award Schedules (MAS), which provide for the supply of usually unlimited quantities over an indefinite period of time; and Single Award Schedules (SAS), which cover contracts made with one supplier for a specific product at a stated price for delivery to a geographical area defined in the schedule. The main advantage of GSA schedules is that they forestall the need to go through complex U.S. federal procurement procedures, because the GSA has in effect certified that is the best value item for its purpose. Effectively, employees of the Federal Government can simply buy GSA scheduled items without needing to obtain bids. Obviously for manufacturers of high technology, particularly software, obtaining a listing on an MAS schedule is hugely advantageous. MAS Schedules will typically cover a wide range of software, small computers and workstations, peripherals, etc.

Guidelines For Examination: statement of the general rules applied by the European Patent Office to patent applications.

H

Hard IP: Although hard IP is usually taken to mean patents and perhaps know-how, it is perhaps better considered as the type of IP that permits or facilitates certain activities, processes and services or the making of tangible goods and refers to ownership of functional ideas as opposed to rights over expression and aesthetic aspects of ideas. Practitioners of what is known as soft IP sometimes regard the distinction as pejorative and belittling. The dividing line between hard and soft IP is difficult to define, software for example being a tricky area.

Hague Agreement: Hague Agreement Concerning the International Deposit of Industrial Designs.

Hague Convention and "Hague Service": usually refers to the Hague Convention of November 15, 1965 on the Service Abroad of Judicial and Extrajudicial Document in Civil or Commercial Matters is the key international agreement for bringing suit against foreign parties, i.e., for a U.S. company or party to sue a company outside the U.S. or an EU company or party to sue a non-EU company or party. It provides the service mechanism for papers initiating a lawsuit and should be followed in order to obtain an enforceable award in the defendant's jurisdiction. There are a large number of Hague Conventions on different issues ranging from diplomatic rights to the rights of combatants, which can lead to confusion.

Hallmark: effectively an early form of trademark and quality-mark. Hallmarks were stamps placed by guilds on goods, which, after inspection met their minimum standards for quality. The use of hallmarks is most commonly associated with silver and goldsmiths and most notably attested to the minimum silver or gold content of an item. Hallmarks were so known because they were applied at the city guildhall or at the hall of the relevant city guild, and thus each hallmark also served to identify the city of manufacture and the actual maker (the maker's mark). Guilds had charters granted by the city or state, which often granted them quite draconian powers to prohibit the counterfeiting of marks. Over time the closed shop tendency of guilds (full membership often became effectively hereditary) caused craftsmen who had completed their apprenticeships to leave for cities which lacked a relevant-guild or where a manufacturing technique was unknown, giving rise to early patents of importation. Hallmarks remain in use today, though access to the right to apply a hallmark is much easier and generally regulated by the city/state directly rather than by the guilds.

Hart-Scott-Rodino Act: *See* HSR.

Harvard Negotiation Project: started in 1979, is a project of Harvard University (the Law and Business Schools), which has developed a "principled" approach to negotiation that is widely taught in law and business courses.

Hatch-Waxman Act: A U.S. law whose full title is the Drug Price Competition and Patent Term Restoration Act of 1984, codified in several places, including 21 U.S.C. §§ 301, 355, 360cc; 28 U.S.C. § 2201; 35 U.S.C. §§ 156, 271, 282. The statute is extremely complex, as it addresses several areas of law including drug patents, drug marketing approval and regulation and Federal Civil Procedure.

Hatch-Waxman is designed to deal with the complex issues that arise when the patent on a drug is about to run out and generic drug makers want approval of their products, for which they would normally file an ANDA. One difficulty in this situation is that applying for approval of a drug while is still under patent might be regarded as technically patent infringement. The Act allows an NDA holder (usually the company that originally developed the drug), to list its patent in a record maintained by the FDA known as the "Orange Book." Once the patent or patents are listed in the Orange Book, a generic company that would like to market the same drug must assert that those patents listed in the Orange Book are either invalid or not infringed by the generic drug the company is filing an ANDA for. The patent/NDA holder then has forty-five days to file an infringement suit, after which there is an automatic thirty-month stay of FDA approval of the ANDA, unless or until there is a court decision in the generic drug company's favor.

One problem with this structure is that because the patent/NDA holder has every incentive to slow the process, it inevitably files suit in the slowest court it can find and does everything it can to slow the litigation (profits per day being potentially orders of magnitude more than legal fees). Another issue is that some drug companies have (allegedly) recorded patents in the Orange Book, which they know do not apply to a specific therapy, specifically to delay generics. One recent change has been to allow the generic drug manufacture to file a declaratory judgment action to speed the legal process, if they argue they have a reasonable fear of being sued for infringement.

The "patent term restoration" phrase in the statute deals with a peculiar problem, which arose temporarily as a result of the TRIPS. Prior to the Uruguay Round, U.S. patent were valid for seventeen years from the date of grant, while in the rest of the world patents were valid for twenty-one years from the date of application—amending U.S. patent law created an issue known as "delta," where depending on how long a patent application had been pending, a patent holder might have a shorter term under one rule than the other. This provisions of Hatch-Waxman in effect created complex rules for restoring the "delta."

Have-Made, Right to: theoretically if a licensee chooses to contract-out the manufacturing of licensed goods or the use of a licensed method to produce goods for the licensee, that subcontract may involve a sub-license. Since the extent of the right to grant sublicenses under a license agreement is often unclear, and indeed sub-licenses as such may be prohibited by the agreement or not automatic under applicable law, it has become standard practice to state whether the licensee has received the right to engage in such contracting-out, and what restrictions are placed on this activity. Such a have-made provision should be understood as having either of three effects, depending on applicable law, it: (a) confers a right the licensee did not have; (b) confirms a right the licensee did have, but perhaps constrains its exercise; or, (c) it simply clarifies the arrangement. A well-written license agreement will, at least in the interest of (c), address the issue.

HDL: Hardware Descriptor Language, a language akin to a programming language used for the conceptual design of integrated circuits. Examples are VHDL and Verilog.

Heads of Agreement, Heads of Terms: in a typical negotiation, key terms are resolved in discussion, such a price, delivery, assets conveyed, term, etc., and are recorded in what are known as the "heads of agreement" or "heads of terms," which often will be in the form of an MOU. The heads of agreement form the foundation around which legal advisors will draft contracts. It is important to discuss with appropriate counsel what issues the heads of agreement should cover before negotiation, as missing an issue may mean that negotiations re-open to resolve it.

Heads of Damages: refers to the categories and basis for the pecuniary damages that may be awarded for IP infringement, usually regarded as an abbreviation for headings, i.e., paragraph titles. *See* Damages.

Healy's Rule (Law) of Holes, First Law of Holes: Dennis Healy, a U.K. Member of Parliament and former Chancellor of the Exchequer, famously commented "Follow the rule of holes; if you are in one, stop digging."

Herfindahl-Hirschman Index, HHI: a standard way of indicating the degree of concentration of an industrial sector. HHI is calculated by summing the square of the market shares of the market participants, usually expressed as a percentage rather than as a decimal. Thus for a given market, it can be expressed:

$$HHI = S_A^2 + S_B^2 + S_C^2 + S_D^2 + S_E^2 \text{ etc.}$$

The maximum possible HHI, one where 100 percent of the market is held by a single monopolist is 10,000, while for example a market with ten participants each with a 10 percent market share would have an HHI of 1,000. In a merger occurs between say, participant A and participant B, the HHI would then be recalculated thus:

$$HHI_{\text{Post Merger}} = (S_A + S_B)^2 + S_C^2 + S_D^2 + S_E^2 \textit{ etc.}$$

HHI is used in particular by United States Antitrust Division and United States Federal Trade Commission to measure whether a merger is unduly concentrative. In particular the "Horizontal Merger Guidelines" issued April 2, 1992, and revised April 8, 1997 set certain criteria for market concentration and allowable mergers, including mergers notified under the

Hart-Scott-Rodino Act. Where the post-merger HHI will be below 1,000 the agencies will regard the market as un-concentrated and the merger is unlikely to attract further scrutiny. Where the post merger HHI is between 1,000 and 1,800 the market is regarded as moderately concentrated and mergers that cause a change in the HHI of more than 100 would normally attract close scrutiny. Where the post merger HHI is more than 1,800 the market is regarded as highly concentrated and mergers that raise the HHI by 50 will attract close scrutiny and those raising it by 100 would be regarded as likely to have anticompetitive consequences.

The EU Horizontal Merger Guidelines (2004 OJ C 31/5) set forth slightly different HHI criteria. Where the post merger HHI is below 1,000, the European Commission regards significant analysis of the merger as usually unnecessary. Also, in general, where the post-merger HHI will be less than 2,000 and the merger caused a change in HHI of less than 250, or the HHI will be more than 2,000 but the change was less than 150, the Commission will normally not engage in significant analysis, except under certain circumstances such as: one of the merging companies is a new or potential entrant with an as yet small market share; one of the parties is a major innovator; there are significant cross shareholdings between market participants or the target company is regarded as an industry "maverick"; there is reason to believe that cartels have existed in the sector in the past; or the acquirer already has a 50 percent market share.

The problem with HHI as a measure is that it depends on what one defines as the relevant market. Take, for example, the market for fruit—if it is defined as say the supply of pears, the market might prove highly concentrated; if it is defined as the market for hard fruit (e.g., apples and pears), moderately concentrated; if defined as all fruit, un-concentrated. Arguably a merger of two of a small number of pear suppliers might result in a highly concentrated market, but if one were to regard apples as a substitute for pears, it would result in only a moderately concentrated market, while if oranges were added as a substitute, the market would be hardly concentrated at all. Much of the antitrust battle in complex mergers lies in addressing this issue of market definition and what are viable substitutes.

The origin of HHI lies with two economists, who working separately, developed a similar mathematical measure of concentration, which was subsequently dubbed with both of their names. Orris Clement Herfindahl was an agricultural economist (and noted ecologist) who developed his version of the index in 1952 at the University of Chicago while studying concentration in the steel industry. Herfindahl died in 1972 while trekking in Nepal. Albert O. Hirschman, a more prolific author, was a member of the Institute for Advanced Study at Princeton University, and is now retired.

Hockey-Stick Effect: term used in three contexts:

> First, to describe the tendency of company sales, particularly in business-to-business sectors to be concentrated at the end of a reporting period, creating a sales revenue graph that is said to resemble a hockey stick laid on its side, i.e., flat for most of the reporting period, but rising rapidly toward the end. The effect is said to arise because of the degree of synchronization of public companies' reporting periods, e.g., in the U.S., quarterly, beginning January 1st, April 1st, July 1st, and October 1st. The fact that companies have synchronized financial cycles in turn affects their budgeting and ordering calendars, creating a tendency for all to make decisions at the end of each reporting period, which cumulatively gives rise to the hockey stick effect.

> Second, used to describe the tendency of sales of certain products to rise rapidly with seasonal demand.

> Third, a discredited term used during the dot-com era in business plans to explain how a company burning money would achieve profitability at the end of the business plan due to a sudden surge in sales, triggered by a wide array of hypothetical factors, e.g., advertising finally proving persuasive, word of mouth bringing in customers, or "late adaptors" finally adopting the technology. In almost all instances the surge in sales never showed up. Indeed, occasionally the hockey stick turned out to be upside down, e.g., when the promotional budget dried up or initial public interest fell, sales collapsed.

Holdback: in development contracts and projects it is common for the customer to be allowed to retain a proportion of the contract price, ranging from 3-15 percent for a period of time after effective completion, which is paid upon a specified condition being achieved, e.g., no observed and un-repaired or un-rectified faults after ninety days; no observed faults during fifteen continuous days of operation; or certification and acceptance of the project product by a third party (for example a prime contractor). *See* Stage Payment.

Hot-Document: litigation and discovery term. Because of the vast amount of document production that litigation discovery, particularly in the United States, can result in, it is common for litigators reviewing document production to create a hot-document file that separates from the dross, copies of those documents that are regarded as useful evidence in a case. Different lawyers will usually have different approaches to organizing the hot-document file.

Hot Patent: refers to a patent, usually new, which is attracting considerable interest and is being frequently cited in pending patent applications. The Derwent Patent Indicators database maintains a list of hot patents.

HSR: Hart-Scott-Rodino (Antitrust) Act, which is Section 7A of the Clayton Act, 15 U.S.C. § 8a - U.S. Antitrust Merger review process required when a company being acquired meets a merger review threshold. The process usually takes 30 days, but can be cut short (early termination), or if subject to a Second Request, could take several months. Administered by either the Antitrust Division of the United States Department of Justice (DOJ) or the United States Federal Trade Commission (FTC). HSR only requires notification if transactions exceed certain transaction thresholds: in 2005 the notification threshold based on the value of the business or assets acquired (the "size-of-transaction test") was set at $53.1 million; the threshold based on party size (size-of-person test) based on the annual net sales and/or total assets of the acquiring and acquired persons was set at $106.2 million and $10.7 million, while the level at which the size-of-person test is eliminated for particularly large deals was set at $212.3 million. The thresholds are indexed to the inflation rate and so new thresholds are set annually. HSR notification is expensive both in terms of legal work and the HSR filing fee.

Human Capital: term that, in the business context, broadly refers to the value of employees in a manner that assesses them as more than fungible units of production. In assessing human capital, what is being considered is the range of benefits and value that employees, by virtue of their knowledge and their relationships both within an organization and in the broader commercial environment, as well as their goodwill and the goodwill of their friends and family, create for their employer. The underlying idea is that if businesses consider their human capital as important, then internal actions that increase human capital, for example, training and education, team-building exercises or benefits and treatment that foster employee loyalty, will be easier to justify; the same businesses will press for broader economic changes that foster the growth of human capital in their economies, such as better education and training, health care, etc. The main problem with human capital is that it is difficult to quantify or value objectively, nor can it be listed as an asset on a company balance sheet. The term is closely related and often used interchangeably with Knowledge Capital and Intellectual Capital, though it is in principle different since knowledge capital can be seen as simply a component of both human capital and intellectual capital. The leading proponent of the concept of Human Capital is the economist/sociologist Professor Gary S. Becker of the University of Chicago, who received the 1992 Nobel Prize for his work and authored *Human Capital* (Columbia University Press, 1964). Professor Becker's work focuses to large degree on the broad importance of Human Capital to economies as a whole, in terms of its impact on economic growth and standards of living.

I

ICANN: the Internet Corporation for Assigned Names and Numbers, the internationally organized, non-profit corporation that has responsibility for Internet Protocol (IP) address space allocation, protocol identifier assignment, generic (gTLD) and country code (ccTLD) Top-Level Domain name system management, and root server system management functions.

Idea/Expression Divide: refers to the principle that copyrights only protect the expression of an idea, but not the idea in-of-itself.

IDS, Information Disclosure Statement: a document that is filed in conjunction with a U.S. patent application. The most important feature of the IDS is that it lists prior art known to the inventor or the result of the inventor's prior art search and explains why they do not anticipate the invention. As a result the IDS is the most fertile field for finding prosecution history estoppels.

IEC: the International Electrotechnical Commission, a Geneva-based organization that develops and sets standards, including terms and symbols used to describe electrical circuits and devices through the International Electrotechnical Vocabulary; safety standards; standards for electromagnetic compatibility; electronic communication standards, etc. The IEC works through National Electrotechnical Committees and also cooperates closely with ISO, the International Standards Organization. As a result, many IEC standards are issued jointly with ISO and these are designated with an ISO/IEC prefix.

IEEE: Institute of Electrical and Electronic Engineers, an organization that among various activities establishes under its auspices committees responsible for setting many important standards used in radio, telecommunications and computing.

Impleader, Inpleader: the mechanism by which a party in a case, usually a defendant, brings into the case a third party on the basis that that party is necessary because its interests are directly at issue or because the defendant argues that the party either shares liability or is wholly liable for the plaintiff's claim.

Implied License: a license that results from the conduct of the intellectual property holder, rather than from a formal written or agreed license. For example, when a patent holder supplies a component only usable in a patented combination, there is an implied license to make the combination; or when a patent holder supplies a product only reasonably usable for an infringing process, there is normally an implied license to use it for that process.

Improvement Patent: *See* Incremental Patent.

Inadequate Description: a patent is supposed to teach a reader (usually of ordinary skill in the art) the invention. If it fails to do so, the description is described as inadequate. In U.S. law there are two major types of inadequate description, lack of enablement [q.v.] and failure to disclose the best mode [q.v.].

Incidental Copying: term used to refer to technically unauthorized copies of a copyright work made in the course of, and for the sole purpose of making an authorized copy, for example, when a copyrighted work is sent via e-mail a copy may be lodged in the e-mail server. Such incidental copying will not normally provide a basis for a claim of copyright infringement, provided the purpose was the making of an authorized copy. The term is also sometimes used to refer to unintentional copies of a work, made because it happened to be present when another work was being made, for example, a picture hanging on a wall in the background of journalist's interview of another subject, or loud music audible in a filmed piece that was not intentionally included by the person creating that filmed piece. Unless the taking was substantial and central to the item that includes the unintentionally made incidental copy, there is usually no basis for a claim of copyright infringement.

Incoterms: abbreviation of International Commercial Terms, a set of standardized trade terms developed by the International Chamber of Commerce or ICC in 1932 and updated regularly. There are thirteen established Incoterms, the most frequently used being EXW (Ex works),

FOB (Free on Board), CIF (Cost, Insurance and Freight), DDU (Delivered Duty Unpaid), DDP (Delivered Duty Paid), CIP (Carriage and Insurance Paid To), and CPT (Carriage Paid To). Great care should be taken using Incoterms in sales contracts, as use of the wrong term can impose significant unexpected handling costs on the vendor or buyer. In addition, because high technology products are typically high value, or are for use in time sensitive contracts, and Incoterms also define who bears the risk of loss of goods at various points in the shipping process, care should be taken to ensure that the insurance arranged matches the Incoterm(s) used.

Incremental Patent: a patent that adds to an existing technological field or improves the design or execution of already existing technologies but is not a fundamental or pioneer patent. Sometimes also referred to as an improvement patent.

IND: Investigational New Drug Application, an application to carry out human testing of a potential new drug, known as an NCE or New Chemical Entity. The IND process has three stages: Phase I, safety testing on a limited number of volunteers (20-80); Phase II, testing for efficacy and side effects on a larger group of volunteers, 100-300; Phase III, testing on 1,000-3,000 or more patients to determine whether the drug meets risk/benefit criteria, i.e., do benefits outweigh potential side effects. Typically less than 27 percent of drugs that enter stage I complete stage III, and not all such drugs are then marketed commercially. *See* ANDA, *Quasi*-Intellectual Property.

Indefiniteness: patent claims are required to clearly identify the scope of a claimed invention. In principle, if a claim is so vague as to be impossible for someone of ordinary skill in the art to understand what falls within the scope of the claims, the claim may be void for indefiniteness.

Indefiniteness, Void for, Invalid on Grounds of: a patent claim can be held void under §112 paragraph 2 of the patent act if it is so vague that it does not properly point what the scope of the holder's patent right under that claim in fact is. In particular, the Federal Circuit [q.v.] has established a standard that "a claim is indefinite if its legal scope is not clear enough that a person of ordinary skill in the art [q.v.] could determine whether a particular product or method infringes or not." An entire patent can be invalid or void for indefiniteness if it is not concluded with claims that adequately point out what is claimed to be the invention.

Indemnity: a promise to compensate another contractual party ("the indemnified" or "indemnitee") for the consequences of a possible event, for example, to pay any intellectual property infringement damages that might be awarded against a purchaser for use of a vendor's products. An indemnity is a form of insurance and indeed an insurance policy is in effect an indemnity agreement. Indemnities are either open or capped. That is to say there may be no ceiling on the amount of the indemnity or more sensibly the grantor of the indemnity ("the indemnifier") will limit its liability. Usually indemnity policies will require prompt notice by the indemnitee to the indemnifier of any claims and will typically provide that the indemnifier can control the legal defense of any claims. In many legal systems an indemnity cannot be granted before-the-event, that would shield the indemnified from the consequences of any illegal or prohibited acts by it, and in many an indemnity also cannot prospectively cover willful misconduct or gross negligence (which will often be excluded in any event, though it may pay damages to third parties over and above what the indemnified can pay). An indemnity is different from a warranty, though the legal consequences for an indemnifier or a warrantor may ultimately be the same. *See* Warranty, Representations.

Indemnity Principle: a term used to describe the rule that ensures that a prevailing party in litigation is compensated for all reasonable costs in securing the vindication of that party's position, i.e., indemnified for all legal costs. Under the indemnity principle the winner in a case should receive enough to put it in the position it would have been in if it had been in, had the case not taken place or not been necessary, i.e., if the defendant had paid the plaintiff's claim without the necessity of bringing suit, or if the plaintiff had not brought an invalid claim against the defendant. The indemnity principle is applied in most common law countries other than the United States, where it is known as the English Rule. It is usually subject to numerous exceptions. The indemnity principle is also sometimes stated as the rule that "costs follow the event." *See* Costs, Attorneys' Fees.

Independent Claim: a claim that does not rely on any other claim for its content, structure, or validity and is usually considered on its own for purposes of determining validity or infringement. The opposite type of claim is a dependent claim. One factor in evaluating independent claims that does relate them to other claims is the doctrine of claim differentiation [q.v.].

Inducement of Infringement: Under §271(b) of the United States Patent Act (35 U.S.C. §271(b)) "[w]hoever actively induces infringement of a patent shall be liable as an infringer." What this means in effect is that if someone is found to be responsible for an infringer's decision to infringe, that is to say to have persuaded or caused the infringer to commit the infringing act, that person is also potentially liable for the infringement. Although, this provision is capable of wider application, it is usually used to pursue the managers of an infringing company. U.S. case law has cut back significantly on inducement, requiring that a plaintiff show that the inducer's "actions induced infringing acts and that [the inducer] knew or should have known [inducer's] actions would induce actual infringement." However, that the inducer had "knowledge of the acts alleged to constitute infringement" is not enough and "[p]roof of actual intent to cause the acts which constitute the infringement is a necessary prerequisite to finding active inducement." Moreover, "[i]nducement requires proof that the accused infringer knowingly aided and abetted another's direct infringement of the patent." Nonetheless, "[w]hile proof of intent is necessary, direct evidence is not required; rather, circumstantial evidence may suffice."

Industrial Applicability: a requirement that an invention be "susceptible" of some industrial application, i.e., it must have some useful purpose, before a patent can be granted. The concept of industry is broadly interpreted. European and Japanese patents are required to have industrial applicability. Article 1 of the Patent Cooperation Treaty (the Paris Convention) sets forth guidance on industrial applicability. United States Patent law has an analogous rule known as the "Utility Requirement."

Industrial Design: ornamental or aesthetic aspects of an article, which can be the shape or surface of an article, features, such as patterns, lines, or color. Industrial designs can be protected using design patents, registered designs, original designs, or copyright law.

Inequitable Conduct: patent offices require applicants for a patent to display a high level of candor with the patent office. Failure to display such candor by, for example, not disclosing relevant information (such as known prior art), is in the United States known as inequitable conduct, which can render a patent unenforceable, or if it involves outright false statements can rise to the level of fraud on the Patent Office for which there can be potentially more serious penalties (including but not limited to cancellation of the patent).

Inevitable Disclosure: a term used in the context of confidential information, i.e., know-how or trade secrets used in manufacturing a product that will inevitably be capable of being determined by examination of the products. The term is also sometimes used when seeking an injunction to prevent an employee leaving to join a competitor, especially when the employee has signed a confidentiality agreement. *See* Lead Time Advantage.

Informational Asymmetry: refers, particularly in negotiation, to the greater level of information about the value of a transaction that one party in the negotiation possesses. Typically, this arises when one party is a more frequent participant in the market than the other, and hence has more knowledge about market prices and values or competitive information, or alternately, when one party participates at more levels of the market than the other. A classic example is in the real-estate market where the real estate agent (or realtor) is regularly selling or offering to sell property, whereas the typical buyer is only an episodic and infrequent market participant. In addition, the real estate agent knows of other potential buyers and the size of their likely budgets, as well as having direct knowledge of the vendor's actual bottom line. This places the real estate agent at a substantial negotiating advantage. Almost all negotiations are effected to a lesser or greater degree by informational asymmetry, the key to successful negotiation is to recognize what the asymmetries are, and to use research and other techniques to reduce their impact.

Infringement: literally means violating someone's rights. In intellectual property terms it means violating the exclusive rights of the intellectual property owner. Infringement is usually treated as a matter subject to strict liability.

Injunction: an equitable remedy [q.v.] that enjoins, i.e., prohibits someone, from doing something, such as selling infringing goods. An injunction is a presumptive remedy for infringement in most IP systems, usually coupled with damages.

Inoperative: a patent (or a claim of a patent) may be held invalid if the claim language and/or the specification describes and/or claims an invention that simply does not work. In particular in the United States such a situation causes the patent (or the claim at issue) to be invalid under the utility requirements of §101 of the Patent Act and the description requirements of §112. Outside litigation, an innocent error in the specifications or drawings of a patent that render the patent nonsensical or inoperative can be corrected by a reissue of the patent with corrections, however the patent holder must surrender the patent during the reissue process.

Insider Trading: the trading (i.e., buying or selling) of securities by a person on the basis of material non-public (or "inside") information. Although a problem for companies' generally, the difficulty with insider trading is particularly acute in mergers and acquisitions. Studies have shown that few items of information are as consistently leaked, particularly in certain economies, as the existence of merger discussions, so that worldwide, almost half of all M&A transactions involving public companies slip-out pre-closing or announcement. Such leaks are problematic for a variety of reasons. First, they drive up the price the acquirer must pay for the target, typically also increasing the control-premium (i.e., the amount over the market price) that the acquirer must pay by a further third. Second, if the merger is "full form," i.e., the acquirer is paying with its own stock, its share price will usually be depressed by a leak. As a result, such leaks can either "kill" a deal, or at least render it much more expensive for the acquirer. Third, target companies also, at least until they are committed to a transaction, have good reason to keep negotiations quiet, as a disclosure may disrupt customer relationship and cause internal morale problems as well as undermining the incumbent target management's own position if the deal does not go through, and damage the value of the acquired business. Fourth, resumés and *curriculum vitæ* can "fly from the target like confetti" if it is known to be in play, potentially seriously devaluing it. Addressing this category of leaks requires that the usual non-disclosure agreements

("NDAs") used to protect confidential business information be extended to all advisors of the target and acquirer and specifically encompass the fact of the contemplated transaction. It is not enough to assume that professional advisor organizations will have such confidentiality policies in place or carefully enforced; studies have shown they often don't.

It should also be noted that the attitude towards enforcement of insider trading laws varies markedly across the world. The rules are most strictly enforced in the United States, where even tiny insider trades are caught. By contrast, some countries with very "reputable" corporate cultures have in real terms enforcement that is so lax and slipshod, that insider trading is conducted in a laughably obvious and blatant manner, underlying participants' certainty that they will not be caught, or if caught, not prosecuted. As a result, if a transaction is price sensitive, it is best to tightly limit the employment of advisors from such jurisdictions.

Insurance Archaeology: refers to a process of reviewing all insurance policies ever held by a corporation to determine whether claims can be made against them for present liabilities based on their genesis in activities that took place when the policies were in force. Insurance archaeology focuses on policies that cover liabilities arising during the term of the policy (i.e., "occurrence policies" [q.v.]) rather than "claims made" [q.v.]. Because under U.S. law, liability for an array of claims, for example environmental liability or product liability (especially asbestos), may arise years and even decades after the events or activities that created them the product of such archaeology can be very valuable. In particular, under the Comprehensive Environmental Response, Compensation, and Liability Act of 1980 (CERCLA, known as the "Superfund"), a broad range of parties can be held jointly and severally liable for environmental cleanup costs, often for pollution that occurred decades before. U.S. courts have repeatedly held that companies can claim under the policies that were in force when the events or acts occurred, even where those acts were not prohibited during that time-frame. Moreover, U.S. courts have also generally held that a corporation that is liable for a predecessor's products or pollution can claim under a predecessor's applicable insurance policies. Further they have also held that an acquired corporation can expressly assign its insurance coverage to its purchaser, even without the insurer's consent after a loss has occurred and notwithstanding "no assignment" clauses. The result has been disastrous for many insurers, most notably syndicates in Lloyds.

Instruction Set: The collection of machine language instructions that a particular micro-processor understands. The term is largely synonymous with "instruction set architecture" or ISA, i.e., the parts of a processor's design that need to be understood in order to write assembly language, such as the machine language instructions and registers. Many aspects of instruction sets may be proprietary, i.e., covered by patents or only disclosed in a know-how license. The best-known instruction sets are the Intel's X-86 set and the ARM set.

Integration Clause: sometimes known as an "entire agreement" or supersedes clause, is a contractual provision to the effect that the document is the entire agreement between the parties and supersedes all other writings and understandings between the parties. The purpose of the clause is to try to strictly invoke the parol evidence rule. Such clauses are usually a standard provision in agreements, to such an extent that the absence of such a clause, especially when an agreement has been drafted by experienced counsel, is sometimes regarded as manifesting an intent to include various extraneous evidence in the agreement and may preclude application of the parol evidence rule.

Integrator, System: refers to a business that does not develop technology, but rather integrates other suppliers' technology, for example supplying computers, software, and network technology from various suppliers as a package, often combined with consulting services.

Intellectual Capital: refers broadly to the intellectual assets of an organization including Knowledge Capital [q.v.] and Know-How [q.v.]. Usage varies on whether other assets such as trade secrets, business secrets, and more recognized intellectual capital such as patents are included in intellectual capital. The term intellectual capital (or IC) was first popularized in Sweden and represented an effort to quantify the intellectual assets of a business in such a way as to include the knowledge capital and know-how not traditionally recognized under accounting rules.

Inter Partes: Latin term that denotes that both parties are present in the course of a hearing or legal proceeding, contrast with *Ex Parte*.

Inter Partes **Reexamination**: refers to a patent office proceeding to re-examine the grant of a patent, usually in light of prior art not before the patent office in the original examination, where third parties, for example competitors, are allowed to be present and argue against the re-grant of the patent or for more limited claims. *See Ex Parte* Reexamination.

Interference: a type of administrative action that takes place in the United States Patent and Trademark Office and arises because the U.S. has a first-to-invent [q.v.] patent system. An interference arises when two parties claim the same invention and is in essence litigation to determine who invented it first.

Interim Rights: When a patent application is published, interim rights start to accrue, which allow the patent applicant to sue for infringement damages, if and when the patent is ultimately granted.

Interlocutory Appeal: refers to an appeal permitted during the course of a lower court or tribunal proceeding, usually on a specific but crucial point of law. Interlocutory appeals are rare in most legal systems.

Internal Marketing: the process of "selling" a new product or service to a company's own employees and managers, or in the company's distribution channel. A failure to ensure internal marketing takes place may be a primary reason for poor performance when distribution agreements are made with fairly large distributors.

Interpleader: a process by which a debtor or holder of an asset, who has two different parties claiming the right to receive payment or the asset, can deposit payment or the asset with the court (or agree to turn it over), but petitions the court to resolve which of the two parties should receive it, in effect forcing the contending parties to fight the issue out between themselves and avoiding any liability that might result from making the choice itself.

Interrogatory: literally a question, but usually refers to the right of a party to a litigation to issue written questions in discovery to other parties on issues relevant to the case, seeking written answers.

Intervening Reference: with respect to an international patent application, a document published prior to the international filing date but later than the claimed priority date. Such a reference is also known as a P-Reference. *See* A-Reference, Y-Reference, and X-Reference.

Intervenor, Third Party, Interested Party: most legal systems allow third parties to intervene in legal proceedings where interests and rights might be directly implicated by the outcome. This is a particularly important right when the outcome of the case might effectively impose liability on the third party, or limit the third party's rights. The constraint on the right of intervention is that the third party must have some reasonably direct connection to the subject matter of the lawsuit, rather than an interest driven by the policy issues at stake in the case or general legal precedents likely to be set by a decision in the case. *See Amicus Curiæ.*

Invalidity: a defense to a case of infringement of an intellectual property right, in particular a patent, trademark or registered design. Invalidity with respect to patents can be found on a wide array of grounds including novelty (non-novelty) [q.v.], obviousness [q.v.], misidentification of the inventor [q.v.], fraud on the patent office [q.v.] (or very severe inequitable conduct [q.v.]), failure to teach the best-mode [q.v.], failure to disclose the preferred embodiment [q.v.], lack of enablement [q.v.], indefiniteness [q.v.], inoperability [q.v.] and failure to pay renewal fees. Trademarks are typically held invalid on relatively narrow grounds such as descriptiveness [q.v.], genericization (genericide) [q.v.], naked licenses and assignments [q.v.], non-use [q.v.], indecency and failure to pay renewal fees. Designs, such as registered designs and design patents are typically argued to be invalid on grounds of functionality [q.v.].

Invented Words (Fanciful Terms, Coined Terms/Words): refers to words made up by a trademark applicant and therefore not in the standard dictionary. Such words are relatively easy to obtain as a trademark.

Invention: in most patent systems an idea that is new (novel), useful, and not obvious to someone of ordinary skill in the art (non-obvious).

Inventor: the person or persons that had the patentable idea, that is to say contributed to its conception and to its reduction to practice.

Inventor's Bonus: in many countries an employee is entitled to some share of an employer's profits from an invention. For example, in the United Kingdom, an employee is in principle entitled to some part of the profits from an employee invention (Sections 39 to 43 of the Patents Act 1977); in Germany, employees should be compensated for an invention according to complex rules that take into account value, the employee's initiative, and position (Employees Inventions Act of July, 25 1957); in France, under a recent *Cour de Cassation* (Supreme Court) decision, the employee should be compensated according to the value of the invention. Most notably in Japan, Shuji Nakamura, whose invention of the blue light-emitting laser diode may yet win him the Nobel prize, claimed that his former employer Nichia Corporation awarded him a mere 20,000 yen (about $200) for an invention potentially worth billions of dollars; a Japanese court awarded him ¥60.4 billion (i.e., about $180 million) in a 2004 decision. Notably the court had ruled that he could have received half the lifetime value of the patent, estimated as in excess of $1 billion; in early 2005, during an appeal of the ruling Nakamura and Nichia settled for ¥840 million (then circa $8.1 million). This situation is in marked contrast to U.S. law. To avoid the risks that such requirements may impose, companies should ensure that employee inventions and other intellectual property is rewarded in a bonus program that is facially and broadly equitable. Such a program should have two components—a general element, which compensates all employees relatively equally for inventions, and a subjective element, which allows for extra bonuses to be paid where an invention turns out to be particularly valuable.

Inventor's Notebook: because of the United States' first-to-invent system [q.v.], it can prove important to show the date of reduction to practice in order to demonstrate priority. As a result R&D departments, particularly in the pharmaceutical sector, have developed a system of inventors' notebooks. Traditionally these notebooks were duplicate books, which made a carbon copy of each page, in which researchers noted all their work.

At the end of each day the inventor would then find a colleague who would countersign and date the pages of the notebook written that day, sometimes with a statement such as "read and understood by me." Researchers would keep the retained carbon copies in the notebooks on their office shelves, but the originals would be archived by the company. Modern inventor's notebooks are often escrowed [q.v.] electronic logs.

IP: (a) an abbreviation for intellectual property, as in IP Law; (b) an abbreviation for Internet Protocol, which in formal terms is the network layer for the TCP/IP protocol suite used in Ethernet networks, the most recent version of which is IPv6; (c) a more broadly used acronym for technical effects and business plans achieved via the Internet.

IPC: International Patent Classification, a taxonomy of patents established by the World International Patent Organisation (WIPO) to assist in searching patents and filing international applications.

Irish Copyright Exemption: Section 195 of the Irish Tax Consolidation Act, 1997 allows the Irish Revenue Commissioners to make a determination that certain artistic works are original and creative works generally recognized as having cultural or artistic merit. Once such a determination is made, earnings derived from these works are exempt from income tax. Classes of works that may benefit from the exemption include:

- Books or other forms of writing;
- Plays;
- Musical compositions;
- Paintings or other similar pictures;
- Sculptures.

However, there are exceptions, for example textbooks and professional works, advertising jingles, and essentially functional works. Not surprisingly, a larger number of popular writers and composers have established a residence in Ireland.

Irish Medicines Board: the Irish regulatory agency responsible for the approval of drugs (human and veterinary) and medical devices for sale in the Republic of Ireland.

Irish Patent Exemption: Irish tax law provides a total exemption from tax for income derived from "qualifying patents" received by a person resident in Ireland and not resident in any other country. A "qualifying patent" is defined as a patent *in relation to which* the research, planning, processing, experimenting, testing, devising, designing, developing, or similar activity leading to the invention that is the subject of the patent was carried out in Ireland. Further, distributions by Irish resident companies of income, which falls within the exemption, are also exempt for tax purposes. A qualifying patent does not have to be an Irish patent.

ISO: the International Organization for Standardization, a network of national standards institutes. ISO is the source of international quality standards, such as ISO 9000, ISO 9001, ISO 14000, etc. ISO 9000/9001 is a generic business processes (or management systems) quality standard, frequently specified in supplier contracts. ISO 14000 is an environmental quality and impact standard, which is from time to time specified in certain supplier agreements. Because ISO 9000 compliance may extend down through the supply chain from the original specifier, it is increasingly pervasive in inter-company contracts.

Issue Preclusion: a legal rule that precludes a party from re-litigating issues (other than on appeal), already addressed in a previous legal proceeding (usually) between the same parties. The application of issue preclusion is highly complex and decisions in one court do not necessarily preclude addressing the issue in another court, in the same or a different way. Nonetheless, in the event that there has been litigation between the same or related parties in the past, relating to the same subject matter, the question of issue preclusion should be considered and addressed. Usually foreign court judgments are not "issue preclusive" but they may be considered as influential on the same facts under principles of comity. In addition, various conventions, for example the Brussels Convention, may give decisions more far reaching issue preclusive effects between EU courts, while other conventions may preclude re-litigation of issues such as child custody. Issue preclusion is sometimes inaccurately referred to as collateral estoppel; the difference is that issue preclusion is usually mandatory while collateral estoppel is at the discretion of the court. The term issue estoppel is also similarly used, although again the word estoppel indicates a mandatory loss of the right to re-litigate an issue.

Italian Torpedo: a term coined by Mario Franzosi in a 1997 article, *Worldwide Patent Litigation and the Italian Torpedo,* published in the EIPR. It refers to the technique of filing a declaratory judgment case in a slow jurisdiction such as Italy, thereby under the Brussels convention [q.v.] precluding under the *lis pendens* rule [q.v.] another EU member state's courts from taking the infringement case, as it is already before another EU court. The result could be to stall the case for years. As a tactic this can be effective, but courts in many EU member states are beginning to reject this tactic and allow cases to proceed in their faster court notwithstanding the existence of an Italian torpedo.

ITAR: the United States' International Traffic in Arms Regulations, administered by the State Department's Directorate of Defense Trade Controls. U.S. regulation promulgated under the Arms Export Control Act, 22 U.S.C. §2778 and set forth in 22 CFR 120-130 with amendments in the Federal Register. ITAR governs primarily weapons and military equipment, while dual-use [q.v.] goods and other sensitive exports are governed by the Export Administration Regulations (EAR).

J

JDA: *See* Joint Defense Agreement.

Jepson Claim: a form of claim in which the preamble acknowledges the prior art and then proceeds to describe and claim an improvement to the prior art. Jepson claims can go so far as to recite "the invention as set forth in patent __, with the addition of ..." but usually they simply recite and reiterate a prior art description or claim damage before adding elements. Jepson claims are frequently used to secure blocking patents and force a cross license.

JFTC: Japan Fair Trade Commission, the Japanese government agency charged with enforcing competition law in Japan. The JFTC has published numerous guidelines, dealing with areas including licensing, merger review, and distribution. It is not unusual for the licensing or distribution guidelines, in particular, to be raised in negotiations, so it may be useful to be familiar with their provisions.

JNOV, JNV: *See* **Motion, to Dismiss, Summary Judgment, Set Aside the Verdict**

Joint and Several Liability: means that a number of people are jointly liable for a debt or claim. Joint and several liability can arise under a contract, but also as a result of certain torts. Where two or more persons or entities act in concert to violate another's rights, they may be joint and severally liable for all of the victim's injuries, regardless of whose conduct caused most of the damage, under a principle sometimes referred to as co-conspirator liability. Thus for example, in some legal systems, all members of a cartel may be held individually liable *in toto* for a victim's damages, regardless of the degree of their individual dealings with that victim. A party held jointly and severally liable in such a way can bring suit against the other "joint obligors" for contribution, i.e., that they should pay to the party held liable the share of the damages they were forced to pay. In most jurisdictions, each of a group of joint and several obligors can be sued separately, i.e., the plaintiff does not have to file a claim against all.

However, a few jurisdictions do require all joint obligors to be named as defendants, while many have a rule that provides that a release of any one joint obligor without reserving the putative plaintiff's rights against the remaining obligors, acts as a release of all the obligors.

Joint Authorship, Joint Work: a work created by more than one author in which the authors' contributions cannot be segregated. In such a work ownership of copyright depends on the relationship between the authors and the work. If they are employees, the copyright usually vests in the employer (subject to shop right). If they are independent, ownership depends on the agreement between the authors, or absent an agreement is typically joint and shared. This can be problematic as in some jurisdictions joint ownership means that the authors can each exploit the work as they wish, while in others, notably France and Germany, the consent of all joint owners is required to any copyright license.

Joint Defense Agreement (JDA): agreement between two parties on the same side of a lawsuit, usually both defendants (but sometimes and indemnifier and the beneficiary of the indemnity (or indemnitee/indemnified)), that allows their counsel to exchange information and discuss strategy, while preserving attorney client privilege. JDA's are particularly important when in U.S. litigation or when U.S. litigation is threatened. If joint parties communicate otherwise attorney-client-privileged information without a JDA, there is a substantial risk that a court will hold the communications non-privileged. For a JDA to be valid there must be a community or commonality of legal interest, e.g., parties should be defending the same or very similar claims, for example the same patent; JDA's can also be executed between a defendant/indemnitee and the indemnifier. Usually a JDA will, especially in the case of an indemnifier-indemnified relationship specifically provide that its sole purpose is the protection of privilege and preclude any other changes in the contractual/indemnity relationships between the parties. It is important to be aware that any statements made or information exchanged between the parties before the JDA is reached do not benefit from privilege. Moreover the parties' counsel should be part of the communication loop.

Joint Inventors: when there is more than one inventor, the inventors are joint-inventors and absent an agreement, each joint inventor usually has equal rights to use and exploit the resulting patent. *See* Un-Named Inventor.

Joint Venture (JV): an agreement of firms or individuals to jointly undertake a specific business project usually under the auspices of an SPV. Joint ventures [q.v.] can range from merger-like arrangements to cooperation in particular areas such as R&D, production, or distribution. Full-function joint ventures are ones in which the SPV is able to operate independently from the parent companies, because they contain all of the key business components such as marketing, distribution, etc. Joint ventures may raise issues under Competition Law, in particular JVs between competitors or potential competitors. The latter, especially if they are full function [q.v.], may be treated as concentrations [q.v.] (i.e., akin to mergers).

Joint Venture Notice: The European Commission in 1998 issued a notice stating which types of joint ventures would be treated as mergers for Competition Law purposes. *Commission Notice on the concept of full-function joint ventures under Council Regulation (EEC) No. 4064/89 on the control of concentrations between undertakings* 1998 OJ C 66/01. This a key document that should be reviewed whenever large companies are setting up a joint venture in the European Union and EEA or which would have substantial effects in the EU or EEA.

JPO: Japanese Patent Office.

Judgment Proof: term used by lawyers to describe a putative defendant who has so few available assets, that were a suit to be brought and won, funds to pay damages even amounting to the cost of bringing the suit would not even be available—i.e., too poor or with assets too sheltered to be worth suing.

Jurisdiction: literally means the right to make law. Its legal meaning is the persons, territory, or activities falling within the authority of a state or court. Obtaining jurisdiction in international litigation is a key issue; you cannot sue someone or a business unless the court you bring suit in has a basis for jurisdiction over the parties. In addition, there is a second problem, subject matter jurisdiction, which relates to the authority of the court or tribunal to consider the specific issues in suit. In the United States, the word jurisdiction is used in a number of ways: Federal Jurisdiction means that a matter falls under the authority of the Federal Courts, which usually arises when the case is under a Federal Law such as copyright, patent, Lanham Act Trademark Cases, Federal Antitrust or cases involving diversity of citizenship (i.e., in-state and out of state parties) and substantial sums of money; State Jurisdiction places the matter in state courts; and jurisdiction is also used in the sense of which Federal Judicial District the case can be brought in. *See* Venue.

K

Kankei: Japanese word for relationships, a core Japanese value. In particular, Japanese business highly values *kigyo-kan kankei,* which might best be described as long-term business relationships.

Kenri no Ranyo: Japanese term for Abuse of Rights [q.v.].

Kernel: The essential core part of an operating system, responsible for resource allocation, low-level hardware interfaces, security, etc. As operating systems are laden with an increasing number of utilities, applications, and bells and whistles, the term has been used to describe those fundamental elements of the OS that are essential for the computer to run. However, the definitional line between what is a kernel and what is the rest of the OS is fuzzy at best.

Key-Man Insurance: an insurance policy obtained by a company, which pays out to the company in the event of the death or disability of a "key employee." Particularly in startup companies, or companies that are beginning to enjoy early success, where a small number of key employees are responsible for much of that success, venture capitalists and lenders may require, as a condition of funding, that the company secure such "key-man" insurance.

Kicker Clause, Royalty: a clause that provides for a royalty rate to increase if the license turns out to be unexpectedly more profitable to the licensee than was assumed when the license was entered into. For example, suppose the license is based at a rate of 5 percent based on a market size of say $100 million, and sunk cost for plant and development of say $40 million (which the licensor must recover before making a profit), but the license parties are aware of another potential market or factor that could drive the overall market size to say $300 million. A kicker clause might be included that raise the royalty rate slightly if this market became accessible. Kicker clauses are very rare in *ad valorum* licenses, since the licensee can argue that the licensee benefits from the additional market based on the royalty rate. They are more common in paid up license situations or where a license fee has been charged, i.e., if the license cost, paid up, $5 million in the above context, a kicker clause might be for an additional $10 million. The upside of a kicker clause for a licensor is that it protects it from the consequences of mistaken assumptions; the downside for the licensee is that the license may cost more, the cost may be uncertain and a that a poorly drafted clause will result in a royalty dispute. *See* Escalator Clause.

Killer-App: colloquialism for a use or application for a technology (or a software application), which so useful and so rapidly adopted that it drives a large increase in sales of that technology. In desktop computers the original killer-app was considered the spreadsheet and especially the first widely used spreadsheet known as Visi-Calc developed by Dan Bricklin and Bob Frankston; later killer apps were easy to use word processing packages such as WordPerfect; networking software such as Novell Netware and most recently the widespread popular adoption of the Internet. In cellular phones, SMS or short messaging service has often been described as a killer app. Many commentators ascribe the post 2000 downturn in the technology industry to a dearth of killer apps, although it has also been noted that excessive reliance on killer apps has caused technology to have a pronounced boom-bust cycle. *See* Nifty-App.

Kind-Code: refers the letter designation placed after a patent publication by a national patent office or WIPO, e.g., B1, B2, A1, A2, A3, etc. These codes are not used consistently by different patent offices, so in the event of confusion is wise to look at the handbook of kind codes published by WIPO. Usually a B1 or B2 designates a published patent, A1 and A2 published applications and A3 a search report. Thus for example a European A1 patent publication is an application with the search report; an A2 is an application without a search report included; and A3 is a stand-alone search report. When a patent is granted, it is usually published as a B document.

Kitchen Sinking: tendency of a product to accrete a huge number of features between early design and the production unit (i.e., "adding everything but/and the kitchen sink") swelling cost, complexity, and reducing reliability.

Knock-Off: slang for counterfeit.

Knock-Out Reference: *See* X-Reference.

Know-How: information used in manufacturing and processes that does not necessarily need to be completely secret, but may include information that it is not readily available. *See* Trade Secrets, Business Secrets, Bigot List.

Knowledge Angel: individual whose assistance to a startup company is primarily in the form of advice and information.

Knowledge Capital: refers to the value to an employer of the on-the-job knowledge gained by long-term employees. Knowledge capital is in essence job or employer specific information on how to efficiently achieve employer objectives, ranging from simple know-how to a knowledge of the business organization itself and the broader commercial environment in which it operates. As a concept it seeks to recognize the idea that employees become more efficient and productive the longer they remain within an organization. Knowledge capital is closely related to intellectual capital [q.v.] and/or human capital [q.v.] and forms a component of both.

Know-Your-Customer Principle: key principle in international export controls and money laundering rules and refers to the idea that with respect to export controls you should affirmatively know who the customer for a service, product or products subject to export controls [q.v.] is, before shipping the goods, transferring information or delivering services; or with respect to money laundering, know the true identity and source of substantial funds used in a transaction.

Kokai: a published but unexamined Japanese patent application.

Kokoku: an examined and allowed Japanese patent application, the strongest form of Japanese patent.

L

Laches: a U.S. equitable defense based on prolonged acquiescence by the patent holder to the infringement, which precludes the collection of damages for past infringement. The infringer does not need to show that it knew of the patent for *laches* to apply, but rather that the patent holder's delay was unreasonable and that the infringer's position changed adversely due to such delay. The burden of proof with respect to such irreparable harm resulting from delay lies with the accused infringer for the first six years of acquiescence, at which point it shifts to the patent holder. *Laches* should be contrasted with equitable estoppel, which is a similar but different defense. For mysterious reasons, *laches* is almost invariable italicized.

Lake Wobegon Effect: the American writer-broadcaster Garrison Keillor presents the radio show A Prairie Home Companion from the fictional place "Lake Wobegon, where all the women are strong, all the men are good-looking, and all the children are above average." The Lake Wobegon effect refers to the tendency of some negotiators to take the position that everything they are offering is qualitatively better than what the counterparty is offering. The Lake Wobegon effect is particularly prevalent in cross-license negotiations where a one party will take the position that all of its patents are valid and infringed, but few or none of the counterparty's patents are valid and infringed. As a negotiating tactic it is usually antagonizing and counter-productive.

Landmine Judgment: an unpaid judgment enforceable only in a territory or territories where a person or company does not operate or have assets, and which it has chosen not to pay, typically a default judgment. So-called because the judgment sits, like a landmine, with the plaintiff waiting for the person or asset to expose themselves in an enforcement jurisdiction, whereupon assets will be seized. Companies early in their lives often tolerate the existence of default judgments, to find that they become commercial landmines in the future as the business grows.

Lanham Act: a United States statute, which includes a Federal (as opposed to State) law of unfair competition, as well as antitrust provisions and which also enacted the modern U.S. Federal trademark law. The trademark portion of the Act is codified at 15 U.S.C. 1051-1157. The antitrust provisions of the Lanham Act are administered by the United States Federal Trade Commission (FTC).

Law and Economics: refers to a movement within the academic law and increasingly the legal profession, which seeks to apply "economic theory and econometric methods to examine the formation, structure, processes, and impact of law and legal institutions." It regards law, or most law, and legal institutions as integral elements within economic systems and considers legal rules and laws as essentially variables within the economy designed to promote certain outcomes, particularly economic efficiency. Law and economics is regarded in some quarters as a conservative or *laissez faire* school of law, though this is not correct; left-wing legal scholars also resort to its concepts of the application of law as an economic act. Law and economics is particularly relevant to intellectual property, competition law, and international trade. A "free-markets" subset of the law and economics movement is known as the "Chicago School" [q.v.].

Layer Cake Architecture: refers to software that has been evolved through various versions (e.g., 1.0, 2.0, 3.0, etc.) by adding an additional software layer to the older version, solving certain bugs, and adding functionality. The result is software that can, over time, become bulky, with multiple layers whose interactions are often poorly understood. Layer cake architectures are common where earlier versions of the software were bought in from a third party or were inadequately documented, making it difficult to change the older version of the software by making direct edits to its code. Each successive layer then becomes equally difficult to change, leading to more layers, until the result is a huge, unstable pile of code.

Lead Time Advantage: refers to the advantage the first mover in a market obtains, by for example, establishing its brand first, making relationships with major distributors, etc. Lead time advantage can be a factor in patent damages, particularly for infringements late in the life of patents. It is also used to justify ongoing running royalties for access to know-how or trade secrets, even after inevitable disclosure, when, for example, products incorporating the know-how are placed on sale.

Legacy Software: obsolescent or old software that companies need to have access to, in order to exploit valuable data originally created or recorded using that software, typically information in databases, often on mainframes. Commonly an issue in the financial sector, but also present in computer reservation systems, yield management systems, etc.

Lemelson, Jerome: *See* Submarine Patent.

Leniency Programme: European Competition Law term. The Leniency Programme is set forth in the Notice on Immunity from fines and reduction of fines in cartel cases, 2002 OJ C 45/3. Under the leniency programme, a member of a cartel who cooperates with the European authorities may benefit from a partial or total reduction of fines. Essentially, the leniency programme is an EU Competition Law plea bargaining system.

Level of Market: refers to the economic level at which transactions are carried out, for example subcomponent supplier, component supplier, manufacturer, importer, distributor, sub-distributor, retailer, or reseller. Identifying a level of market is important in licensing and litigation, as the royalty base (which may establishing infringement damages) will vary by market level, increasing say as components are incorporated into finished goods or as each level adds its profit margin, but at the same time sales may become more fragmented and dispersed among the usually larger number of market participants at lower (closer to consumer) levels.

Lexicographer: refers to a phrase of U.S. origin to the effect that a patentee "is his own lexicographer," i.e., that the applicant for a patent can define the terms used in the patent to suit itself, and only if the patentee has not defined a word, will it be given its normally accepted meaning. A lexicographer is the author of a dictionary.

Licence/License: literally an agreement to refrain from asserting a legal right, thus for example a landowner can grant a license to another person to enter their land in a way which would otherwise be trespassing. Similarly, an intellectual property owner has exclusive rights to do certain things, but can license others to do what otherwise would be infringement of those exclusive rights. A license is sometimes described as a covenant not to sue. However, it can be argued that a license goes further than simply an agreement to refrain from asserting a right, but is in fact affirmative permission to do the acts licensed. A license is usually governed by the choice of law rules applicable to contracts and not to the law of the jurisdiction that conferred the IP rights at issue. It is important to specify the exclusionary rights the license is granted under. Absent such a definition the license will usually be taken to apply to all exclusionary rights held by the licensor. In European English licen**C**e is the noun, licen**S**e the verb; in north-American English licen**S**e is the more commonly used form, both as a verb and noun, and licen**C**e usually regarded as an alternate spelling. *See* Non-Assert.

License-Back Clause, Provision: in intellectual property licenses involving standards it is common to require licensees to license back to the licensor (or the standard setting group), on a non-exclusive basis, with rights to sublicense, any essential intellectual property, in particular patents, necessary to practice the standard as it may be evolved. This is done so as to preserve the integrity of the standard. The term grant-back clause is synonym.

Licensing Executive Society: the LES is an organization for in-house counsel and business executives involved in licensing.

Lifestyle Firm: a company that will provide a reasonable income for its founders and early participants, but is unlikely, either because of the desires of the founders or the nature of the business, to provide a satisfactory rate of return for investors who are not employees of the business.

Lingual Mark: mark that is expressed in a word or words, as opposed to a symbol or drawing.

Lisbon Agreement: Lisbon Agreement for the Protection of Appellations of Origin and their International Registration. *See* GDO.

***Lis Pendens* Notice**: a notice that may be filed in a registry of property ownership (i.e., where the property has "record title" recording the fact that a legal dispute exists concerning title to the property). The effect of such a notice is to preclude a buyer of the registered asset from being a bone fide purchaser as against the litigation-claimants listed in the notice. Usually, the prerequisite for filing such a notice is that a case must have already been filed. An inappropriately filed *lis pendens* may give rise to damages and not all registries provide for the filing of a *lis pendens* notice.

***Lis Pendens* Rule**: rule that in principle precludes one court from considering a case (*lis*) that is already pending before another court that also has proper jurisdiction over the matter. *Lis Pendens* can be based on principles of judicial comity (harmony) or alternately on actual strict rules such as Article 19 of the Brussels convention, which typically applies between EU member state courts, or in the United States, State, and Federal civil procedure rules. The purpose of the rule is to try to avoid the proliferation of litigation or contradictory rulings on the same case. The principle of *Lis Pendens* can drive a forum shopping race to court in intellectual property cases, with accused infringers seeking to file declaratory judgment cases before an infringement suit is filed.

Literal Infringement: refers to infringement of a patent claim by a product or process that fulfils without resort to the doctrine of equivalence, each of the claim elements or limitations.

Litigation Hold: under U.S. law, a duty to preserve relevant records, in any existing form, is triggered once a party is aware that litigation, or a government investigation is pending against it, "reasonably anticipates" such litigation, or is put on notice of an imminent suit or prosecution. Once the duty to preserve has been triggered, a party must take affirmative steps immediately to preserve information that they know or reasonably should know to be relevant to the action; reasonably calculated to lead to the discovery of admissible evidence; reasonably likely to be requested during discovery; or is the subject of a pending discovery request. It was the breach of this duty that caused the collapse of the accounting firm Arthur Andersen; breaches may also be sanctioned by fines or even by prohibiting the breaching party from mounting defenses to which the destroyed records may have been relevant as well as penalties for counsel. Jurors may also be advised by the judge that they can draw an adverse inference from the destruction of records, i.e., that they were destroyed to conceal something—usually as bad as possible.

To avoid these consequences a "litigation hold" should be placed in effect suspending the destruction of potentially relevant records including e-mails and computer files that otherwise would be routinely disposed of in the ordinary course of business under whatever document and record-retention policy is in force, and all employees who might have potentially relevant records should be formally advised not to delete, destroy, or otherwise dispose of them.

Little Lanham Act: refers to an unfair competition law enacted at the U.S. state level, which is analogous to the Federal Lanham Act. Little Lanham Acts are often broader and/or more broadly interpreted than the Federal equivalent.

Little Sherman Act: refers to certain antitrust laws enacted at the U.S. state level, the best known of which are New York's Donnelly Act, New York General Business Law § 340[6] and the various Cartwright Acts adopted in several states including California Bus. & Prof. Code 16720. These laws are typically analogous to §1 of the Sherman Act, and prohibit price fixing and other anti-competitive activities.

Lock-in: refers to the economic phenomenon that results when consumers or commercial users of a product or service are faced with high costs of switching ("switching costs") to an alternative technology. Lock-in may occur when the consumer or user incurs an outlay of high fixed costs, such as purchasing a particular technology (e.g., game console) that is not interchangeable with similar competing technologies, or where an alternate technology would require discarding substantial assets. The existence of substantial target customer lock-in may be a factor recommending an acquisition; it may also be a factor that is considered adversely by competition and antitrust authorities in reviewing a merger as it suggests an ability to abuse a resulting dominant position [q.v.]. *See* Legacy Software.

Lockout Device: embedded code or device, usually in software, that disables the software when the license is no longer valid. Lockout devices are often used on mainframe software, which is essentially leased; if the software vendor does not suspend the lockout periodically, the software is disabled. Similarly, some software samples are provided under a license, which allows a fixed period of use or fixed number of users. At the end of this period an unlocking key must be entered or the lockout device takes effect. Lockout devices are potentially illegal and may in some jurisdictions give rise to criminal liability, if the licensee is not informed of their presence and effect. It is also *highly inadvisable* to use lockout software in mission critical or safety applications. The lockout function should not normally be used if there is a dispute about license terms, rather than a clear violation, since this might in some jurisdictions give rise to serious legal liability.

Long-Arm Statute: U.S. legal terminology for a state statute which provides that the state may exercise jurisdiction over out-of-state persons based on certain "minimum contacts" with that state. The minimum contacts required for such a long arm statute to be applicable were first set forth in detail in a U.S. Supreme Court Case *International Shoe Co. v. Washington*, 326 U.S. 310 (1945) and widely known as *International Shoe*. It sets forth three bases for jurisdiction—which have been expanded on by later cases: (1) the defendant has had purposeful continuous and systematic contact with the jurisdiction and the case arises out of those contacts; (2) the defendant has had such a high level of continuous and systematic contact with the jurisdiction that even though the case did not arise out of those contacts, it is not unreasonable to bring suit there; (3) although the defendant's contacts are admittedly only sporadic or casual, the case arose out of one or more of those contacts. However, mere sporadic or casual contact with the jurisdiction, if the contact has nothing to do with the case, is usually insufficient to support jurisdiction.

Long-felt Need, Proof of: demonstrating that there has long been a recognized need for a purported invention, can, in the United States, support the non-obviousness [q.v.] requirement for a patent on the premise that given the need and an obvious solution, persons of ordinary skill in the art would have fulfilled it without the need for invention. U.S. commentators typically defend the use of long-felt need as evidence by the argument that true genius may lie in spotting an simple solution overlooked by others.

Loyalty Rebates: rebates paid to customers (particularly retailers) for not purchasing competing products. Loyalty rebates can be highly problematic under competition law [q.v.] particularly where the supplier holds a dominant position.

Lugano Convention: *See* Brussels Convention.

M

MAC Clause: *See* Material Adverse Change.

Machine Code: The representation of a computer program which is actually read and interpreted by the computer, often also called "object code." A program in machine code consists of a sequence of machine instructions, frequently interspersed with data. Modern programmers almost never write programs directly in machine code. Instead, they use a programming language to write source code, which is translated by a compiler specific to the source code and the machine code of the computer they are programming into the applicable machine code.

Madrid Agreement, Madrid Protocol, Madrid Union: the Madrid Agreement Concerning the International Registration of Marks, a system which allows for the multi-jurisdictional registration of trademarks through WIPO. The Madrid Agreement was made in 1891 and revised at Stockholm in 1967; the revised agreement is known as the "Madrid (Stockholm) Agreement." A number of countries found it difficult to become members of the Madrid Agreement and hence a separate Agreement, the Protocol Relating to the Madrid Agreement, which became effective December 1, 1995 was negotiated. The United States and European Union are notably signatories to the Madrid Protocol, but not the Agreement (though many EU member states have signed the Madrid Agreement too). The membership of both the Madrid Agreement and protocol are referred to as the Madrid Union.

Magill: refers to a famous 1995 European Court of Justice decision (*Radio Telefís Éireann (RTÉ) and Independent Television Publications Ltd. (ITP) v. Commission*, Joined Cases C-241/91 P and C-242/91 P), upholding an earlier 1989 decision by the European Commission (*Magill TV Guides* 1989 OJ L 7 8/43) in an essential facilities case and compulsory license case. In the case Magill, an Irish magazine, wished to publish a comprehensive weekly program guide in competition with the guides in magazine format (TVGuide, RTEGuide) available from the broadcasters then covering the Republic of Ireland, i.e., the BBC, RTE (Radio Telefís Éireann), and ITV

(Independent Television). However, the programmers only made their schedule information available to newspapers subject to a publishing embargo that meant they could only publish daily schedules on the day of broadcast (with two days' schedules on Saturday). The European Commission ordered the broadcasters to make the schedules available to their competitor as an essential facility, and since the Irish High Court had upheld the broadcasters' claim of copyright in the schedules (albeit a claim some commentators regarded as dubious), thereby compelled a license of the copyright in the schedules. Although regarded as a major precedent in compulsory licensing, Magill has not been frequently applied.

Mail Fraud: U.S. Federal law contains an immensely broad antifraud provision, 18 U.S.C. §1341 (Part I Chapter 63) which, because it was enacted when the power of the Federal Government was more limited, was confined to acts that in some way used the U.S. Mail (a Federal agency). A huge number of actions may provide a basis for mail fraud, if a single letter or package has been sent via U.S. Mail to an address in the United States, including under the statute:

> "devis[ing] or intending to devise any scheme or artifice to defraud, or for obtaining money or property by means of false or fraudulent pretenses, representations, or promises, or to sell, dispose of, loan, exchange, alter, give away, distribute, supply, or furnish or procure for unlawful use any counterfeit or spurious coin, obligation, security, or other article, or anything represented to be or intimated or held out to be such counterfeit or spurious article, for the purpose of executing such scheme or artifice or attempting so to do . . ."

Subsequently a similar provision, known as Wire Fraud (§1343) was enacted, which made criminal such acts if they used the "interstate wires," i.e., the telephone, radio, or television systems including faxes and probably e-mails and a third known as Bank Fraud (§1344), which now applies to defrauding any bank or obtaining by fraud any funds in the custody of the bank. In each case, the penalty for the fraud is a fine of up to $1 million and a jail sentence of up to thirty years. It should be recognized that these Federal fraud statutes are extremely broad and it is very easy to become liable under them even based of relatively incidental contacts with the United States. *See* RICO concerning potential civil liability for the fraud.

Maintenance Fees: fees that must be paid periodically after the grant of an intellectual property right such as a trademark, patent, etc. to maintain its validity. No maintenance fees are payable for copyright.

***Mareva* Injunction**: also known as a "Freezing Injunction," is an order obtained in an English, Irish, Canadian, or Australian court or court of another jurisdiction following English precedents, freezing specified assets of a defendant that are at issue in a case, where the plaintiff has demonstrated that there is a risk that such assets may be removed from the jurisdiction. Named after a well-known case, *Mareva Compania Naviera S.A.* v. *International Bulkcarriers S.A.*, [1975] 2 Lloyd's Rep. 509 (C.A.). It is usually applied for on an *ex parte* basis, in England known as an Application Without Notice.

Marriage Contract First: an aphorism used to remind people of the necessity of getting a deal in writing before conditions change. It is particularly relevant to arrangements with consultants or outside contractors to develop intellectual property, since an agreement once valuable contractor IP exists can prove expensive or difficult. *n.b.,* the aphorism is often regarded as quite rude and sexist.

Marketing Authorization: the official document or license issued by a national or trans-national drug licensing and approval authority, which renders a drug legal for sale in that authority's jurisdiction. It will specify the sales name of the product (if different from any generic name), the pharmaceutical dosage form(s), the quantitative formula per unit dose, the shelf-life, storage conditions, and packaging characteristics. It will also specify the information on which authorization is based (e.g., "The product(s) must conform with all the details provided in your application, as modified by subsequent correspondence.") It will also contain a list of the product information that can be provided to health-care professionals and to the public and will state the name and address of the holder of the authorization, and the term of the authorization. Marketing authorization is reviewed periodically, usually every five years. Drugs that have marketing authority are described as registered and the list of such drugs as the register.

Marketing Rights: term used broadly to describe intangible rights used in the process of selling or promoting goods. They would include such things as ownership or control of advertising, Rights of Endorsement, Rights to Endorsement, rights to use trademarks, etc. The term is also use to describe exclusive distribution agreements and/or exclusive licenses for a territory or field of use.

Market Level: *See* Level of Market.

Marking Requirement: United States patent law has a provision that requires a patent owner or licensee to mark goods with applicable patents. The requirement is fulfilled by marking the product with the word patent or an abbreviation (e.g., U.S. Pat) and the patent number. If it is not feasible to mark the product, the packaging can be marked. Falsely marking a product with a patent or using an expired patent may be punishable by a fine and other sanctions. Failure to comply with the marking requirement reduces the remedies available to the patent holder, and in particular can preclude the recovery of damages for patent infringement for activities before an infringement case is filed or to those arising subsequent to an explicit warning letter. *See* Symbol with respect to Copyrights and Trademarks.

Markman Hearing: one result of the United States Supreme Court Case, *Markman et al v. Westview Instruments, Inc. et al*, 517 U.S. 370 (1986), was to clearly place the responsibility for claim construction [q.v.] in the hands of the judge rather than the jury. As a result in a U.S. patent case, before trial, the court holds what is known as a Markman hearing at which the Judge determines the meaning of the claims and the claim terms and issues a "Markman Ruling." The hearing is usually hotly contested, since both infringement and validity of the patent may turn on its outcome. A high proportion of U.S. patent cases settle after the Markman ruling issues. *See* Claim Chart.

Markush Claim: covers a chemical compound with symbols replacing certain chemical groups. Various chemical groups, which can then be substituted for the symbols, are then listed. For example it could list C_2H_5R as the compound and then state that R can be either chlorine, bromine, a hydroxyl group, etc. They can also be written as hardware claims or claims on products whose novelty lies in their ability to combine various items from a list, e.g., "a product which combines two or more of the following features: a, b, c, d …"

Maskwork: refers to Semiconductor Chip Topography Protection, a widely adopted form of copyright-like protection for the design of the circuitry on semiconductor devices. Such circuitry is etched using a photolithographic process in which the negative is known as a mask. In principle it used to be easy to uncover the circuitry of a microchip, photograph it, and create a new mask. However, by the time maskwork laws were enacted in most countries, this type of crude copying was no longer practical due to the shrinking size of circuits and the use of multilayered circuitry.

MAS Schedule(s): *See* GSA Schedules.

Material Adverse Change: because public company (and other business) acquisitions can take a protracted period to close, a merger or acquisition agreement will typically contain a clause that permits the acquirer or merger partner to abandon the transaction or renegotiate price in the event of a material adverse change at the target in the course of the transaction. Because the term "material adverse change" is open to interpretation and an acquirer as the transaction closing approaches would be in a very strong negotiating position, such clauses are often closely negotiated with certain likely MACs being specifically defined (especially as to materiality). MACs can also include untoward facts brought to light in due diligence.

Material Misstatement: U.S. securities law term describing false or inaccurate statements, or omissions of important information, concerning a company's business or prospects which can lead buyers of its shares to over-estimate their value or the company's likelihood of success. Inaccurate or deceptive statements about intellectual property rights have been held to be material misstatements, for example:

- Statements that a company had a pending patent and trade secrets for its technology in the United States, when in reality the patent had already been assigned to another company.
- Stating that a company had a patent when it had only made patent applications and was in fact reliant on third-party technology;
- Falsely stating a company owned patents or patents-pending on Internet-related inventions;
- Misstating the value and extent of a business' copyright assets;
- Implying a company had U.S. patent protection when it in fact only held a Russian Patent;
- Concealing the rejection of a patent application;
- Concealing an adverse court ruling relating to intellectual property;
- Falsely stating that technology was not subject to third party IP rights because it had been developed in a clean room [q.v.]; and
- Misleading statements about the FDA approval process or status of a drug or medical device.

Because many senior managers poorly understand intellectual property rights, the risk of a material misstatement in this area is high.

Means-Plus-Function Claim: a claim, which contains elements written in terms of "means for," and identifying a function. In U.S. patent law such language is permissible under 35 U.S.C. §112, but such claims are "construed to cover the corresponding structure, material, or acts described in the specification and equivalents thereof" i.e., they are usually limited to the means described in the specification employed for the same function.

Mechanical Royalties: refers to royalties for mechanical recordings i.e., records, tapes, and CDs, paid to the songwriter and composers at a fixed rate per unit. Many countries' copyright statutes provide for a fixed rate to be paid in the absence of agreement between the songwriter and the record company, but usually a lower rate is agreed.

Mediation: a usually non-binding form of dispute resolution where a neutral third party seeks to help the parties reach a mutually satisfactory settlement. In many legal systems a judge will require parties in a case to submit to mandatory non-binding mediation before trial.

Memorandum of Understanding: *See* MOU.

Memory Footprint: the memory available in most computers is not infinite and computers typically simultaneously run multiple programs. Moreover in mobile battery powered devices the addition of more random access memory (RAM) to run programs increases power consumption. For this reason it is common to specify in software development contracts that the delivered product, when compiled, should use less than a specified amount of memory, i.e., the memory footprint shall be less than X bytes.

Merchandising (Merchandizing) Rights: usually refers to the right to manufacture, sell, and distribute goods based on a copyrighted work, e.g., music, film, play, book—and more specifically individuals, events, images, or things found in it. Typically such rights would be to things such as toys, tee shirts, posters, etc. The term has no strict legal definition and so such rights in contracts must be very carefully defined.

Merger Doctrine: although the term is widely used in law, including criminal and property law, in intellectual property it refers to a concept of U.S. copyright law that where an idea is inextricably tied up in an expression of the idea, such that the idea cannot be repeated without using the expression, no copyright can subsist in the expression. The best example of the merger doctrine in action would be a mathematical equation.

Merger Regulation, European, European Community (ECMR) : Council Regulation (EC) No 139/2004 of 20 January 2004 on the control of concentrations between undertakings, the European Regulation governing the review of mergers and other "concentrations" affecting the EU. The EU has adopted a merger regime that is intended to only provide a "one-stop-shop" review of mergers large enough to effect a substantial part of the Single Market. Mergers without such a "Community Dimension" are still potentially subject to review in Member States, most of whom have adopted regimes broadly similar to that provided under EU law and may also be reviewed under a "Dutch Clause" [q.v.] referral. Before a merger is viewed as having a "Community Dimension" so that the regulation automatically applies, the merger must meet certain turnover thresholds:

Either

(a) the combined aggregate worldwide turnover of the business involved is more than €5,000 million, _and_
(b) the aggregate turnover in the EU aggregate of two ore more of the businesses involved is €250 million (except where two-thirds of the turnover in the EU of each of the businesses concerned is in the same single member state).

Or

(i) the combined aggregate worldwide turnover of the business involved is more than €2,500 million, _and_
(ii) in each of at least three Member States, the combined turnover of all the businesses concerned is more than €100 million;
(iii) and in each these three Member States the aggregate turnover of at least two of the businesses is more than €25 million;
(iv) the aggregate turnover in the EU aggregate of two ore more of the businesses involved is €100 million (except where two-thirds of the turnover in the EU of each of the businesses concerned is in the same single member state).

Under the Merger Regulation the European Commission must normally complete its review of a merger within 25 working days, unless it decides that the merger must be exempted under Article 85(3) in which case it must normally complete its review within 90 working days.

Metering: a term used in licensing to describe methods for trying to work out the extent of the licensee's use of the licensed technology, by, for example, looking at the number of unique components purchased. Running royalties should usually be tied to something that can be metered easily and reliably.

Method Claim: a claim that describes the invention in terms of a process for achieving a result. By contrast, see Apparatus Claim; _see also_ Claims.

Mezzanine Finance: Refers to venture capital financing for a company in the period between the business being reasonably stable, but before its IPO.

Mezzanine investors are taking a lower risk of loss than those investors who have invested in an earlier round, because they invest once it seems highly likely that the company will be the subject of an IPO.

MFN: acronym for most favored nation rights. A trade law term that refers to the language used in freedom, commerce, and navigation agreement (FCN) under which countries agree to trade with one another. Most favored nation usually means that trade with that country will attract the lowest possible tariff and other trade terms applied to any other trading country. All parties to the General Agreement on Tariffs and Trade (the GATT) are obliged under to apply MFN treatment to one another under Article I of the GATT.

MFN Clause: refers to a provision in a contract or license agreement that provides that one party shall grant the other terms at least a favorable as those granted to any other business partner. MFN clauses are highly problematic for a number of reasons. First, they are often agreed to by startup companies and act as handcuffs for them in future dealings. Second, their actual interpretation and effect is often hard to determine since different agreements can be *sui generis* [q.v.] with for example a running royalty offset by say an upfront fee or other financial compensation. For this reasons lawyers often advise against their inclusion in an agreement. Also known as a NLF or Not Less Favored Clause or sometimes as an MFP or Most Favored Party clause.

MHRA: the United Kingdom Medicines and Healthcare products Regulatory Agency, the agency responsible for the approval of drugs and medical devices for sale in the United Kingdom.

MILSPEC: abbreviation for military specification. It is the minimum acceptable requirements for products procured by the United States Department of Defense. Use of the term MILSPEC indicates that the product meets applicable military specifications. To reach MILSPEC, a product may also be required to include certain features or MILSPEC quality components. Qualifying for MILSPEC can confer many of the features akin to intellectual property rights in terms of product differentiation, especially where only a limited number of suppliers can reach the required standards. *See also* NATO-STANAG.

Minefield Strategy: expression often used to describe a patent strategy that seeks to cluster patents rather than having a diverse scattered patent portfolio. The analogy is typically to that of laying a minefield. There are in principle two choices that can be made, scatter the mines at random, or alternately place them around the most logical paths for an opponent to follow; the latter is more likely to be an effective obstacle.

Minimum Contacts: *See* Long-Arm Statute.

Minimum Sales Requirement: clause, usually included in an exclusive license or distribution agreement, which requires the licensee or distributor to make a minimum amount of sales in the exclusive market(s) or face loss of at least the exclusivity rights under the agreement, if not termination *in toto*.

MIPS-Based License: a type of license used with mainframe software, which limits the size of the computer or CPU the software can be used on. MIPS means million instructions per second and is a unit commonly used to give the rate at which a processor executes instructions. IBM uses a similar benchmark called MSU or measured service units. The advantage of a MIPS based license for a mainframe that acts as a server for a large number of terminals is that MIPS bears a relationship to the use that those terminals are making of the software running on the server. The difficulty is that minor upgrades can push the licensee past the MIPS limit or that with legacy software, mainframe power is increasing steadily in such a way as to render it difficult to replace an old system with a mainframe of similarly small capacity. *See* Power-by-the-Hour.

Misappropriation: term used for theft, particularly the theft of know-how, trade secrets, or business secrets.

Missing Inventor: *See* Un-Named Inventor.

Misuse: refers to commercial strategies that seek to extend the economic benefits of an item of intellectual property beyond is lawful scope. Typically misuse involves a violation of antitrust or competition law, such as illegal tying.

Monetize (Monetise): two meanings. The classic meaning in economics is to allow inflation to effectively eliminate or drastically reduce the real value of a debt, in particular where a government prints money to inflate its currency, lowering the absolute value of the parts of the national debt denominated in the home currency. Alternately, it is sometimes used as a way of describing converting intangible assets, especially patents, into revenue and value, usually by seeking royalty-paying licensees.

Monkey Analogy, the: an analogy sometimes used in copyright law, to the effect that an infinite number of monkeys, left in front of typewriters for an infinite period of time, would eventually type out Hamlet (or alternately the entire works of Shakespeare). In such an event, it is usually suggested that the work would not infringe Shakespeare's copyright or that the monkeys would enjoy copyright in their work.

Although initially appealing, the analogy is a legal nonsense. First, Shakespeare has been dead for hundreds of years—since copyright in a work endures only for life plus seventy years, it is self-evident that Shakespeare's works are in the public domain and copyright could not be infringed, either by intentional retyping or simian hammering. Second, in principle, the random typings of monkeys are so devoid of aesthetic and literary intent, that whatever resulted, even Hamlet, would not likely be entitled to copyright. Third, how would one prove infringement (assuming the monkeys did have copyright) given the existence of an identical version of the work already in the public domain?

How the analogy came to be used (usually verbally) in copyright law is obscure, as indeed is the origin of the analogy. The mathematician Emil Borel, in a 1909 book on probability theory surmised that "dactylographic monkeys" left in front of a typewriter keyboard long enough would eventually type every book in the French National Library. Later the physicist Arthur Eddington suggested in *The Nature of the Physical World: The Gifford Lectures* (Macmillan 1929) "If an army of monkeys were strumming on typewriters they might write all the books in the British Museum."

This scale of this challenge has in theory reduced since the library of the British Museum (the then British National Library) has been since been transferred to a separate institution, the British Library (but more books have been published). However, the origin of the migration of the work recreated by the monkeys from assorted libraries to either Hamlet or all of Shakespeare's works is, as yet, unknown. What is known is that in 2003, scientists from the University of Plymouth working at Paignton Zoo in Devon, England, decided to practically test the theorem by leaving a computer keyboard in the enclosure of six Sulawesi Crested Macaques for a month. At the end of this period the monkeys had produced five pages consisting mostly of the letter S, had attacked the keyboard with a stone, and then urinated and defecated on it. It should be recognized though, that the experiment did not disprove the theorem; rather it was inconclusive due to the failure to use sufficient time, and indeed the use of macaques—maybe they should have used more-intelligent chimps—although technically chimps are apes rather than monkeys.

Monopoly: a market where there is only one potential supplier.

Monopsony: a market where there is only one potential purchaser.

Moot, Issue is: most commonly used in U.S. law to describe a situation where the outcome of a court ruling is no longer of practical relevance, i.e., any ruling could no longer alter the facts. For example, a death penalty appeal is rendered moot by the defendant's death, since the outcome of the case can no longer affect his fate. Where a case is "moot" a U.S. court may be unable to hear it because of the absence of any "case or controversy" as required by the U.S. Constitution.

Moral Grounds: in many patent systems a patent can be denied on "moral grounds," if it for example, would be used primarily for an illicit purpose such as taking illegal drugs. In some countries patents on sex toys and even contraceptives were sometimes also refused on moral grounds. *See* Scandalous Mark.

Moral Rights: rights that are granted to the authors of literary, dramatic, musical, and artistic works and to film directors that allow them to:

-        be identified as the author of the work or director of the film;

-        and to object to derogatory treatment of the work or distortion
         or mutilation that is prejudicial to the honor or reputation of
         the author or director.

Moral rights usually do not normally apply to computer programs, articles
in   newspapers   or   magazines,   reference   works   (dictionaries   or
encyclopedias), or works where the original copyright was vested in the
author's employer. In many countries (such as France and Germany) moral
rights arise automatically in literary and artistic works and are usually non-
assignable; in others such as the U.K. and United States the author must
expressly reserve such rights.

Motion, to Dismiss, Summary Judgment, Set Aside the Verdict: a
motion is a request filed before the court that it issue a particular order or
take a particular course of action. Most legal systems provide that early in a
case, a defendant can file a *motion to dismiss* the plaintiff's claims on grounds
of legal insufficiency, a type of motion also sometimes called a "demurrer."
To explain, if a plaintiff is bringing a claim that requires it to show factual
elements a+b+c+d to succeed and the factual assertions made by the
plaintiff support on a+b, but not c or d, the case is incomplete and should
be dismissed. Normally the court will offer the plaintiff the opportunity to
re-file its claims, if it can assert the missing elements.

Motions to dismiss can be based both on the asserted factual bases of the
underlying claims or on issues such a jurisdiction. By contrast a *summary
judgment* motion usually occurs later in the case, once evidence is before the
court. In a summary judgment motion, the defendant argues that while the
plaintiff is required to show elements a+b+c+d for its claim to succeed, the
plaintiff has failed to advance evidence on which a reasonable person could
find for example that c or d were present and the action would therefore
necessarily fail. In such a case that specific issue does not proceed to trial.

In common law courts with juries, the usual principle is that the judge
controls the law and juries make factual findings based on the evidence
before them. However, after a jury has rendered a factual verdict, if the
judge regards the conclusions of the jury as unfounded, the judge may set
aside the factual findings, i.e., the verdict. In particular if for example a
party needed to show factually a+b+c to succeed on a point in a case and

the judge felt that the jury's verdict had been reached despite a lack of adequate evidence of say fact b, the judge could *set aside the verdict*. This power is designed as a check on runaway or biased juries. Lawyers often refer to this motion and decision as a JNOV, an acronym for *Judgement Non Obstante Verdicto* or JNV, Judgment Notwithstanding the Verdict.

MOU, MoU: acronym for memorandum of understanding. An MOU is in principle a non-binding agreement between two parties, typically written in the course of contract negotiations as a preliminary to drafting a definitive agreement. Typically an MOU will contain a clause specifying some or all of the MOU as not binding—though most commonly that clause makes an exception of choice of law and forum provisions and frequently confidentiality provisions as well. The practical legal effect of MOUs is typically poorly understood. While in principle the MOU is non-binding, it can as practical matter become part of the contract; for example; if the definitive agreement is vague on a point, depending on the application of the *parol* evidence rule, the MOU is likely to be consulted to help interpret the definitive agreement. More significantly, if no definitive agreement is in fact made and the parties go forward with the business arrangement contemplated in the MOU, it will almost inevitably be considered as strong evidence as to what the unwritten contract between the parties in fact was. In this way, MOU's can come to bind the parties.

Mouse-trapped: generally refers to a business agreeing to contract provision(s) that unwittingly lock it into a particular long-term commercial relationship (usually dependent) with a counterparty, in a manner highly beneficial to the counterparty and harmful in the long term to the business. Usually, this involves the offer of a facially very attractive proposal to a company that needs a business relationship, for example a startup company's first significant deal. The analogy is to a mouse entering a trap attracted by very attractive bait. Three areas that present a high risk of mouse-trapping are ownership of rights to use intellectual property, MFN Clauses, and options or rights to future developments.

MPEP: the Manual of Patent Examining Procedure, a list of rules developed by the USPTO for the examination of patent applications before it.

MPP: Manual of Patent Practice a list of rules developed by the U.K. patent office for the examination of patent applications before it.

MTF: Merger Task Force, a division of the European Commission's Competition Directorate General that reviews mergers which meet European merger review thresholds.

Multi-Sourcing, Multi-Sourcing Agreement: in some industries, major companies often seek to ensure that there are multiple sources of supply of key strategic components. To achieve this objective they often press a key supplier to license a second source manufacturer to supply the component. Agreeing to such an arrangement can be very high risk for the supplier, since it may in effect be creating its own competition.

Munitions List: lists maintained by countries implementing export controls [q.v.] identifying those items that are considered munitions or components of munitions and therefore subject to export licensing.

N

Naked License or Assignment: In the United States, trademark licenses (or assignments) that do not contain provisions to ensure that the quality associated with the mark is maintained may be regarded as "naked," i.e., not clothed in any meaningful quality standard; as a result the mark can be treated as abandoned and thereby lost. A naked assignment is also known as an Assignment in Gross.

Naming Rights: refers to the right to put a name on a building or event, for example, the Pan-Am building in New York (now the Met-Life building), Enron Field (now Minute Maid Park), the Budweiser Irish Derby, etc. *See Quasi*-Intellectual Property.

Nasty-gram: slang for a warning letter [q.v.], i.e., a cease or desist letter or a letter threatening some course of action (pun on telegram).

National Agency for Medicines: *Lääkelaitos Läkemedelsverket*, the regulatory agency responsible for the approval of drugs and medical devices for sale in Finland.

National Institutes of Health: Prestigious U.S. Federal government medical research organization.

National Phase: after a PCT application is received in a national patent office, the inventor must elect to convert that PCT application into a national application for that specific country, by for example, paying national filing fees, translating the application and redrafting it to match local rules. This step is known as entering the national phase.

National Treatment: most commercial treaties, especially involving intellectual property, for example the TRIPS, the Berne Convention and the WIPO treaties as well as FCN agreements, provide that citizens of signatory countries are entitled to the same legal treatment in other signatory countries as that countries nationals would receive, i.e., that they shall not be discriminated against in law.

NATO Patent: refers to a patent that has been classified as secret for security reasons. Various agreements, particularly between NATO countries allow for such secret patent to be granted and mechanisms exist for compensating their inventors.

NATO-STANAG: Term for the North Atlantic Treaty Organization Standard Agreement, which established a NATO-wide form of MILSPEC.

NDA: acronym used for two purposes, New Drug Application and Non Disclosure Agreement.

Negative Clearance: a ruling by the European Commission in response to an application (made essentially on the same Form A/B as a notification) that an agreement or practice does not violate Articles 81 and/or 82 of the Treaty of Rome (Amsterdam) [q.v.] and therefore raises no issues under Competition Law [q.v.]. Although the Commission can issue negative clearances, in practice it rarely does so, since each may be regarded as establishing a legal precedent.

Neighboring Rights: refers to copyright rights in music of recording artists, record producers, and broadcasters, and encompass copyright in performances, and sound recordings and communication signals of those performances.

Net Participation, Share of the Net: entertainment and movie industry jargon for a really bad deal with respect to participation. Net receipts usually means revenue minus expenses. The problem lies in the definition of expenses, which might for example include taxes, allocated overhead for the studio and production company (including losses made on other films), arbitrary fees charged by the studio and production companies' related companies; actors' and producers' salaries and their share of the revenues (i.e., their participation), and their (and their entourages') hotel rooms, Winnebagos, apartment and house rentals, travel expenses (usually first class or private aircraft), and as any remotely chargeable extravagances; bonuses for studio executives, promotional costs, crew salaries and expenses, catering, parking tickets for everyone connected with the production, amortization of the studio lot, and whatever else the studio or production company's bookkeepers and accountants can think of. As a result, such an arrangement means that when a recipient gets a share of the net receipts, it typically means zero (or indeed less). Hollywood is replete with stories of authors of blockbuster movies, which took huge sums at the box-office, who received nothing because they had agreed to receive net participation, or their participation was not calculated from "dollar one." Such a proposal is usually worthless to the recipient, unless he or it is looking for tax losses. Contrast with Gross Participation. *See also* Adjusted Gross Participation.

Net Receipts: entertainment and movie industry jargon for the revenue a production generates after the deduction of expenses. Through the "wonders" of entertainment industry accounting, this amount is almost inevitably zero, or indeed less, whether the production was a blockbuster or not. Usual basis for calculating net participation [q.v.].

Network Effects: value that is generated by widespread adoption of a technology. The term was coined by the American technologist Robert Metcalf, a key pioneer of the Internet, who coined Metcalf's law, that states that the value of a network is approximately equal to the square of the number of users of the network (i.e., n^2). Recent analysis has postulated that the real value of a network is in fact: $n.\log_e n$ (or $n.\ln(n)$). In any event, the basic point is that the value of a network rises dramatically as the number of users increases. The classic example used to describe this effect is the advent of the telephone and later the fax (tele-facsimile) machine. Assuming, *arguendo* that only one person has a fax machine, it would be useless; once two people owned fax machines, the value would increase substantially, but each machine's utility would be limited to sending messages to just that one other machine. However, as more people acquire a fax machine, the value of a fax machine to the owner of each existing machine rises because of the rising number of potential communication partners their device has. Standards are said to be particularly valuable when they drive network effects.

New Drug Application: application to a drug-licensing agency for approval to sell a new drug for a specific treatment.

New Headquarters/Office Syndrome, Shiny: anecdotal experience tends to lead many people in the technology industry to suggest that growth (or newly "sexy") companies rapidly head into difficulties at about the same time as they move from the seedy garages and crumbling buildings they started in to shiny new office buildings. The evidence has not been the subject of any formal study and so remains anecdotal, but instances are sufficiently frequent to render it difficult to discount the syndrome. Suggested underlying reasons include, growing corporate bureaucracy and vanity with an attendant lack of close focus on the business and rising internal politics, distraction associated with the move, or the dispersal of employees (not all of whom may get desks in the shiny new office) and the segregation of management from the operative end of the business, harming communications and eliminating the coffee-pot effect/water-cooler channel. Another suggestion sometimes made is that "when your office is a dump, you're inclined to go out and look for business; when your office is pleasant and comfortable, why not sit back and enjoy it?" Numerous instances of the syndrome were set forth in C. Northcote Parkinson, *Parkinson's Law: The Pursuit of Progress*, London, (John Murray, London 1958, Houghton Mifflin, New York, 1962).

New York Convention: popular name for the United Nations Convention on the Recognition and Enforcement of Foreign Arbitral Awards, done in New York, June 10, 1958. All significant economies are parties to the New York convention which now has 135 signatories. The most important provisions of the New York Convention are Articles III, IV and V. Article III sets forth the general principle that arbitral awards wherever rendered shall be recognizable and enforceable in any signatory state. Article IV sets forth what a party must do in order to enforce an arbitral award in country or jurisdiction other than that in which the arbitral tribunal sat. Article V sets forth the limited list of grounds under which a court in a signatory country can decline to recognize or enforce a foreign arbitral award.

Nichia **Case, the**: *See* Inventor's Bonus.

Nifty-App, Nifty-Feature: in contrast to a killer-app [q.v.], a nifty-app or nifty-feature is a very useful application that, in of itself, does not drive sales, but when combined with other nifty-apps may collectively, over a longer time-frame, have the same effect as a killer-app. The term is used in the context of an argument that the technology sector would be healthier if its sales were driven by a steady accretion of nifty-apps, which would lead to steadier growth than the boom-bust cycle ascribed to killer-apps.

NIH: acronym for National Institutes of Health or Not-Invented-Here Syndrome [q.v.].

NLF Clause: abbreviation of no-less-favored or not-less-favored, contract clause with the same effect as an MFN Clause [q.v.].

No-Action Letter: an letter sent by the SEC [q.v.] in response to a written query as to the legality of an activity under Securities Law [q.v.], indicating that no civil or criminal action will be taken against an individual engaging in that particular activity.

***Noerr-Pennington* Doctrine**: a legal doctrine in antitrust law that provides that companies or individuals cannot be held liable for anticompetitive conduct that was required of them by law in, even in a jurisdiction that did not impose the requirement. The doctrine finds its origin in two U.S. antitrust cases: *Eastern R. Conf. v. Noerr Motors*, 365 U.S. 127 (1961); and *United Mine Workers v. Pennington*, 381 U.S. 657 (1965). Thus companies sometimes lobby governments in connection with certain issues, for example standards, with a view to getting the government or an agency to enact decisions or regulations that are competitively beneficial to the lobbyist and indeed may violate competition law; both the lobbying activity (absent corruption) and complying with the resulting decision or regulation is not a something the company(ies) can be held liable for. Although many countries outside the U.S. recognize the *Noerr-Pennington* doctrine as a defense, it has context specific exceptions—for example, EU prohibitions on state aids.

No-Challenge Clause: provision in licensing agreement that prohibits the licensee from challenging the validity of the underlying intellectual property right, usually a patent. No-challenge clauses for patents have often been held illegal or void as against public policy. One major exception to the prohibition, illegality, or void-ness usually arises when the no-challenge clause is part of a license granted as part of a settlement of litigation with respect to the non-challengeable patent.

No-Hire, Non-Hire Clause/Agreement: agreement akin to a non-solicitation agreement where a party (usually a company disposing of a business or a departing senior manager) agrees not to hire specified persons. Thus, for example a large company selling part of its business to another might agree for a period of time not to hire any of the employees who changed employers in the transaction. Although such clauses have the immediate facial advantage that a violation is easily provable as compared to a non-solicitation provision, they may be more difficult to enforce as they affect the interests of a third party, the prohibited-from-hiring employee, who is not a party to the no-hire clause or agreement.

No-Horse, No-Dog, or No-Skin Plaintiff: derived from the phrases "no horse in the race," "no dog in the hunt" or "no skin in the game" and refer to a plaintiff (usually a patent holder) who has no commercial presence in the industry from which the infringing product emerges or where it is used. Defense lawyers perceive such parties as much more difficult to deal with as they have little to lose by pursuing the action to the "bitter end" and are usually invulnerable to counterclaims. Their litigative behavior is frequently different from litigants from within the relevant industry, i.e., industry participants.

No-Less-Favored Clause: also expressed as a not-less-favored clause or NLF clause, contract clause with the same effect as an MFN Clause [q.v.].

Non-Assert: an agreement not to assert a patent or patents against the recipient for a period of time or indefinitely. Many recipients believe that it is the equivalent of a license [q.v.], but this is not the case. Unlike a license, a non-assert *may arguably* leave the recipient liable for damages during the period it was in force, in the event that it is terminated, although the recipient may be able to raise equitable defenses such as *laches* [q.v.] or *estoppel* [q.v.]. The other key difference between a non-assert and a license is that while a license can be argued to be affirmative permission to do something, a non-assert is a passive agreement not to take prohibitive action, at least for a period of time. Fundamentally, with a license, the recipient knows what it has received; with a non-assert, what is received is unclear. As with licenses, a non-assert is usually governed by the choice of law rules applicable to contracts and not the law of the jurisdiction that conferred the IP rights at issue (except with the possible exception of acquiescence[q.v.]-based defenses).

Non-Compete Agreement: an undertaking, usually obtained from an employee or the seller of a business not to compete with the employer or purchaser for a period of time. Such agreements are usually required to be reasonable in time and scope and can be held invalid if they go too far, i.e., they effectively render the signer unemployable in their profession within his or her existing community or are otherwise unreasonable in temporal, geographic or commercial scope. Indeed, in a number of U.S. states they are illegal and unenforceable when applied to individuals, for example California. Non-compete agreements between companies are also legally risky and can raise antitrust and competition law issues in many jurisdictions. Non-compete agreements should usually be tailored to protect specific interests and it is wise to establish some internal process for each and every agreement in which the interests the non-compete is intended to protect are identified and the non-compete's duration and scope are established and justified.

Non-Disclosure Agreement: a term for a confidentiality agreement. In most jurisdictions such NDAs need to be reasonable in time and scope and cannot survive the loss of confidentiality of the underlying information used to support them. In employment law in particular, an NDA which renders it difficult for someone to obtain work in his/her profession without moving will often be considered an illegal non-compete agreement [q.v.].

Non-Liability Opinion: an opinion obtained from legal counsel to the effect that a product or process does not render the recipient liable for infringement of certain third-party intellectual property rights. In U.S. law, such an opinion can provide a good faith basis for a belief that a product is non-infringing (i.e., that there was no willful infringement) and is therefore highly relevant evidence in determining whether a prevailing plaintiff should received enhanced damages and attorneys' fees. Such an opinion must be "competent," which can mean a number of things, but for example precludes a simply conclusive opinion written in essence by a "hired gun," but rather requires that the opinion be a considered application of the law to the patent, that the opinion writer be independent (i.e. outside counsel), and have considered the file wrapper of the patents and should credibly and logically explain, based on a review of relevant facts the reason no liability arises, e.g., invalidity, unenforceability or non-infringement. Privilege [q.v.] is usually waived in such opinions in the course of a patent infringement suit, as well as related communications with the opinion writer. Formal legal opinions may also be sought on antitrust issues so as to provide a good faith basis to believe in the legality of agreements, understandings, and practices.

Non-Solicitation Clause: a clause found in many contracts and non-disclosure agreements prohibiting one party from seeking (soliciting) to hire the other employees, or in some instances from hiring an employee who approaches that party for a period of time. Although the latter type of clause is justified on the basis that who initiated the hiring process may be difficult to identify, such clauses may be legally suspect in some jurisdictions, especially if they render employees unemployable in their professions within their own community (i.e., an area defined by reasonable commuting distance). In addition such clauses should usually be reasonably limited in time and not perpetual or so long as to make them effectively perpetual; typically lawyers will advise no more than three years. The best advice is not to make such provisions broader than they objectively need to be. Some jurisdictions, regarding such clauses as unfair to an employee who was not a party to the agreement may also require the employer invoking such a clause to compensate the employee (even if employee has left) for any financial consequences. It is also difficult to enforce such a clause if the employee was dismissed (fired) by the first employer, before the clause was invoked.

Non-Use: refers to the failure to offer relevant products or services bearing a trademark in a given jurisdiction, which after a prolonged period, can result in cancellation of the trademark.

No-Patent Clause: clause prohibiting a sponsored researcher from patenting the results of the sponsored research without the sponsor's consent. Such clauses are not uncommon where: (a) it is believed that the best form of protection for the research results may be secrecy (i.e., to treat them as know-how); or (b) the research is sponsored by a philanthropic organization or certain government agencies.

No-Shop Clause: clause in a merger agreement, which precludes the incumbent management of the target from looking for a higher bid from other companies. Since they may prevent the maximization of the purchase price, prohibitions on target management listening to, or considering unsolicited bids is usually unenforceable and contrary to directors and management's fiduciary duties [q.v.] to shareholders and thus most prevailing corporate laws. Even though prohibitions on actively soliciting higher bids are generally legally acceptable, they can also under certain circumstances be a breach of managements fiduciary duties, where for example the offer that management has accepted is not vary favorable to shareholders and a real prospect would exist of securing a higher offer if one was sought. *See Revlon* Duties.

Notice of Allowance: a written notice from a patent office indicating its intent to grant a patent on at least some of the claims in a patent application. The notice of allowance usually precedes the issuance of a patent by a period of time and may specify a fee to be paid before the patent issues.

Notice of Intent to File Suit, Issue Proceedings: in a number of jurisdictions a putative plaintiff must send the intended defendants a demand letter stating the nature of an intended claim and the plaintiff's intent to file suit if no settlement is reached by a given date. Failure to do so may expose the plaintiff to sanctions including a requirement to pay some or all of the defendant's legal costs. This is for example the case in the United Kingdom. The main risk of serving such a notice is that the potential defendant will file a declaratory judgment [q.v.] case.

Notification: in principle, refers to any formal or semi-formal process of informing a third party of a fact or event. However, it generally refers to a formal requirement that an official body be notified of certain facts or events. In particular, in competition law [q.v.] it refers to the formal notification of a competition authority of an agreement that may have anticompetitive effects, seeking approval or exemption of the agreement. This notification system was until 2004 an important aspect of European Competition law. A Form A/B [q.v.] was normally filed on a potentially anticompetitive agreement. Notification in EU law still applies to concentrations (e.g., mergers, full function joint ventures) using a Form CO [q.v.] (short form or long form).

Not-Invented-Here Syndrome: the tendency of organizations to reject competing ideas or technology that comes from outside. NIH is a major reason technology mergers fail, since it leads companies to reject acquired technology in favor of their own. A classic example of NIH would be where a company buys a rival for its technology, but continues to develop its own internal rival while ignoring the acquired company's solution.

Novelty: refers to the requirement for a patent that an invention be new. Thus for example under United States law (35 U.S.C. §102) a patent may not be granted if the same device if created by a third party was described or in use before its priority date, or if it was described in a publication by the inventor more than one year prior to the application date for the patent. In U.S. law novelty is a different issue from obviousness [q.v.]—an invention is only non-novel if it was wholly and essentially identically described (i.e., all claim limitations met) in a single publication the prior art, whereas an invention is obvious under 35 U.S.C. §103 if the invention would have been obvious to someone of ordinary skill in the art, especially someone who had knowledge of the prior art, even if that person needs to combine items of prior art. In other words, novelty asks if someone has *actually* made it before, obviousness asks if a reasonably skilled and educated person *could have made it before.*

No-Waiver Clause: clause that provides that the failure of a contract party to exercise a right under a contract when an opportunity to do so first arises, does not preclude the invoking of that right at a later date, because of claimed acquiescence. For example, a clause that says that should the other party breach the terms of the agreement and the holder of the right does not sue, cancel the agreement or use any other remedies, it can still at any point choose to do so (i.e. it has not waived its rights) and it may also exercise the rights in the event of a repeated breach of the same type. Strict no-waiver clauses are common in financing agreements, to protect the lender. They can be problematic in development agreements where plans may be frequently changed.

NSG: acronym for Nuclear Suppliers Group, an organization of countries that manufacture technologies necessary for the manufacture of nuclear weapons, which seeks to cooperate in the implementation of export controls for such technologies. Members include: Argentina, Australia, Austria, Belarus, Belgium, Brazil, Bulgaria, Canada, China, Cyprus, the Czech Republic, Denmark, Estonia, Finland, France, Germany, Greece, Hungary, Ireland, Italy, Japan, Kazakhstan, the Republic of Korea, Latvia, Lithuania, Luxembourg, Malta, Netherlands, New Zealand, Norway, Poland, Portugal Romania, the Russian Federation, Slovakia, Slovenia, South Africa, Spain, Sweden, Switzerland, Turkey, Ukraine, the United Kingdom, and the United States. The European Commission participates as an observer.

Nuisance Suit, Nuisance Value: lawsuit brought by a plaintiff who does not seek to bring the suit to trial, but rather is willing to settle it for "nuisance value." The amount of nuisance value can vary. At the low end it may be a fraction of the cost of litigating the suit; at the high end it may reflect a timing problem, for example, it may have been brought immediately pre-IPO, and seek a settlement that reflects the likely cost of a delayed IPO. A nuisance suit is potentially abuse of process [q.v.].

O

Object Code: computer program expressed in machine code. Source code is translated by a compiler into object code. Software is almost always sold in object code format and source code retained by the software company as confidential.

Obviousness: in almost all patent systems an invention must not be obvious to someone of ordinary skill in the art. In U.S. law novelty [q.v.] is a different issue from obviousness—an invention is only non-novel if it was wholly and essentially identically described (i.e., all claim limitations met) in a single publication the prior art, whereas an invention is obvious under 35 U.S.C. §103 if the invention would have been obvious to someone of ordinary skill in the art, especially someone who had knowledge of the prior art, even if that person needs to combine items of prior art. In other words, novelty asks if someone has *actually* made it before, obviousness asks if a reasonably skilled and educated person *could have made it before* had they considered the problem and the then existing art.

Obvious-to-try: an obviousness argument with respect to an invention that, given what was existed in the prior art, what the inventor added was a variation that was "obvious to try." The argument is more successful in some jurisdictions such as the U.K., than in others such as the U.S., and it also usually requires showing that some thing in the prior art would have impelled someone skilled in the prior art to try.

Occurrence Policy: An insurance policy that indemnifies the insured for claims against it where the events or actions by the insured, that give rise to the claim occurred during the policy period. Occurrence policies, which are also some times known as "claims arising" policies, can be used many years after the term of the insurance policy has expired. Moreover, significant U.S. case law has held that the right to indemnity arising under such policies are not limited by a non-assignment provision, even where the insured's liability is for activities that were legal and not-actionable during the period that the policy was in force such as asbestos or environmental liability. *See* Claims-Made Policy.

ODM/OEM: the latter, original equipment manufacturer is the better known term and refers to a third party manufacturer who manufactures either subassemblies or entire items to be sold by a vendor, usually under the vendor's brand. OEM equipment is usually made to a specification or design supplied by the vendor. By contrast, an ODM or original design manufacturers, refers to a manufacturer who develops a design on its own account, which it owns, and then supplies products of its manufacture to a vendor who sells it under the vendor's brand name. The underlying agreements in such an arrangement are usually referred to as Originate-Design-Manufacture arrangements.

OEM Agreement, Rights: the acronym stands for Original Equipment Manufacturer. An agreement pursuant to which a third party product is offered in conjunction with a primary product as either standard item or an option. Thus for example, particular application software might be offered in conjunction with certain systems, or alternately say a particular brand of tire with new cars from a particular manufacturer. In the context of a durable optional item, the advantage to the OEM supplier is the opportunity to have its optional item offered at the moment when a customer of the primary product is buying additional items. With respect to consumables, especially non-optional consumables, the advantage is that the customer will often replace or renew the consumables with products of the same brand, e.g., he or she will buy the same tires for his car as it originally had. OEM suppliers typically either: pay a commission to the primary product vendor; supply items at a deep discount, or agree to make items specially tailored to the primary supplier's needs. These rights are also sometimes known as "bundling rights." *See* Right-of-Endorsement, Right-to-Endorsement.

Office Action: term used to describe decisions made by patent offices with legal consequences, though most typically to decisions to reject a patent application.

Official Journal (OJ): the European Commission publishes information in a journal known as the OJ. There are two Official Journals, the Legislative Journal, where documents that have a legally binding effect are published, and the Notices Journal, in which information, notices, and draft EU legislation is published. The Legislative journal is designated by the letter L, the Notices by the letter C. In Europe there is a standard format for citing OJ's YEAR OJ SERIES EDITION/PAGE, e.g. 2005 OJ L 6/59 refers to the 6th legislative OJ published in 2005 at page 59. The European Patent Office also issues an Official Journal, which is published periodically with some special editions.

Off-Patent: refers to products, particularly drug compounds, upon which the patent term has expired.

Offsets: refers to requirements often included in major public procurement contracts, especially for military equipment, that the contractor place some of its own purchase contracts in the procuring country or make investments, offsetting the foreign exchange value of the procurement contract. Offsets are usually designed to results in the creation or expansion of industrial capacity in the purchasing country and usually involve co-production, licensed production, subcontractor production, capital investment, or technology transfer.

OHIM: Office for Harmonization in the Internal Market, the official name for the European trademark office based in Alicante, Spain. The marks granted by OHIM are known as Community Trademarks. OHIM is widely regarded as an unfortunately "Eurocratic" choice of name and many people call it the Community Trademark Office, EU Trademark Office, or some variant thereof. Community Designs (i.e., European Registered Designs or design rights) are also registered at, and managed by OHIM.

OJ: *See* Official Journal (OJ).

Oligopoly: a market where there are so few suppliers that each can anticipate the others' likely conduct and adjust its commercial and marketing activities accordingly.

Oligopsony: a market in which there are so few buyers that each can anticipate the others' likely conduct and adjust its commercial and purchasing activities accordingly.

Omnibus Disclosure: refers to a big patent application, often filed as a provisional application, which contains a large amount of information about multiple inventions combined in a single product. It usually results in divisional applications. *See* Big Book Application.

One-Legged Chinamen Fallacy, the: cautionary tale sometimes told to admonish executives not to base investment decisions in China solely on the putative size of the Chinese market based on its population alone, or to assume that their products or services will be automatically attractive or profitable in China. In the 1970s, an Irish trade mission visited China. On the delegation was a senior Irish diplomat as well as representatives of a number of large Irish companies and industries. One of the delegation was a representative of the Irish footwear industry, who was able to do little or no business, especially when compared to the success of executives from Irish power generation, aircraft leasing, and other businesses and industries; finally the perplexed diplomat asked the footwear "rep" why he had bothered coming on the trip. He replied "well there's over a billion Chinese; imagine if we could sell them all just one shoe." Over the following years, low cost imports from, amongst other places, China, devastated the mass-market Irish shoe industry; one-legged Chinamen buying Irish shoes have yet to appear in serious numbers.

On-Sale-Bar: most patent systems prohibit an inventor from applying for a patent once he has offered the product for commercial sale. There are jurisdictionally specific exceptions to the "on-sale bar," for example tradeshows and experimental use and some jurisdictions offer limited grace periods [q.v.], the United States for example twelve months, while Japan offers six months for experimental or academic use. However, because these exceptions are often hedged with conditions, are different from one country to the next, and often do not apply at all, inventors should not rely on them. Rather they should assume that a patent should always be applied for before a product is offered for commercial sale or use, advertised, or presented at a trade show.

Open Claim: a patent claim that recites a series of limitations or elements, but by its language means that the addition of new un-recited elements to a product or process would not prevent infringement, e.g., if the claim is to a+b+c, a product or process consisting of a+b+c+d would still infringe. Most patent claims are drafted as Open Claims. *See* Claims, Closed Claim, Comprising, Consisting of.

Open Source: software for which the source code is made available to users so that it can be modified and customized. Open source software is usually subject to a simple "public license" or a disclaimer of intellectual property rights. One meaning for "open source" is that the source code that would normally be kept confidential by the software house is disclosed to the public; open source should not therefore be regarded as automatically subject to a public license or free.

Operating System: in principle, the low-level software that handles the interface to peripheral hardware, schedules tasks, allocates storage, and presents a default interface to a user. The term OS has burgeoned to include applications, utilities, and "bells and whistles" sold or supplied with the OS and usually integrated into the OS package. As a result, the OS may be split into a kernel which is always present and various system programs which use facilities provided by the kernel to perform higher-level house-keeping tasks, and graphical user interfaces, low level applications, etc. Thus for example Windows was originally an interface application that ran on top of the MS-DOS operating system, but now is referred to, colloquially at least, as an operating system in its own right. Much of the Microsoft antitrust litigation concerned this integration as well as the integration of applications such as Explorer into the operating system.

OPIC: the United States Overseas Private Investment Corporation, an entity that provides assistance to U.S. companies investing in various countries. The most important form of such assistance is political risk insurance.

Opinion: *See* Non-Liability Opinion.

Opposition: a term used to describe a legal objection to the grant of a patent or trademark filed in the relevant trademark or patent office. In the European Patent Office an opposition can be filed for up to nine months from the issue date of the patent.

Ordinary Skill in the Art: a term found in the United States Patent Act that relates to the concept of obviousness. An invention is obvious if it would have occurred to someone of ordinary skill in the art presented with the technical problem the invention purports to solve. In U.S. patent litigation, a considerable amount of dispute can center on what the hypothetical person of ordinary skill in art is, i.e., should it be a Ph.D. scientist, an ordinary technician, etc. A person of ordinary skill in the art is presumed to also be someone who would be familiar with all the prior art in the inventor's field of endeavor and of common prior art solutions to the particular problem presented used in other fields.

Original Designs: Section 1301 of the U.S. Copyright Act extends ten years of protection to "original deigns," i.e., "an original design of a useful article which makes the article attractive or distinctive in appearance to the purchasing or using public," which "provides a distinguishable variation over prior work pertaining to similar articles, which is more than merely trivial and has not been copied from another source." The statutory subsection also includes protection for boat hull-forms.

Originality Requirement: most key forms of intellectual property have an originality requirement. Thus copyright will usually only protect a work that has a modicum of originality on the part of its author or creator. The originality requirement in terms of patents is usually expressed as novelty. A trademark can only be obtained for something that is not already in use to describe or identify the same class of good or services and is not a word that is merely descriptive. The originality requirement is often expressed in the context of copyrights and design rights.

Original Work: some countries, most notably Germany, set high standards for the originality that a work must display before it is entitled to copyright protection. Thus in Germany, normally only personal intellectual creations that have attained a high level of creativity will satisfy the originality requirement, i.e., a work must rise above skilled craftsmanship. Similar concepts are found in the copyright law of France, Spain, and Italy.

Ornamental Design: synonym for Registered Design [q.v.] and Design Patent [q.v.].

Orphan Drug Rights: exclusive rights to sell known, unpatented, or off-patent compounds, for particular therapeutic purposes, typically for five to ten years. These rights were developed in both the United States and Europe to encourage the development of drug therapies from compounds without patent protection, particularly where the therapeutic market is small and therefore does not usually justify the cost of extensive trials. There is some controversy about the application of these rules in Europe.

Orphan Product, Orphan Ware: *See* Abandonware.

Orphan Work: term used to refer to a work protected by copyright, whose ownership is unknown or very unclear. Because the owner cannot be identified in order to obtain legal rights to use the work, it can languish unused and become forgotten. The orphan work problem is particularly prevalent where there has been a copyright term extension [q.v.] under the TRIPS [q.v.]. The problem of orphan works with unidentified owners has been recognized by various copyright offices, who are discussing solutions, which will likely consist of compulsory licensing at a fee set by the copyright office or another agency, with fees and royalties held in trust for the putative owners. Resolving the issue where ownership is disputed, presents a more complex problem.

Output Restraints: agreement(s) between manufacturers to limit their output of certain goods or services, so as to reduce competition and raise prices. Usually illegal under Antitrust [q.v.], Competition [q.v.], or unfair trade/competition laws, but most countries provide a mechanism where such restrictions can be legally imposed with government consent (under the *Noerr-Pennington* Doctrine [q.v.] and its analogues) usually for a limited period of time to allow an industry to restructure, commonly accompanied by international trade safeguards.

Over-Lawyering: activities by lawyers that may waste time and money and create obstacles to contracts or other business arrangements by seeking terms or clauses to deal with very unlikely or remote possibilities, or seeking promises or commitments from the counterparty that would be difficult or not cost-effective to enforce. Over-lawyering does happen, but it is difficult to identify as lawyers, through experience, generally have better information than clients as to the actual magnitude of a given risk. On the other hand, risks are often context specific and this factor should be considered when determining the amount of effort that should be applied to obtain a specific contractual provision.

Oversell, Oversold: the terms are *not usually* an antonym for undersell or undersold. Both terms are commonly used in two different ways. First, to describe a sale obtained by over-promising or overstatement by the vendor of the item to-be-supplied's capabilities, or where the item is to be developed, the time to delivery or the likely capabilities of the product when delivered. Alternately, where a vendor has a limited capacity to supply goods or services, overselling means selling to one or more customers more of the goods and or services than the vendor can actually deliver from the resources in its control.

P

P-Reference: a classification for prior art references established by WIPO in Standard ST. 14 for patent search reports. A P reference is a document published prior to the international filing date but later than the claimed priority date (commonly called an intervening reference). *See* A-Reference, Y-Reference, and X-Reference.

PACER: Public Access to Court Electronic Records, an electronic public access service that allows subscribers to obtain case and docket information from most United States Federal Courts at a low cost-per-page. An account is necessary to access the service. Most good international law firms, whether in the United States or not, have established an account to allow them to track cases of interest to their clients.

Package License: license on a bundle or portfolio of patents, which may be charged at a single royalty rate or based on a royalty formula that does not take account of the number of patents used. Package licenses are often used to license essential technology [q.v.] in patent pools [q.v.]. Where a single royalty rate is charged for the entire package, regardless of the level of use, there is a risk that the arrangement will be regarded as illegal tying [q.v.] under competition [q.v.] and antitrust law [q.v.], especially where the patents may not be licensed separately and the package includes substitute technologies [q.v.] rather than complementary technologies [q.v.].

Paid-Up License: means a license under which all royalties have been paid in advance, i.e., there are no running royalties [q.v.]; alternately, a paid-up (or pre-paid) license can be for a certain fixed number of units or period of time, usually at a substantial discount to the usual running royalty. Partially paid-up licenses have the advantage to the licensor of placing pressure on the licensee to rapidly exploit the technology, since non-use would mean writing off the sum used to acquire the paid-up component. The disadvantage for the licensee is that certain money is traded off against uncertain, i.e., the more paid up a license is, the lower the running royalty. A paid up license is typically irrevocable, i.e., the licensor's remedy lies in damages and not in cancellation of the license. *See* Certainty/Uncertainty Trade Off.

Parallel Imports: refers to the resale of goods legally sold pursuant to parallel intellectual property rights granted in another state or territory in a different country, for example purchase of Levi's Jeans in the United States for resale in the U.K. The legality of such imports is very complex and depends in part on who sold the goods in the first country of sale and what that vendor's legal rights were with respect to the IP. Also known as "Grey Market" imports.

Parallel Patent, Trademark: refers to essentially the same patent or trademark in another country.

Parens Patriæ, in, (parens patriae): the United States Congress, pursuant to 15 U.S.C. §15(c), known as the Parens Patriæ Act, has given to state attorney generals the right to bring claims on behalf of their states' citizens, under 15 U.S.C. Sections 1-7, i.e., the Sherman Act and the merger provisions of the Clayton Act. This is the reason some cases, for example, cannot easily be settled without the consent of the states attorneys general participating in the case. The best-known example of this type of suit was the Microsoft antitrust case where the states were participants *in parens patriæ*. In the context of currently relatively lax Federal government enforcement of U.S. antitrust law, this provision is of increasing importance. The origin of the term was a legal rule that allowed courts (as an organ of the state) to make decisions on behalf of those who were incompetent or unable to make the decisions on their own behalf, e.g., minors and the mentally ill. The words *in parens patriæ* mean literally "as the father of his country" and signified that the state was regarded as the ultimate guardian of all its citizens and could act as a parent or guardian for one, where no one else was willing or able to serve in that capacity.

Parent Company Guarantee: a guarantee from a parent company that certain obligations of a subsidiary, affiliate, or SPV will be carried out. Parent company guarantees are usually sought where the contracting entity might not, of itself, have the resources to make enforcing the obligation against it worthwhile, or where the subsidiary or affiliate is close to bankruptcy or may be sold or spun-off.

Pari-Passu. literally means at an equal rate or pace. The term is often used in financing and shareholder agreements to indicate that obligations and benefits will de distributed equally in accordance with some measuring factor, e.g., shares held.

Parking-Lot Briefing: a last minute briefing just outside a customer or counterparty's premises immediately prior to a meeting. The term is used critically, to describe poor preparation and planning, as in "all they do are parking-lot briefings." *See* 3-to-1 Rule.

Parol **Evidence Rule**: evidentiary rule in common law countries (e.g., U.S., U.K., Ireland, Australia, etc.), which, in principle, provides that a court should only consider the "four corners" of a contract to determine its meaning and effect. *Parol* evidence is such extraneous evidence. The *parol* evidence rule is not as broad in application as is often presumed. As it is generally applied in the United States, it prevents the parties to a complete written agreement from introducing evidence of negotiations and understandings prior to or contemporaneous with the written agreement, which varies the terms of or is inconsistent with the later executed written agreement; *parol* evidence may be considered that is ***consistent*** with a possible interpretation of the agreement. Under English law, in principle, the rule provides that evidence cannot be admitted (or even if admitted cannot be used) to add to, vary or contradict a written instrument; i.e., neither party can rely on extrinsic evidence or the terms alleged to have been agreed, i.e. on evidence not contained in the contract. However, under English law *parol* evidence can be used to establish the matrix of circumstances surrounding the contract, i.e., what the parties' understanding and intent was when the contract was entered into. For curious reasons, the word "parol" in *parol* evidence is frequently italicized in text.

Participation: movie industry and entertainment jargon for a share of the revenue generated by a production. *See* Gross Participation, Net Participation.

Passing Off: selling a product in a manner calculated to persuade the purchasers that it came from a third party source, usually the normal vendor or supplier.

Patent: in principle refers to the governmental grant of a right, privilege, or authority. In practice it has come to mean the exclusive right to sell an invention, provided it is novel and non-obvious, for a period of years, subsisting twenty years from the filing date of an application for a patent.

Patent: a right granted by a government, providing the grantee with the ability to prevent others from engaging in a particular activity or selling particular goods or services without the patent holder's consent. In the modern context, patents are exclusively granted on new and useful inventions and grant the holder the sole right to practice the invention for a set period of time, which under the TRIPS is twenty years from the date on which the patent was applied for. Holders of patents may themselves exploit the sole right or alternately license others to practice the invention.

Patent Annuity Company, Agency: a third party company or agency that can be retained to ensure that patent renewal fees (and trademark fees) are paid on time. The patent annuity company will typically track a portfolio of a person or company's patents and ensure that the relevant patent and trademark offices worldwide are paid on time.

Patent Bar: a collective term for the admitted patent agents (in the U.K. patent attorneys) in a jurisdiction; the term member of the patent bar is also used to describe someone who is a patent agent. The patent bar is also used to describe the exam taken to qualify as a patent agent or patent attorney.

Patent Clustering: *See* Clustering, Thicket.

Patent Family: refers to all the patents that derive from a single original patent application, including foreign or PCT [q.v.] patents, continuations [q.v.], divisionals [q.v.], and CIPs [q.v.].

Patent Pool: a broad cross license [q.v.] usually negotiated by two or more members of an industry to deal with a large number of potential blocking patents. Patent pooling arrangements can raise complex antitrust [q.v.] and competition law [q.v.] issues. The existence of patent pools or cross licenses involving two merging companies has sometime been considered relevant by competition and antitrust authorities when reviewing mergers, suggesting that the companies may, by virtue of their intellectual property, have a collective dominant position [q.v.] that would be exacerbated if the merger is allowed.

Patent Thicket: *See* Thicket.

Patently Ambiguous: a term that does not refer to patents, but rather denotes a contract that contains provisions that are inherently ambiguous, for example because they are contradictory. If a court finds that a contract is, on its face, patently ambiguous, this may justify the consideration of *parol* evidence [q.v.] in order to interpret it.

Patents County Court: a U.K. court established in 1990 as an alternative to the English High Court, for hearing less complex and lower value patent cases. The Court has been relatively inactive, but has recently been revived by the appointment of a specialist judge. U.K. patent practitioners are interested to determine if the Patents County Court will prove more patentee-friendly that the High Court (the Patents Court) which is perceived as hostile to patent holders and very disinclined to uphold patent validity.

Patents Court: a specialist part of the Chancery Division of the English High Court that hears U.K. patent cases (except for cases now brought before the Patents County Court [q.v.]).

Patstats.org: group operating under the auspices of the University of Houston Law Center which maintains an Internet accessible database dating to 2000 of current U.S. patent cases and outcomes on various legal issues that may arise in such cases, e.g., invalidity on various grounds, non-infringement, etc. The database is useful in assessing the potential effectiveness of various legal defenses.

PCA: acronym for per customer acquired.

PCI: two meanings, a widely used standard developed by Intel for connecting peripherals to a personal computer; an acronym for per customer influenced.

PCT: the Patent Cooperation Treaty an international treaty that provides for the international recognition of patent applications and for their transmittal between patent offices to create parallel international patents. It is managed by WIPO.

PCT Application: a patent application filed under the PCT. Under PCT rules an inventor filing a national patent has twelve months to decide whether to turn that application into a PCT Application. The PCT application is then communicated to the relevant national patent offices where the inventor translates the applications or does what other things may be necessary under the local patent law in what is known as the national phase.

Peg: refers to fixing the price of a commodity or instrument, typically an input (e.g., steel) or an exchange rate either in international trade or for purposes of a contract price. *See* Currency Peg.

Pendent Jurisdiction: U.S. litigation term. Federal Courts have limited jurisdiction based on either: (a) diversity of citizenship; or (b) Federal Questions, i.e., cases arising under Federal law such as Copyright, Patent, Federal Trademark and Federal Antitrust (and others). Where a state law claim is based on a "common nucleus of operative fact," i.e., the same facts or events are at issue, Federal Courts can hear the claims based on state law, if they are simultaneously hearing a case based on Federal Question jurisdiction.

Per Customer Acquired, Cost: Sometimes expressed as "PCA," a measure of the total cost effectiveness of marketing and sales efforts. It usually includes the cost of advertising per customer, sales effort in closing a deal with the customer, gifts or other promotional items and commissions paid to a sales force.

Per Customer Influenced, Cost: Sometimes expressed as "PCI," a measurement of the effectiveness of advertising, which measures the cost of specific advertising or marketing activity per customer gained as a result of that advertising or marketing. Measuring the effectiveness of advertising is notoriously difficult and therefore methods of advertising that allow marketers to readily determine their effect on sales are very attractive.

Performing Rights Society: because it would be economically inefficient to the point of infeasibility for individual owners of music copyrights or recording artists to police every public playing of their record in order to recover a small royalty, almost all are members of performing rights societies who charge license fees to bars clubs, night-clubs, etc. and monitor radio stations for use of the music of the societies members. Radio monitoring is increasingly carried out by computers or other automated means. The performing rights societies then distribute the collected money according to formulae that reflect the level of airplay and usage of members works, usually based on statistical sampling. There is typically at least one performing rights society per major economy. Occasionally, the societies split, the most common issue being revenue distribution or arguments that flat fee-based royalties over-reward less popular artists and undercharge for the more popular. The best-known societies are ASCAP (American Society of Composers Authors and Publishers. USA), BMI (Broadcast Music, Inc., USA), Performing Right Society (U.K.), Mechanical Copyright Protection Society (U.K.), SACEM (Sociéte Des Auteurs, Compositeurs et Editeurs de Musique, France), IMRO (Irish Musical Rights Organisation). Similar organizations (often formed as corporations), usually referred to as collecting societies also exist to recover royalties for professional photography, printed material, artistic works (e.g., the Design and Artists Collecting Society, U.K.), characters (e.g., cartoon characters), broadcast material and TV listings.

Periodic Review: *See* Market Authorization.

Per-Processor License: refers to a type of license formerly used by Microsoft under which it charged computer manufacturers copyright royalties for Windows and MS-DOS-based on the number of computers using compatible processors they shipped (i.e., x86-type processors) regardless of whether Microsoft's software was installed or not. The result was to discourage manufacturers from installing any competing operating system since they would have to pay for the Microsoft product in any event. This type of license was ruled illegal. The term per-processor license has come to be used for any license form in which royalties are metered based on sales of an item, which might or might contain the licensed IP, as if every unit sold did indeed contain the IP. It does not require the metered item to be a processor, software, or even computer technology. Such license arrangements are potentially illegal and should be avoided.

Per-Use License: a type of license agreement used in connection with intellectual property that may be used in a host of different products. Such a license provides that a fixed fee be paid with respect to each use of the IP for a new product (as an alternative to a per unit running royalty or in addition to a per unit royalty). A per-use license may also be written as a framework agreement, with only the fee per use (and potential running royalty) to be agreed before each use. The most complicated issue with a per-use license is defining in the license what is a "use." For example, is the re-creation of a microprocessor (containing a per-use licensed component) using a different manufacturing process, so that physical elements change, but the processor otherwise behaves identically and is used for the same purpose, a second "use" or still the original "use"?

Petty Patent: *See* Utility Patent.

Phase I, II and III Human Drug Trials: *See* IND.

Pioneer Patent: (also termed a "Fundamental Patent") is one of the most overused terms in intellectual property law. A pioneer patent discloses an invention that creates a new technical field or new technical direction in an existing field. The term is a hackneyed expression in litigation—everyone seems to want to dub theirs a "pioneer patent," no matter how prosaic, derivative, or un-pioneering it might actually be. Nonetheless, it is fair to say that pioneer patents do exist. Contrast with Incremental Patent.

Plant Variety: most major economies have enacted laws protecting plant breeders from having new plant varieties they develop cultivated by other plant breeders and seed merchants. The system is similar to patent protection, and under the UPOV Conventions [q.v.] of 1961, 1978, and 1991 is typically granted for twenty years for most plants and twenty-five years for trees and vines.

Pollution, Intellectual Property: describes the inclusion of third party intellectual property in a product, e.g., code pollution is the intentional or inadvertent copying of third party code into what would otherwise be the code-writers (or his employer's) proprietary code. The difficulty is that such IP pollution is an infringement of the third party's rights for which the third party may be able to sue, or alternately demand payment or other benefits under an existing license agreement. *See* tar baby license, clean room, derivative work, code-napping.

PMDA: Pharmaceutical and Medical Devices Agency, centralized Japanese agency responsible for drug and medical device approvals.

PMI: the Project Management Institute, an organization that seeks to promote professional project management, with specific qualifications and certification. A requirement that some or all project managers be PMI certified sometimes appears in project contracts.

Poison Pill: refers to an array of anti-takeover defenses that a company may put in place including, for example, the issue of preferred stock that allows shareholders special rights after a takeover or change of control, for example the right to buy additional shares of their own company (a flip-in) or the acquiring company (a flip-over) at a discount; change of control provisions in key license agreements; issuing stock options, particularly to employees that all vest on change of control; etc.

Posthumous Work: a work published after the author's death. Being a posthumous work can effect the copyright term in various ways that varies between legal systems.

POTS: acronym for Plain Old Telephone(ny) Services, i.e., analogue voice telephony.

Power-by-the-Hour: refers to a type of contract. The first widely reported general use of power by the hour was in connection with a high wing four-engine regional jet then named the BAe 146. Despite certain advantages, in particular, short take off capabilities (it was the only jet initially allowed to fly out of tiny city centre airports such as London City), the aircraft was initially unsuccessful due to the higher maintenance costs of its four engines and their perceived reliability problems. In response, the engine manufacturer devised a contract in which they did not sell engines to the owner of the aircraft, but rather sold engine usage time, which to the airlines was attractive because liability for maintenance and service rates fell on the engine manufacturer and was not specific to a particular engine (i.e., the manufacturer needed to have spare swap out engines to hand). The contract was known as a "power-by-the-hour" agreement. Since then, power-by-the-hour has come to be used in a wide array of applications including the supply of mainframe computer time and other services. Metering is not necessarily by time, it may be on a wide array of usage metering bases, for example, IBM uses a similar benchmark called MSU or measured service units that are akin to MIPS [q.v.].

Predatory Pricing: the selling of key products at a loss to win market share, primarily by forcing competitors out of business. Some law and economics advocates claim that predatory pricing is economically irrational and thus either does not exist or should be a concern of competition and antitrust law; others respond that this is a fallacy somewhat like saying that since playing roulette or other games of chance is a broadly a losing proposition, such gambling therefore does not exist and neither do casinos, and anyway, since roulette players ultimately lose, why regulate gambling. Predatory pricing if demonstrated, may violate competition law [q.v.], but it can be a difficult case to prove. In some sectors though, various governments prohibit below cost selling—e.g., "loss leaders." *See* Discipline Pricing.

Pre-Emptive Concessions, Don't Make, Signaling: aphorism that refers to a common negotiating error—making a concession without obtaining a clear concession from the counterparty; alternately behavior that signals the existence of additional concessions that the counterparty could get if they just negotiated long enough and hard enough, thereby forestalling a deal.

Preferences: bankruptcy term. Most bankruptcy statutes seek to ensure that all creditors of a bankrupt are treated equitably. However, realistically, most insolvent companies, as bankruptcy approaches, tend to treat some creditors better than others, perhaps because they can apply more pressure, moral, personal, or otherwise. To solve this problem, bankruptcy statutes usually provide that payments made within a certain period before a party files for bankruptcy be "clawed back" by the bankrupt and then redistributed to creditors equitably, (e.g., if you received "dollar for dollar," you may need to give the money back and join the queue for "cents on the dollar.") Pre-bankruptcy payments that are treated this way are called preferences. To be a preference the payment usually has to be within a time period (Sixty or ninety days) before the bankruptcy filing for ordinary creditors, or a much longer period for creditors with some connection with the bankrupt (i.e., shareholders, relatives, senior employees etc.), typically at least a year. Payments in the ordinary course of business can often avoid being treated as preferences. When in a dispute to recover debt from a company that may be heading into insolvency, it is important to be aware that a later win of a larger amount may be pyrrhic, if that puts the settlement into the ninety/sixty-day preference window. Since bankruptcy trustees, receivers, and administrators tend to automatically send out letters demanding returns of payments made during preference period without determining whether the payment meets other legal criteria to be considered a preference, re-payment of alleged preferences should not be automatically made before qualified, specialist legal advice has been obtained.

Preferred Embodiment: under many patent systems the inventor is not just required to disclose how to practice the invention, he or she is required to disclose what he or she believes is the best way to practice the invention, which is referred to as the preferred embodiment. Failure to do so, by, for example, disclosing a way to practice the invention that works, but gets worse results than another known to the inventor, is inequitable conduct. *See* Best Mode.

Preliminary Examination: *See* Examination.

Presumption: an evidentiary term that refers to who in litigation has the burden of proving a fact; thus for example, intellectual property rights are usually presumed legal and it is for the challenger produce evidence to show them invalid, while the holder of the rights has the burden of showing infringement. Sometimes referred to as "burden of proof." The burden of proof can shift back and forth in a case. For example, if one party has produced initial evidence that amounts to *prima facie* evidence of a claimed fact, the burden then shifts to the other party to rebut that evidence with evidence of its own.

Price-Fixing: agreement between a group of parties typically on the same side of a transaction to charge the same prices, e.g., vendors agreeing to charge no less than the same minimum price for comparable goods or purchasers agreeing not to pay more than the same maximum price for comparable goods (sometimes camouflaged by insignificant differences on slightly different goods); almost always illegal under antitrust, competition, or unfair trade/competition laws. Price-fixing is often a crime, for which any business executives involved may go to prison (for example in the United States).

Prima Facie: literally means at first sight. The term is used to describe initial evidence that suggests that a question or issue in litigation (for example with respect to claim element) has been answered. Thus, for example, a *prima facie* proof of negligence can be made out by showing certain facts—but that case can be rebutted by the defendant. Usually *prima facie* proof of an issue by a first party shifts the burden of showing that the issue is not proven to the other party. *Prima facie* evidence does not mean that a fact is proven unless the evidence is not adequately rebutted.

Prior Art: refers to disclosures and publications in the field of the invention that predate the filing date of the patent in first-to-file countries and the date of invention in the United States. Prior art is not necessarily invalidating, though the term is often loosely used to refer to invalidating references; it can be and usually is simply technical background. The question of what is prior art is closely tied to the priority date for a patent application.

Priority Date: the date with respect to a patent or patent application, of which pre-existing publications and disclosures are regarded as prior art for purposes of novelty and obviousness. In most jurisdictions the priority date is the filing date of the patent application. However, in U.S. law, the question of what is the priority date of an invention is complicated by the fact that the United States applies the first-to-invent principle. What is regarded as prior art is set forth in considerable detail in 35 U.S.C. §§102(a), 102(b) and 103(c). Under normal circumstances in order to qualify as "prior art" a reference must have existed as of the date of invention, which is normally presumed to be as of the filing date of the application until an earlier date is proved. There are two types of prior art, §102(a) prior art and §102(b) prior art.

§102(a) prior art is third party art, that is the work of parties other than the claimed inventor. For such art, all that must be shown is that it anteceded the date of invention. §102(b) usually applies to disclosure by the inventor; for such art to preclude the grant of a U.S. patent, it must antecede the date of the patent application by more than one year. Further, §102(b) is also described as a "statutory bar" in that whether or not an inventor can show a date of invention earlier than one year prior to his or her application date, the inventor is not entitled to a patent if published prior art more than one year old existed as of that application date. The purpose of the statutory bar is to force inventors to the patent office. Under §102(e) U.S. patents, if granted to an entity other than the applicant, are prior art as of their filing dates, regardless of whether they issue after the patent they are alleged to antecede. Section 103(c) refers to whether certain foreign applications filed on behalf of the same applicant can qualify as prior art for obviousness purposes.

Private Copying Levy: some countries (e.g., Canada), in an effort to compensate recording artists for private copying of their works have a hypothecated tax on recording media, e.g., blank cassettes and recordable DVDs, the revenue from which is then redistributed to copyright owners, usually through performing rights societies.

Private Placement: a sale of shares in a company, which is not to the public, but rather to venture capital companies and high net worth individuals. In the United States such a private placement is under SEC Regulation D and is required to only consist of sales to Accredited Investors [q.v.] and certain other "sophisticated" investors.

Privilege: refers to the confidential nature of the advice of a lawyer or patent agent. Legal advice and the right to obtain it, is protected in most countries by making lawyer client communications confidential (known as Attorney-Client Privilege or Legal Professional Privilege). Also usually covered by privilege is the work of a lawyer for a client and the lawyer's thought processes (work product privilege).

Generally lawyers cannot be compelled to disclose privileged communications and are in most circumstances professionally prohibited from disclosing it without the client's consent, while clients cannot be compelled to disclose such communications with their counsel. Selective waiver of privilege is usually not allowed, that is to say a client cannot disclose some of its lawyer's advice, but conceal other information. The exception in the U.S., usually subject to agreement, is the disclosure of non-liability opinions [q.v.]. Since the privilege rules are stronger and more extensive than in a typical Non-Disclosure Agreement, it is often regarded as unwise to require one's own lawyer to sign an NDA, as this may be regarded as detracting from, limiting, or otherwise reducing the scope of the lawyer's professional obligations.

When two parties are on the same side of a legal dispute or court case and wish to cooperate with one another, especially in the United States, it is wise to execute a Joint Defense Agreement or JDA before they start exchanging information. There are a number of exceptions to privilege including: a lawyer may usually disclose privileged information in order to defend himself or herself from claims by the client (i.e., in response to suggestions of malpractice or poor representation); where the lawyer is providing purely commercial advice (i.e., acting as a businessman), rather than legal advice, the communication is usually not privileged; the co-conspirator rule, i.e., where a lawyer is a co-conspirator in a criminal or illegal action with the client, privilege usually does not attach; and where the existence of a legal opinion is used to limit liability (e.g., a non-infringement opinion), privilege in the opinion will usually need to be waived, along with any related communications with the opinion writer.

Process: a method of doing something, or achieving some effect or making something.

Product-by-Process: before analytical chemistry was well developed it was common to describe and define products by the process used to make them rather than trying to describe their underlying chemical structure—such patent claims were known as product-by-process claims and are still used. The treatment of product-by-process claims is complex and varies from jurisdiction-to-jurisdiction, and they can be used to claim an existing product by a novel process. In some instances it has been held that a product-by-process claim only covers the product made by the process, in others it has been held that where the product is novel, making it by an alternate process will not avoid infringement. *See* Claims, Method Claim, Apparatus Claim.

Product-Placement: arranging for a product to be prominently used in a production, e.g., a move or television show, thus gaining an implicit endorsement. The product is usually supplied as a free prop and increasingly a fee may be paid to the production company.

Prohibited Mark: most trademark registration systems have "prohibited marks," that is to say words or symbols which are not permitted in a trademark, for example because they are reserved to the government or might imply governmental approval. This term may also be used in reference to scandalous marks.

Propriété Industrielle: French law and the law of many other civil law countries makes a distinction between intellectual property that can be used for primarily industrial or commercial purposes and "la propriété littéraire et artistique," i.e., literary and artistic works. One major distinction is that the latter class of rights benefit from moral rights.

Prosecution: the process of pursuing a patent or trademark application.

Prosecution History: the history of an application for a patent, including the patent application and all relevant correspondence and arguments made to and by the patent office.

Prosecution History Estoppel: a quasi-equitable doctrine of claim construction, which refers to statements made by a patent applicant in order to secure the grant of a patent. Where an applicant says that the scope of claims in a patent is limited in a particular way, that statement will usually bind the applicant with respect to the subsequent patent. The basic principle is that a patentee should not, in litigation, recapture scope for a patent that the patentee had given up during the application (prosecution) process of the patent application. Classic prosecution history estoppel in U.S. law occurs when a patent applicant make a statement or argument so as to overcome rejection. However, more modern precedents hold that any statement disclamatory of claim scope should be regarded as giving rise to presumption of preclusive effect," i.e., an estoppel. Prosecution history estoppel is sometimes referred to as file-wrapper estoppel. As a doctrine it is usually described as a limitation on the doctrine of equivalents [q.v.] though in practice disclamatory language in the prosecution history is also applies to claim construction [q.v.] for purposes of literal infringement [q.v.]. *See* Teach-Away.

Prospectus: a formal written offer to sell securities to investors, which sets out relevant facts that the investor should have in order to make an informed purchasing decision. Under United States Securities Law such a prospectus must be approved by the SEC and must be accurate. If not the promoters of the company (i.e., the managers, bankers and lawyers) are subject to serious civil and criminal liability. The only exception to the prospectus requirement is a "private placement" under Regulation D, where shares are only sold to accredited investors. A prospectus is sometimes referred to as an SEC Form S-1.

Protective Notice: One problem with freedom of information laws such as the United States Freedom of Information Act, 5 U.S.C. § 552 is the risk exists that trade secrets and confidential information disclosed to governments pursuant to a contract or bid for a contract will be disclosed in response to such a request. Most freedom of information provisions contain specific exceptions shielding certain classes of confidential information from disclosure, including trade secrets and confidential know-how owned and supplied by government contractors. Nonetheless, to avoid the risk of an accidental disclosure, such material should have a notice, known as a protective notice, stating that the information is: (a) confidential; (b) the property of the supplying private entity, developed by that entity (noting if possible that the development was at the entities expense); (c) that it is not subject to disclosure under the Freedom of Information Act (or other relevant provisions); and (d) that inadvertent or intentional disclosure could cause grave commercial harm to the entity that supplied it to the government. In the U.S. the notice should also cite to the applicable sections of the Freedom of Information Act that excepts the information from disclosure, i.e., 5 U.S.C. § 552(b)(1)(A), 552(b)(4), as well as Executive Order 12600 and also note that unauthorized disclosure may be an offense under 18 U.S.C. §§ 1831-39 and 1905.

Protective Order: an order, common in U.S. commercial litigation and especially intellectual property and trade cases, which provides that certain commercially sensitive and confidential information produced in discovery be kept confidential and usually only provided to party's counsel rather than to party's themselves. Usually when there is a protective order, public and non-public versions of pleadings and other records of court proceedings are produced—with the confidential information redacted (deleted) from the public versions.

Proto-droits, proto-rights: French term analogous to quasi-intellectual property [q.v.].

Provisional Application: patent application filed in a hurry, usually without claims, because of the risk of a publication, on-sale bar violation or intervening prior art if there was undue delay. Some systems, such as the United States, allow provisional applications as a special class, others simply treat them as incomplete applications. Waves of omnibus disclosures precede major trade shows such as COMDEX or the GSM World Congress because of the number of product announcements at those events. Many provisional applications are also essentially articles filed by the author immediately prior to publication. *See* Omnibus Disclosure.

PSTN: Public Switched Telephone Network, acronym used to refer to the worldwide voice telephone network.

PTO: abbreviation commonly used for the United States Patent and Trademark Office and other countries' national agencies which have responsibility for both the examination and issuance of patents *and* trademarks.

Publication: has three meanings: first, in copyright law in certain circumstances the term of copyright is measured from the date of first publication; second, a publication (i.e., a publicly available description) is typically is usually required to show prior art [q.v.]; and third, with limited exceptions and some grace periods [q.v.] (e.g., 1 year in the U.S., six months in Japan), publishing an invention before filing for a patent loses the inventor the right to a patent.

Public License: a license that allows the public to freely use the underlying intellectual property. The best known is the GNU General Public License [q.v.].

Puffery: superlatives used in advertising, that it is presumed the public know to be unverifiable or of dubious accuracy, for example "the greatest," the "world's best." Ordinary commercial puffery is usually not open to legal challenge, *however* where it crosses the line into asserting specific verifiable facts (e.g., "best on-time performance") it usually becomes legally dubious if not illegal and sanctionable under unfair competition laws [q.v.] or consumer protection statutes.

Pull Strategy: a method or strategy for introducing a product to the market that focuses on creating consumer demand by direct marketing, used as a way to drive retailers and distributors to stock the product.

Punitive Damages: the strict legal term is exemplary damages [q.v.].

Push Strategy: a method or strategy for introducing a product to the market that focuses getting retailers and distributors to stock the product and largely promote it themselves.

Put Option: the right to require a party to purchase an asset at a fixed minimum price at a particular time.

Q

Qualitative Restrictions, Qualitative Tying: tying the sale of goods or of services together (i.e., you can only buy a if you also buy b) is in general prohibited by all antitrust and competition law systems. However, it is permitted to make such ties where it can be demonstrated that the tied goods or services are necessary to maintain the quality of the primary product under a license or distribution arrangement.

Quality Assurance Clause: a clause typically found in a trademark license, but also franchise agreements and selective distribution arrangements. In the context of trademark licenses (which are typically incorporated into franchises), lack of such provisions can lead to a mark becoming naked [q.v.] under U.S. law.

Quality Mark: a brand name used on array of largely fungible goods from a single supplier that indicate that the goods are of a higher or more reliable quality than the normal run of goods of their type or class.

***Quasi*-Intellectual Property (*Quasi*-IP), *Quasi*-Rights**: certain legal rights and licenses have come to possess many of the qualities and aspects of intellectual property, although they are not statutorily or by definition regarded as intellectual property rights, for example aircraft supplemental type certificates and airline slots; new drug applications; box-rights; naming rights; drug marketing authorizations, etc. Such rights are often referred to as quasi-intellectual property.

R

Ratchet: *See* Anti-Dilution Clause

Reasonable and Non-Discriminatory (RAND) Terms: terms used with respect to essential facilities and in standards that refers to the terms under which licenses should be granted subsequent to the adoption of the standard, guidelines, exemption, etc. For example in a European Competition Directorate "comfort letter" on a standards agreement, parties may be required to license "all comers" on reasonable and non-discriminatory terms. Similarly, IEEE in its patent policy with respect to standards policy requires essential patents to practice a standard to be made available to participants:

> "that a license will be made available to all applicants ... under reasonable rates, with reasonable terms and conditions that are demonstrably free of any unfair discrimination."

However, the term "reasonable" is in legal terms somewhat of a nightmare, since reasonableness is very much "in the eye of the beholder"; i.e., an offeror's reasonable may often be an offeree's unreasonable. Non-discriminatory is an easier term. It essentially means that the offer should be available to all on terms, conditions and at a cost that do not vary substantially. It does not usually mean that the terms have to be identical, though identical terms are *perforce* non-discriminatory. Thus for example, a license scheme that steps royalty rates with volume would be non-discriminatory if the steps are reasonably accessible to most similarly situated licensees. However, if they were written in such a targeted way that only one (or tiny proportion) of potential licensee(s) might benefit, they would probably be discriminatory.

Reciprocal Exclusivity: refers to a supplier conditioning its exclusive supply of goods to a vendor on a condition that the vendor (e.g., a distributor or retailer) does not carry competitors' goods. Such provisions can raise issues under antitrust or competition law, especially where the supplier enjoys a dominant position and/or the available distribution/sales channels are limited.

Reciprocal Rights: term used in reference to cross-licenses to refer to the idea that each party has the same rights with respect to specified intellectual property of the other.

Recitals: terms in a contract, which are agreed statements of facts about the contract and the circumstances in which the contract was entered into. Recitals are frequently preceded by the term "*whereas*" and should be regarded as similar to representations. Recitals are more legally significant than most contract parties realize, since they are in effect signed declarations of fact which it will be difficult for a contracting party to argue were false at a later date.

Reckless Trading: *See* Trading while Insolvent.

Recorded, First, in a Tangible Medium: *See* Fixed.

Record Title, Recordation of Title: ownership of and interests in certain classes of assets such as land, cars and ships, patents, trademarks, etc. is capable of being recorded on an official register of title. Such recordation may be compulsory or voluntary depending on the applicable legal regime. In any event, failure to record such interests, when recordation is possible, can create significant legal risks. *See Bone-Fide* Purchaser.

Category	Recorded?	Category	Recorded?
Land	Normally	Automobiles	Always
Patents	Always	Know-how	Never
Copyright	Usually not, Can be in US	Plant varieties	Always
Trademarks	Usually, but not always	Business Names	Can be, but not always
Naming Rights	Never	Rights of Publicity	Generally never, except by legislation for certain events (e.g., Olympics)

Category	Recorded?	Category	Recorded?
Trade Dress	Can be, often not	Registered Designs	Varies by jurisdiction
Orphan Drugs	Must be	Architectural Designs	Rarely, except as a U.S. Copyright
Service Marks	Can be, but often are not	"Tag" and "Strap" Lines	Can be as Trademarks, often not
Domain Names	Always	Colors, odors	Sometimes as trademarks

Red Herring: a draft prospectus, which has not been approved by the SEC. So called because it is required to be printed and circulated with a pink cover.

Reduction to Practice: patent term meaning that the invention is essentially complete. There are two types of reduction to practice, constructive reduction to practice, which means that the invention is completely conceived and described in such a way that it can be practiced by someone of ordinary skill in the art without undue experimentation, and physical or actual reduction to practice in which the invention is applied or physically embodied. In most patent systems, constructive reduction to practice is sufficient to secure a patent.

Re-Examination: refers to a patent office proceeding to re-examine the grant of a patent, usually in light of prior art not before the patent office in the original examination. There are two types of re-examination, *Ex Parte* and *Inter Partes*. Despite the view sometimes expressed in the media that a reexamined patent is somehow flawed, or of questionable validity, in fact a patent that has survived reexamination is considerably strengthened, and usually much more difficult to challenge on the basis of the art considered in the reexamination. While reexamination does not exist in the European Patent Office, there is a somewhat analogous procedure known as opposition [q.v.]. In principle, the Director of the USPTO can also order a reexamination, but this is a very unusual procedure, usually only applied to controversial or joke patents [q.v.] although there are recent anecdotal suggestions that political lobbying has given rise to such reexaminations in high-profile patent cases.

References: in scientific and scholarly articles, means references to the article by other articles. Similarly, in patent law, references refers to the publications, including patents, referenced by the patent office in considering a patent and as forward references to subsequent patents and patent applications in which the patent office looked at a specific patent.

Refusal to Deal, Concerted: *See* Group Boycott.

Register: refers: (a) to the list of trademarks recognized in a given jurisdiction, which can be divided into a primary register and a secondary register; (b) to the list of drugs in a give jurisdiction that hold a valid Marketing Authorization.

Registered Design: design patents and registered designs are a form of IP protection that falls between patents and copyrights. These rights essentially protect the aesthetic aspects of product design rather than functional technical aspects.

Registered Mark: a formally registered Trade Mark (or Trademark), denoted by the use of the Symbol ®.

Registered Office: an official address of the company to which legal documents may be sent. There is often a legal requirement that companies doing business or certain classes of business within a country establish a registered office in that country to receive legal process.

Registration, Copyright: although under the Berne Convention, it is not required for any formalities, including copyright registration, to take place for a copyright holder to enjoy the basic rights and entitlement to damages available under the Berne convention, copyright registration still exists and can gain the registrant significant additional rights, particularly in the United States.

Registration States: those U.S. states that require franchisors to register and maintain with the state government a Uniform Franchise Offering

Circular or UFOC [q.v.]. At the time of writing Registration States are California, Hawaii, Illinois, Indiana, Maryland, Michigan, Minnesota, New York, North Dakota, Rhode Island, South Dakota, Virginia, Washington, and Wisconsin.

Regnal Year: official dates in Japan are often given by reference to the number of years the then current Japanese emperor has or had reigned. The current era is Heisei, which began in 1988. Thus 2006 is the fourteenth year of the Heisei era and patents granted in this year will be given a prefix 14 or He14, followed by a hyphen. The previous era was that of the Emperor Showa (known in the west as Hirohito) which ran from 1926-1988.

Regulation D: refers to United States securities law regulation (17 CFR §§ 230.501-230.508) setting forth under safe harbor exemption of section 5 of the Securities Act of 1933 (15 U.S.C. §77a *et seq.*), to the need to avoid the expensive process of filing a registration statement with the SEC. Regulation D is usually used for selling shares in startup companies and closely held businesses. *See* Accredited Investor.

Reissue: a patent that has been reissued after errors in the original patent were corrected and the original patent surrendered. In the United States reissues are usually designated by the letters "Re" before the patent number.

Rejection: the refusal to grant an applied for patent or trademark. In the context of a patent rejection, it may apply to some or all the claims of a patent. Rejections may or may not be final—if they are not final the patent office is leaving open the possibility that it may after some argument and explanation accept claims as drafted, if it final only an amendment or appeal may overcome the rejection.

Relevant Market: refers to the market analyzed by courts and/or competition and antitrust agencies in evaluating whether a competitor is dominant [q.v.] or has market power, which is the first step in analyzing the potentially anticompetitive effects of allowing a merger to proceed and often a key step in determining whether such a competitor has violated a competition or antitrust statute, such as abuse of a dominant position [q.v.]. Given its central importance in the analysis of competition and antitrust issues, determining the relevant market is often characterized by the divergent views of "dueling" economic experts. In controversial mergers it also often ends up being a "football" that the competition and antitrust authorities, the merging companies and those opposing the merger kick back and forth, each pressing a definition that suits their purposes and objectives. Because the definition of "relevant market" is very mutable and small and subtle changes can dramatically change the competitive analysis of a case, whether a current set of U.S. Federal Trade Commission [q.v.] Commissioners or the Antitrust Division [q.v.] define markets broadly or narrowly is a key way of loosening or tightening antitrust enforcement and therefore whether they are pro or anti-consolidation, and so reflects the views of an incumbent administration. *See* HHI.

Repair, Right of: one element of exhaustion of rights is that a purchaser of a product covered by an intellectual property right usually has the right to repair and restore the item without infringing the IP rights (but not to build individual components covered by a separate IP right).

Repatriation: the process of taking an "outsourced" function back as an internal business function, usually because outsourcing has proved unsuccessful. Repatriation can raise serious intellectual property issues, for example obtaining ownership over IP created by the outsourcing company such as databases [q.v.] and other records. *See* Contractor IP.

Representations: in a contractual situation, the first party to a contract may require that second party state or recite certain facts, which that second party has asserted to the first party and which were key factors in persuading the first party to enter into the contract; these statements are called representations and are often found in a preamble to the contract (often preceded by the word "*whereas.*") Sometimes there will be a specific "representations" clause or section, which will usually state that the representations therein are the sole representations and no further are made or implied by either party. If a representation in a contract can be shown to be false the party to whom the representation was made may use the false statement as a basis for seeking damages or rescission (canceling) of the contract. *See* Warranty, Indemnity.

Representative Director: a number of corporate jurisdictions, most notably Japan, require companies, especially local subsidiaries of foreign companies, to appoint at least one or two representative director(s) who is normally resident in the jurisdiction. The purpose is to ensure that there is at least one senior manager or officer of the local company who is easily amenable to legal sanctions in the event of a violation of local laws, especially company law.

Resale (Retail) Price Maintenance (RPM): agreements, arrangements, activities, or practices between supplier and dealer/retailer to establish a minimum price or price level to be observed by the dealer when reselling a products or services to customers. RPM can be achieved directly or indirectly. RPM arrangements and activities are almost always regarded as serious violations of competition and antitrust law.

Rescission: a legal remedy that effectively nullifies the contract and allows the party exercising it to demand that the other party restore it to the position it enjoyed prior to the contract. Rescission is usually available as a remedy for fraud or concealment of key relevant information, which one party knew or reasonably should have known would have militated against the other party entering the contract.

Residuals: two meanings

(1) a term for fees paid to actors and writers when movies, television and radio programs and advertising are rerun on the networks, cable and satellite stations, and internationally. The increasing number of channels available through cable and satellite broadcasting has created a rising demand for programming to fill the time, much of which is repeats and re-broadcasts. As a result residual rights are becoming quite lucrative. In the United States the right to residuals was and is primarily negotiated and administered by the Screen Actors' Guild. Residuals on movies are calculated as a percentage of the gross. The rate for residuals set in U.S. productions for television broadcasts of movies are 3.6 percent of broadcaster license fees; video and DVD is 4.5 percent on the first million copies and 5.4 percent thereafter; for television shows residuals are calculated by episode, based on a percentage of the performer's original pay rate and the number of times the episode has been shown; writers earn 2 percent. The right to residuals outside the U.S. is inconsistently present and typically much more limited.

(2) In the context of a residuals clause in a non-disclosure agreement or know-how license, a provision designed to protect the ability of employees to use the skill developed from experience, including working on the licensed technology. Typically such a clause defines residuals as:

> "any information that is retained in the unaided memory of one or more or the recipients employees who have had access to the confidential information pursuant to this NDA/License/Agreement. An employee's memory is "unaided" if the employee has not deliberately memorized the confidential information for the purpose of retaining and later using or disclosing it. . ."

linked to a provision to the effect that:

> "employer and/or its employees may use "Residuals" for any purpose; provided that the foregoing right does not grant any license or licenses under any of [counterparty's] copyrights or patents, other than as provided elsewhere in this NDA/License/Agreement."

Residuals Clause: *See* Residuals.

Res Judicata: legal principle that disputes already adjudicated in one court should not be re-litigated in another. Generally, *res judicata* only applies against a party that had, or could have availed or, an opportunity to appear in the prior case and argue its position. *Res judicate* does not apply to appeals of the prior ruling within the judicial system that the order was issued in.

Restraints on/of Output: *See* Output Restraints.

Returns: term found in licensing, agency, and distribution agreements. It refers to sales made by the licensee, distributor, or agent where the product is subsequently returned and usually provides that commissions or royalties be reduced in respect of such returns.

Revenue Recognition: publicly traded companies must comply with revenue recognition rules before they can accrue revenue, i.e., declare it as income in their public reporting. Revenue recognition rules are very important drivers in sales transactions and purchasers who are aware of the rules can often use them to their advantage in bargaining. Under U.S. (FASB) rules there are two tests that revenue must fulfill before it can be declared:

(1)   Completion of the earnings process, i.e., the vendor must have no significant remaining obligations to the customer, so if under the sales contract some major element remains to be delivered, the revenue cannot be recognized—in addition if there is a return period, i.e., the customer can return the goods for refund for a certain period of time, the revenue cannot be recognized until that time has elapsed;

(2)   Assurance of payment, i.e., the vendor must be reasonably that it will be paid.

Under International Accounting Standards the rules are expressed somewhat differently. IAS 18 makes provision for goods and services. With respect to goods, revenue can be recognized once:

- the vendor has transferred to the buyer the significant risks and rewards of ownership, which also requires that
  o the vendor retains neither continuing managerial involvement to the degree usually associated with ownership, nor effective control over the goods sold;
- the amount of revenue the vendor will derive from the transaction can be measured reliably, i.e., reasonably accurately;
- it is probable that the economic benefits associated with the transaction will flow to the vendor, i.e., that it is the vendor who will receive payment; and
- the costs incurred or to be incurred, by the vendor, in respect of the transaction can be reliably measured.

With respect to services, IAS 18 provides that revenue can be recognized once:

- the amount of revenue the vendor will derive from the transaction can be measured reliably, i.e., reasonably accurately;
- it is probable that the economic benefits associated with the transaction will flow to the vendor, i.e., that it is the vendor who will receive payment;
- the stage of completion of the delivery of services at the balance sheet date, for which revenue is being recognized, can be measured reliably; and
- the costs incurred, or to be incurred, by the vendor, in respect of the transaction can be measured reliably.

Reverse Doctrine of Equivalence: U.S. legal doctrine that was expressed in U.S. Supreme Court Cases as:

"Where a device is so far changed in principle from a patented article that it performs the same or a similar function in a substantially different way, but nevertheless falls within the literal words of the claim, the doctrine of equivalents may be used in reverse to restrict the claim and defeat the patentee's action for infringement."

Graver Tank & Mfg. Co. v. Linde Air Prods. Co., 339 U.S. 605, 608-09, 70 S.Ct. 854, 856, 94 L.Ed. 1097 (1950) and:

"The patentee may bring the defendant within the letter of his claims, but if the latter has so far changed the principle of the device that the claims of the patent, literally construed, have ceased to represent his actual invention, he is as little subject to be adjudged an infringer as one who has violated the letter of a statute has to be convicted, when he has done nothing in conflict with its spirit and intent."

Boyden Power-Brake Co. v. Westinghouse, 170 U.S. 537, 568, 18 S.Ct. 707, 722, 42 L.Ed. 1136 (1898).

The doctrine is intended to cut back on overly expansive claims. It is relatively rarely applied today. *See*, Doctrine of Equivalence.

Reverse Engineering: the process of examining a product to determine how it works or was made, so as to enable the examiner to either make a compatible product or indeed copy the product. Reverse engineering may involve technical dismantling, input output probing, and decompiling of software. If performed with publicly available materials, reverse engineering is not strictly illegal. However it may place its practitioners in a weak position if accused of patent infringement.

Revlon Duties: in *Revlon, Inc. v. MacAndrews & Forbes Holding, Inc.*, 506 A.2d 173 (Del. 1985), the Delaware Supreme Court held that incumbent management, pursuant to its fiduciary duties to the company, must not play favorites when a bid has been made for the company. Rather, management has a duty, a *"Revlon* duty," or *"Revlon* duties" to consider all bids for the company when it has effectively been put up for sale and to award the sale of the company to the bidder that maximizes shareholder wealth. In particular, excessive "break fees" [q.v.] and too-restrictive "no-shop clauses" [q.v.] have been held to violate these *Revlon* duties.

RICO: acronym for the Racketeer Influenced and Corrupt Organizations Act, 18 U.S.C. § 1961 *et seq.* RICO creates an offence predicated on a pattern of illegal activities, i.e., at least *two* similar acts and lists a wide array of such "predicate acts" including Mail Fraud and Wire Fraud. Most importantly, the statute provides for civil suits to be brought by victims of racketeering and for those victims to automatically receive treble damages and attorney' fees, and the civil suit does not require a successful criminal prosecution. Although originally targeted at organized crime, e.g., the Mafia, RICO has been successfully used against otherwise respectable companies who have transgressed against civil plaintiffs repeatedly in a similar way. State RICO laws also exist.

Right-of-Endorsement: allows a company to put its logo on the item, for example Michelin® on a Formula 1 racing car. *See* Box Rights, Right-to-Endorsement.

Right-of-Publicity: term typically used to refer to endorsement by a celebrity or fictional character. Rights of publicity are not recognized in principle in a number of jurisdictions such as the United Kingdom, but well established for example in the United States, where Section 46 of the Restatement of the Law Third, Unfair Competition states:

> "One who appropriates the commercial value of a person's identity by using without consent the person's name, likeness, or other indicia of identity for purposes of trade is subject to liability for the relief appropriate."

Rights Offering, Rights Issue: an offering of "rights," usually to existing shareholders to buy additional shares. Usually the term is a bit of a misnomer since if shareholders to not take up the "right" they are penalized by being diluted to the extent that other parties do utilize the rights to subscribe.

Right to Continued Employment: *See* At-Will Employee, At-Will Employment.

Right-to-Endorsement: allows a vendor to put the grantor's trademark or logo on the box, for example the logo of the American Dental Association on a toothpaste package. *See* Box Rights, Right-of-Endorsement.

Right-to-Have-Made: *See* Have-Made.

Robinson-Patman Act: 15 U.S.C. §13, United States antitrust law, in particular an amendment to Clayton Act that forbids any person or firm engaged in interstate commerce to discriminate in price to different purchasers of the same commodity when the effect would be to lessen competition or to create a monopoly. The statute is primarily designed to protect small shops from the buying power of big chains.

Rocket Docket: largely U.S. legal jargon that refers to a very fast U.S. Federal District Court. (A docket is a court's schedule or timetable.) The life of cases in the United States Federal Courts can vary dramatically, slow courts typically taking three to five years to complete a case through trial (though there are even odd notorious cases that have been pending for more than a decade). Fast courts typically take a little over a year, but a few districts, notably the Eastern District of Texas and the Eastern District of Virginia, typically hear cases within seven to nine months, have very tight scheduling rules, and rarely allow any delay by defendants. However, these courts do have drawbacks, including in E.D.Va. and E.D.Tx. a reputation for pro-local or anti-foreigner chauvinism. In terms of speed the courts of the Netherlands are regarded as Europe's rocket-docket. *See* Forum Shopping.

ROM: Read Only Memory, a type of data storage device which is manufactured with fixed contents, usually inserted by "burning in." ROM is often used to hold programs for embedded systems, as well as for mobile devices such as cell-phones and handheld computers to store the operating system. Some software and databases are sold on detachable ROMs known as dongles (the word dongle is also used to describe as detachable adaptor for computers).

Rome Convention: usually refers to a European community agreement, the Rome Convention on the Law Applicable to Contractual Obligations (1980 OJ L 266/1), known as Rome I (a new convention the Rome Convention on the Law Applicable to non-Contractual Obligations, known as Rome II, is pending and likely to be adopted on or about the time of publication of this glossary). In general the Rome Convention seeks to settle what law will apply, where there is *no choice of law* provision in the contract. In such circumstances it governs what law will apply to contracts agreed between parties in more than one EU member state, and broadly requires that the law of the country with which a contractual obligation is most closely related shall be applied. However, it also includes two major exceptions limiting the applicability of contractual choice of law clauses that would deprive a party of rights under consumer protection law or employment law.

Royalty Base: The total value of the goods or services upon which a license royalty can be charged. *See* Level of Market.

RPC: Revenue per Customer, the average amount that each customer spends with a business. Sometimes expressed on a *per annum* or per transaction basis.

Rule 11: short for Rule Eleven of the [United States] Federal Rules of Civil Procedure, which provides that in signing a pleading (especially a complaint or defense) a party's lawyer is certifying that the pleading (or case) is: (a) not being filed for an improper purpose; (b) that the claims, defenses, and other legal contentions in the pleading have a reasonable basis in law or can be justified by a "non-frivolous argument" for a new legal principle or extension of existing law to be made; (c) that the factual assertions either have evidentiary support or will likely have such support after discovery; or (d) that denials of facts (as in a defense) are justified. Violations of Rule 11 can result in sanctions being imposed on a party's lawyer(s) up to and including the counterparty's attorneys' fees. Rule 11 motions should be filed with care. It is not unusual for an ill-judged Rule 11 motion to itself attract Rule 11 sanctions.

Rule of Reason: Competition Law and Antitrust principle first articulated by the United States Supreme Court in the 1911 Standard Oil case and repeatedly reiterated under the same name, but in varying and not necessarily consistent ways since. The basic premise of the rule of reason is that an agreement or business arrangement that on its face appears to conflict with competition law may be treated as legal if its actual effect is to promote competition or the public welfare and the gains thereby outweigh any anti-competitive impact. Generally the applicability of the rule of reason is determined by a three-part test:

1. does the agreement or arrangements under examination, *prima facie*, reduce or restrain some aspect of competition;
2. does the agreement or arrangements have "pro-competitive" (or other) benefits that outweigh the harm resulting from (1);
3. are the agreement or arrangements the least restrictive or anticompetitive way to achieve the benefits identified at (2) or it there a "less restrictive alternative."

The European Equivalent of the Rule of Reason is sometimes referred to as the "Appreciability Test," [q.v.] i.e., that a restraint on competition and its effects on commerce within the EU must be "appreciable" for it to violate Article 81(1) of the Treaty of Rome. The appreciability test is not absolutely equivalent, but it does examine the overall effect on economic activity. It could also be said that the Article 81(3) [q.v.] conditions for exemption are essentially the same as the Rule of Reason.

Running Royalty: a royalty that is charged over the life of the license either as a percentage of sales (usually to the first unrelated party), a fixed amount per unit, or a fixed amount per calendar period. *See* Metering, Certainty/Uncertainty Trade Off.

Runoff Insurance: an insurance policy purchased to cover future claims related to past liabilities. Typically used in two contexts: (a) mergers and acquisitions where the acquiring company usually buys a policy, paid for out of the purchase price, to cover any acquired liabilities, or liabilities of a particular class such as intellectual property infringement; (b) in the context of professional indemnity insurance for lawyers, accountants and doctors, it refers to the requirement that after a practice ends, they continue paying insurance until the applicable statutes of limitations have run, or make a one time buy of insurance to cover claims that may be made in the future. Runoff insurance is also sometimes referred to as "Closeout Insurance."

RWA: short for résumé (*curriculum vitæ*) writing activity, as in there is "too much RWA going on; I'm worried." *See* CVQ.

S

S-1, Form: *See* Prospectus.

Saisie-Contrefaçon: also referred to simply as a *saisie*, an order in French and Belgian law which an intellectual property holder may seek on an *ex-parte* basis to have a bailiff (a *huissier*) search an alleged infringer's premises and seize evidence of the infringer's activities including allegedly infringing goods. Evidence gathered in a *saisie* may then be used in court cases not necessarily limited to France. A *saisie* is similar to an English Anton Piller order.

Salami Slicing: two meanings. The analogy is to the way in which a salami that is being sliced gets barely perceptibly shorter with each slice, until there is little or no sausage left. In fraud, particularly computer-based fraud, it usually refers to embezzling tiny amounts from the system, by, for example, taking fractional amounts of currency in transactions usually rounded out and accumulating them in a bank account. The sums involved are usually so small that no party really misses them, but over time and done frequently enough, they can accumulate to huge amounts. In negotiation, it refers to a tactic of slowly accruing concessions from a counterparty, until that counterparty finds that it has in fact been left with a poor deal. This tactic is often accompanied by the counterparty making the mistake of buying the same horse twice [q.v.], or allowing the "blame God" [q.v.] tactic to be deployed.

Sales Base: synonym for Royalty Base.

Sandbagging: a sandbag or sap was used by some "muggers" to hit victims over the head, temporarily stunning them and rendering resistance difficult. In law, the term has come to mean the filing of motions or delivery of documents at a time that makes it very difficult for another lawyer to respond, for example 5:30 p.m. on the Friday before a holiday weekend or just before Christmas etc., or on the eve of a meeting. As a tactic sandbagging is often used by large firms against small firms, or lawyers they perceive to have fewer resources. Sandbagging is an unwise practice for a number of reasons. First the legal motto "one good sandbagging deserves a worse one" means that retaliation can be expected and it is likely to be much worse than the original sandbagging; the end result is simply to cost the clients money. Second, sandbagging tends to anger the other party and its lawyers, rendering civil relations between counsel difficult, which also raises costs for all parties with little legal gain. Third, judges and courts are not naïve and tend to recognize sandbagging when they see it, while the sandbagging may also spoil the judge and his or her clerk's weekend; this usually is very counterproductive for the sandbagging party. An unsubtle and obvious form of sandbagging in negotiations is to deliver documents late and converted into printed, i.e., non-data format or "locked" image files, thus rendering editing and response difficult.

Sarbanes Oxley Act: also known as SOX and SarbOx, 18 U.S.C. § 1514A was enacted in the wake of a series of U.S. accounting scandals to both increase management's liability for false accounting and inaccurate reporting and to impose meaning quality standards on public company's internal controls. Much of the legislation, and the record-breaking number of rules promulgated by the SEC in implementing the act, addressed the increasing lack of independence perceived in the activities of public accountants. It has been heavily criticized in some quarters for the burden it places on companies, though others have suggested that there are some tangible benefits to improved internal controls. Section 302 of the Act requires the company to certify the accuracy of its quarterly financial reports and certain company officers (CEO and CFO) to certify that financial reports that, in addition to personally reviewing all financial reports, the reports present a fair and truthful picture of the company's finances. Further, Section 302(a) requires that the signing officers establish, maintain, periodically review and report changes, deficiencies, and corrective actions in the effectiveness of the corporate internal controls necessary to provide financial reports that comply with these requirements. Section 404 establishes a requirement for companies to state in their public annual reports the responsibility of corporate management to establish and maintain such internal controls as are necessary to provide financial reports that comply with the Act's requirements and also that the external auditors also provide an assessment of the effectiveness of the company's internal controls.

Saving Clause (Savings Clause): a clause in an agreement (or law) designed to protect the overall agreement should a provision of the agreement be held invalid or illegal under applicable law. Such a clause usually provides that such a provision will be excised from the agreement, but the remainder of the agreement will remain valid. Although the inclusion of such clauses is quite automatic, it may be wise to exclude certain provisions from its scope, if their invalidity would fundamentally undermine a party's interests in continuing the agreement.

SBA: the United States Small Business Administration, a Federal agency that seeks to assist small companies, including startups, with low cost loans and other assistance.

SBIC: a Small Business Investment Company, a business licensed by the SBA to receive government funds as leverage in order to raise funds to use in venture capital.

Scale Fees, Scale Costs: in a number of legal systems, for example Germany, lawyers charge for certain services, particularly litigation and property transactions, based on a fixed fee schedule established under local law or by the local bar associations. Such a fee schedule takes into account the level of court and the amount at issue or the value of the transaction. There is considerable debate about the benefits of such fee scales. Where the fee scale is set to high, it may be regarded as resulting in overcharging— this was the basis for prohibiting such scales in property transactions in some countries as a form of price fixing by the legal profession. Where the fee scale is set too low, it may limit the amount of effort that a lawyer is willing to put into a difficult case. There are also at least anecdotal suggestions that where fee scales are set too low, various means are used by clients to circumvent the scale, such as sending the lawyer a number of high fee but simple projects—this may be the case, but public confirmation is, not surprisingly, impossible to find. Moreover, if the system does provide for a winner to recover its costs, all a court will usually award are the "scale costs." It is fair to say that lawyers from jurisdictions that have a "scale fee" system support this approach, lawyers from jurisdictions that do not have, or have abolished such a system are very skeptical.

Scandalous Mark: applications for trademarks that are outrageous, e.g., overtly sexual, scatological or simply use crude language, can in many trademark systems be refused or alternately held invalid, or held not capable of being damaged by infringement (precluding damages). *See* Prohibited Mark, Moral Grounds.

Search Report: the results of a prior art search. The search report usually specifies the field of search and may, if it is an international search report or EPO search report classify references as X, Y, and A.

Seats: term in software licensing, which usually refers to the number of computers in an organization that can simultaneously either use or have loaded a software program or package.

Secondary Meaning: a word, which is not fanciful or is even descriptive, can be trademarked if it can be shown that it has come to have a secondary meaning in the eyes of the public, which as a result associates it exclusively with the applicant's goods or services. The term "acquired distinctiveness" is also used for this purpose.

Secondary-Source License: *See* Multi-Sourcing.

Secondary Use Rights: rights sometimes granted to a licensee that allows it to use one primary copy of the software on one machine and a second copy on for example a personal laptop or spare computer.

Secret Patent: *See* NATO Patent.

Securities Law: United States term for the laws that govern the sale of shares, bonds, and other instruments that might be considered securities, to the public. The scope of what are considered securities and are therefore in principle regulated is defined in Securities Exchange Act of 1934, as including:

> "Any note, stock, treasury stock, bond, debenture, certificate of interest, or participation in any profit-sharing agreement or in any oil, gas, or other mineral royalty or lease, any collateral trust certificate, preorganization certificate or subscription, transferable share,

investment contract, voting-trust certificate, certificate of deposit, for a security, any put, call, straddle, option, or privilege on any security, certificate of deposit, or group or index of securities (including any interest therein or based on the value thereof), or any put, call, straddle, option, or privilege entered into on a national securities exchange relating to foreign currency, or in general, any instrument commonly known as a "security"; or any certificate of interest or participation in, temporary or interim certificate for, receipt for, or warrant or right to subscribe to or purchase, any of the foregoing; but shall not include currency or any note, draft, bill of exchange, or banker's acceptance which has a maturity at the time of issuance of not exceeding nine months, exclusive of days of grace, or any renewal thereof the maturity of which is likewise limited."

U.S. securities law is enforced on the basis of "strict liability," that is to say ignorance of the law is not an excuse, though if nit willful, it may reduce the penalties applied.

Security for Costs: in legal systems that apply the indemnity principle a litigant, usually a plaintiff, may be required to provide "security" to show that it can pay the other party's costs in the event that it fails to win its case. However, as security for costs is regarded as potentially making it impossible for someone to bring a suit, even if well founded, it is usually only ordered where the plaintiff has a very weak case and there is some sound reason to believe it will not pay costs if it loses the case, e.g., it is a foreign party that could dodge paying costs or it is teetering on the edge of bankruptcy. Orders requiring security for costs are usually very rare.

Selective Distribution: the use of a distribution network where sales outlets are required to meet certain criteria, e.g., quality, staff, premises, etc. Selective distribution systems are permissible under competition law provided they can be objectively justified.

Selling the Same Horse Twice: *See* Don't Buy the Same Horse Twice.

Servicemark: a trademark that covers services rather than goods. Some trademark agencies used to keep servicemarks on a separate register.

Settlement Discussions, Admissibility of: *See* Without Prejudice (Rule).

Sherman Act: 15 U.S.C. §1 *et seq.*, enacted in 1890, was the first U.S. Federal antitrust law. The act declares illegal every contract, combination (in the form of trust or otherwise), or conspiracy in restraint of interstate and foreign trade. It has been variously-amended, by the Clayton Act and the Robinson Patman Act. The Sherman Act has quite severe sanctions. Violating it is a felony (i.e., a crime), which can result in a prison sentence on an individual of three years and fines of up to $350,000 per violation, while companies can be fined up to $10 million per violation. Violations can also give rise to civil suits, including class actions, that can result in enhanced, treble damages. State Attorneys General can also bring suits under this legislation under the *Parens Patriæ* Act.

Shop Right: a term commonly used to describe certain employers' rights with respect to IP created by employees in the course of their employment. The key dangers with shop right are:

- first, that is often poorly understood, even by IP lawyers;
- second, that the nature of shop right can vary depending on the form of IP;
- third, that it varies with each jurisdiction that the right arises in; and
- fourth, that "choice-of-law" rules vary, so that sometimes the law of the place of creation or employment applies and sometimes the law of the jurisdiction in which the IP right is asserted applies.

Under the United States copyright statute, works of authorship made for hire by employees working within the scope of their employment automatically become the property of the employer (work made for hire or "work for hire.") However, patent rights do not automatically become the property of the employer, rather the employer may own the rights based on complex case-law based rules and factors including whether the employee was "directed to invent." Indeed in the United States it is possible, depending of the facts of the situation, that an employer's shop right may be limited to a royalty-free license to use the patented invention, without assignment or licensing rights, while the employee/inventor might be able to resign and go into competition with a former employer or sell or license the patent rights to a competing company. A key exception to shop right in most jurisdictions is that it does not apply to contractors or consultants.

Short-Name Mark: Refers to the greater value of shorter words used as trademarks. Generally the public prefers brand names with fewer syllables, thus one syllable is very valuable (e.g., Dell, Coke), two also quite valuable (SONY, Levi's), but the value (and memorize-ability) declines, as the name gets longer. Notably, Coke is an abbreviation of a four syllable mark, Levi's of a three syllable mark, both were commonly used by the public for some time before their owners recognized their value. *See* Two Syllable Rule.

Short-Swing Profits Rule: U.S. securities law contains a provision (in what is known as the Williams Act, §16b of the Securities Act of 1934, 15 U.S.C. § 78p(b)), which prohibits a company insider from making a profit from transactions in shares of the company held for less than six months, i.e., the purchase and subsequent sale of shares or the sale and subsequent purchase of shares. Under the short swing profit rule the insider is usually required to disgorge any such profits to the company. The statute creates strict liability for insiders engaging in short-swing trading without regard to the trader's intent and regardless also of whether the trading results in a profit or a loss. The statute aims to deter insiders from taking unfair advantage of confidential company information to realize short-swing profits on trades in the company's stock. Other jurisdictions have enacted similar rules and they are also sometimes written into insider's employment agreements. Compliance with the rule has the advantage of immunizing insiders to a degree from accusations of insider trading, which can be particularly useful for executives who have a high proportion of their net worth "tied-up" in company stock. There is no short-swing profits rule in the UK, which for such executives can present a serious problem, as they may be disbarred from selling any stock, except in short, uneventful periods of time for the business.

Show-How: term used for showing a third party to carry out a process or make a product. Show-how can present tricky issues in some legal systems, as it sometimes will not be treated as licensable intellectual property—in which case service contracts should be used rather than license agreements.

Showstopper: colloquial term used to refer to a bug that causes a program to stop or crash. *See* Class A Bug.

Shrink-Wrap License: a copyright, know-how or trade secret license which accompanies the work (typically software and occasionally a book) and provides that if the purchaser opens the "shrink wrap" in which the work is packaged, they have accepted the terms of the license. Typically the license is in the form of an End User License Agreement. *See* Click License.

Simplified Procedure: EU Competition law term that refers to a faster, streamlined review procedure for mergers and concentrative joint ventures that do not raise significant competition concerns and are eligible to be notified using the Form CO Short Form [q.v.]. The simplified procedure was formalized in Commission's Notice on a simplified procedure for treatment of certain concentrations under the Council Regulation (EC) No. 139/2004 2005 OJ C 56/32. A review under the simplified procedure will normally be completed within 25 days. Assuming the turnover thresholds (*See* Merger Regulation, European) are met (if not the merger of joint venture is not subject to review, the simplified procedure will be applied to:

> (a) Full Form Joint Ventures [q.v.] where the JV has negligible impact in the EEA, i.e., the turnover of the JV in the EEA is less than €100 and the total value of the assets in the EEA that the parent have transferred to the JV is less than €100 million;
> (b) Mergers and joint ventures where none of the parties are participants in the same markets, or markets upstream or downstream;
> (c) Mergers and joint ventures where,, although the parties are present in the same market, their combined market share is less than 15 percent;
> (d) Mergers and joint ventures where, although the parties are present in upstream and downstream markets their combined or individual market shares at any level of market [q.v.] is less than 25 percent.

Sisyphus: either an effort to pronounce the acronym CFIUS [q.v.] or a classical allusion to the founder of the city of Corinth and son of Aeolus, king of Thessaly and Enarete, who instituted the Isthmian Games. He was allegedly prone to waylaying travelers and murdering them. He also betrayed the secrets of the gods and chained Thanatos, the god of death, preventing the dead from reaching the underworld, an act for which he was punished by Hades, Lord of the Underworld, by being forced to roll a block of stone against a steep hill, which rolls back down again when he reaches the top, forcing him to repeat the process into eternity (hence the term a "Sisyphean task.") He is also alleged to be the father of Odysseus by Anticlea, who subsequently married Laertus.

Site License: a license that is limited to use by the licensee to a particular site. Such licenses are very common in the chemical industry.

SJ: letters designating someone as a member of the Society of Jesus, i.e., a Jesuit priest or alternately an acronym for summary judgment. *See* Motion, to Dismiss, Summary Judgment, Set Aside the Verdict.

Sleeping-Dog License: comes from the English phrase "let sleeping dogs lie" and is another term for a tacit license [q.v.] based on a decision by a patent holder not to pursue an infringer because of its own possible infringement of the infringer's patents and lack of desire to engage in expensive and potentially pyrrhic litigation.

Slots, Schedule: the right to conduct a specified activity at a specific repeated time, usually daily. Such rights frequently become legally vested by passage of time or by contract and since they have gained many of the attributes of intellectual property are known as quasi-intellectual property [q.v.]. Most slots arise in the transportation sector, and include airport takeoff slots, ferry terminal slots and railway line and platform slots. A major pitfall of these rights is that they are not universally recognized.

Small Entity: most patent and trademark systems provide that "small entities" can obtain a substantial discount on application and maintenance fees. Small entities are defined by the number of employees the business has, according to quite complex rules that vary both as to employee number and employment conditions (i.e., part-time, full-time) from country to country. Companies claiming small entity status should be careful not to inadvertently continue to do so after they grow over the threshold as this can have adverse effects on patent or trademark enforceability or validity.

Soft IP: a term usually used to describe intellectual property which is intangible and consists of rights over expression and aesthetic aspects of ideas, i.e., trademarks, literary copyrights, etc. It is sometimes also used to describe IP transferred in an intangible form, for example microprocessor designs in RTL (Register Transfer Level) format. Some soft IP practitioners consider the term pejorative and belittling. The dividing line between hard and soft IP is difficult to define, software for example being a tricky area. *See* Hard IP.

Software Directive: properly titled the Council Directive 91/250/EEC of May 14, 1991 on the legal protection of computer programs, the directive established the basic requirements for the legal protection of software throughout the European Union.

SOL: acronym for "S**t out of luck," as in "if your PCA is more than your RPC, sooner or later you're going to be SOL." It usually means an irreversibly bad outcome for the party that is SOL.

Source Code: a program expressed in a high level language (e.g., C++) before it is compiled into machine code (object code). Software companies usually treat the source code version of a program as highly confidential and laced with business secrets and know-how.

Source Code Escrow: *See* Escrow.

Source Code Visibility (Clause): clause in a contract that provides that a purchaser of software can see or inspect the source code as well as receiving the object code. Clauses providing for source code visibility usually restrict access to inspection at the licensor's premises or alternately require the source code to be kept in a secure manner (e.g., on a non-networked computer, with drives and media/data transfer ports disabled). Source code visibility is usually sought when the software is to be integrated with a device or other software, so as to facilitate debugging and problem solving.

SOX: *See* Sarbanes Oxley Act.

Special 301: refers to the so-called "special section 301" Omnibus Trade and Competitiveness Act of 1988. The ordinary section 301 of the U.S.

Trade Law allows the U.S. to take retaliatory measures against countries applying "unfair" trade practices to U.S. trade. The special 301 authority is designed to enhance the U.S. administration's ability to negotiate improvements in foreign intellectual property regimes either bilaterally or multilaterally. The statute requires the United States Trade Representative ("USTR") to annually identify those foreign countries which deny adequate and effective protection of intellectual property rights or fair and equitable market access for Americans relying on intellectual property protection. Those countries not making improving such conditions or entering into good faith negotiations may be identified as "priority foreign countries" and may be subject to further investigation and various trade consequences. The legality of special 301 under international trade agreements has often been questioned.

Specialization Agreement: an agreement between multiple businesses to each specialize in the production of a narrow or specific range of goods or services. The general rationale is that the market for such goods cannot support the sunk cost or investment necessary for parties to the agreement to compete effectively in the space and that specialization thus leads to greater efficiency and cheaper supply of the specialized products. Such agreements are often reached with respect to component parts, which are then supplied to non-manufacturing parties at close-to-cost. Specialization agreements are divided into agreements whereby: (a) one party gives up a manufacturing activity or services area in favor of another party (unilateral specialization); (b) each party gives up a manufacturing activity or services area in exchange for a like commitment form another party (reciprocal specialization); and (c) the parties agree to jointly manufacture or provide services (joint production). Specialization raises significant issues under competition law [q.v.] and in the EU is the subject of a Block Exemption [q.v.].

Specification: two meanings:

(a) it is usually used to refer to the part of a patent in which the invention and how to practice it is described in detail, although technically it also includes the claims;

(b) a statement of criteria that an intended product, project or process must achieve. Specifications are prospective and in principle aspirational and may be highly detailed, laying down key requirements for the product, process or project to be successful, including operating successfully in the intended environment. All technology contracts usually include a specification.

Spectrum: abbreviation of "electromagnetic spectrum," which is usually taken to mean the range of electromagnetic frequencies (or wavelengths), which can be used to transmit radio signals. Spectrum is regarded as a public commons, which governments then allocate through a licensing process to particular users. Thereafter, allocated spectrum is usually regarded as a property right or *quasi-IP right*. One method of allocation is auctioning of parts of the available spectrum, for example to cellular telephone operators—in the latter case the operators in recent cellular auctions in the U.S. and Europe are regarded as having catastrophically overbid (overpaid) for spectrum.

SPV: acronym for special purpose vehicle, a limited liability company, usually a subsidiary of a larger company, established to carry out a single business role or "special purpose," thus insulating the parent from potential liability. SPV's are often established in international tax havens such as the Virgin Islands, Bahamas, Isle of Man, or Channel Islands.

Stage Name: actors' unions, for example Actors Equity or the Screen Actors Guild, administer a system whereby a person joining the union must identify a stage name, which they will use professionally. The union will typically require the actor to select a name different from their actual name if there is a risk of confusion with another actor. Separately, an actor may be able to assert claims based on trademark and passing off.

Stage One, Two, Three Drug Trials: Alternate term for Phase I, II, and III Human Drug Trials. *See* IND.

Stage Payment, Stage Completion: in long-term development contracts or projects the contractor may, if payment is "on completion" of the contract, find itself with significant cash flow problems as well as substantial risk in the event of customer default or bankruptcy. To reduce this risk, the development or project is divided into stages and upon completion of a stage, payment for work performed on that stage is made. Customer holdback [q.v.] is usually withheld from stage payments.

Standard of Review, Appellate: a key question in legal appeals is how closely the decision of the lower court, tribunal, or agency will be scrutinized. Faced with the possibility of a legal appeal, the first question a lawyer will ask will be what are the grounds for appeal—but the immediate second will be what standard of review is applied to each "ground." Appeals will normally always consider whether the lower court made a fundamental error of law. However, the factual findings of a lower court can be considered in a number of different ways. *De novo* means that the higher court, should, in principle, ignore any factual findings of the lower court and review the evidence again, reaching its own factual conclusions. While this is the strictest standard of review, it should be recognized that the appellate court is usually influenced, to a lesser or greater degree by the lower court's decision. At each successive level above *de novo*, the lower court's ruling is granted greater levels of deference. The next level of review is usually described as "clear error" or "clearly erroneous," where the appeals court will consider the evidence before the lower court and if there simply was not enough evidence to support the lower courts decision, and/or the factual conclusions appear to be unambiguously at odds (not justified or contradicted) by the evidence, will reverse. The next level of review is usually described as lack of "substantial evidence," which requires a finding that the ruling of the lower court was unsupported by any substantial (i.e., credible and convincing evidence); this standard is difficult to reach because, by its nature the winner in a case usually has presented at least some evidence in support of its positions. Finally abuse of discretion requires a showing that the lower court judge or the agency acted in an arbitrary and capricious manner, i.e., did not in fact apply discretion or judgment. Another key factor in appeals, that is almost never publicly stated, is the opinion the broad legal community, and appeals judges in particular, hold of the appealed from lower court judge or agency—if it is poor, successful appeals will often arise; further, the more often a judge or agency is reversed, the less trust, deference and respect it will attract from the appellate court.

Standards, Mandatory, Compliance: standards that certain products must comply with to be legal for sale. Most such standards are safety related and goods that meet the standards display a compliance mark. The best-known compliance markings include:

> CE: for European Union Standards;
> FCC: U.S. Federal Communication Commission Standards;
> CCC: Products for sale in China;
> Ek: Products for sale in Korea.

Companies engaged in international sales of technology products frequently experience problems with complying with the testing regimes required by such standards, usually because not enough time has been allocated for testing and compliance or because substantial modifications have been carried out to the product without considering the possible need for recertification.

Standard, Technical: common specifications established to ensure interoperability of technology. For example, early and now largely ubiquitous standards were established for light bulbs and light-bulb sockets, or railway gauges. Technical standards fall into two categories: (i) multilateral standards established by committees or groups drawn from across an industry (often described as technical experts groups), usually under the auspices of an organization such as the Institute of Electrical and Electronic Engineers (IEEE); or (ii) unilateral or *de facto* standards (the best known of which include DOS and Windows), which develop because market externalities favor companies making their products compatible with those of major product manufacturers in a given industry sector. Standards and standard setting can raise significant antitrust [q.v.] and competition law [q.v.] issues. Staple Article of Commerce: *See* Contributory Infringement.

State Trademark: in the United States, state trademarks exist in thirty-six of fifty states. Such marks provide on a state-by-state basis essentially the same rights as a federal trademark, but are subordinate to (pre-empted by) federal trademarks and may grant rights contradictory to those provided under federal law.

Statute of Anne: a British "Act for the Encouragement of Learning, by Vesting the Copies of Printed Books in the Authors or Purchasers of such Copies, during the Times therein mentioned" (8 Anne c. 19), enacted in 1710 during the reign of Queen Anne and usually described as the first modern copyright law.

Statute of Monopolies, The: usually described as one of the first modern patent laws, was "[a]n Act concerning Monopolies and Dispensations with Penal Laws, and the Forfeitures thereof" dated 1623 (21 Jac. 1, c. 3). Prior to the Statute of Monopolies, patents in England had been monopolies of products sold by the government to raise revenue or given to court favorites. The system had come to be seriously abused, particularly by Elizabeth I, who was often chronically short of funds. The power to grant such patents was severely abused, with patents (which then meant monopolies) being granted on items ranging from salt to playing cards and the patent holders being granted extraordinary powers to enforce those rights. The Statute of Monopolies reformed the patent system, adopting the continental or "Venetian" system of only granting patents for inventions (including imported technology). The Statute of Monopolies is often inaccurately, described as the first modern patent law, notwithstanding the existence of earlier such laws, for example the Decree of 1474 on the Protection of Inventions in the Republic of Venice, whose principles it largely copied.

Statutory Bar: usually refers to one of the statutory grounds for denial of the grant of a patent, i.e., novelty [q.v.], obviousness [q.v.], on-sale bar [q.v.], etc. *See* 102, 103.

Statutory Damages: damages for intellectual property infringement, which are provided for in the applicable intellectual property statute. These usually are applied in situations where damages would be difficult to quantify or where actual damages per defendant are tiny, but a deterrent effect is required. The most notable example of statutory damages is in the United States where they are available for infringement of a registered copyright and are a minimum of $750 per infringement (i.e., per infringer, per work) rising to a potential $30,000, while willfulness of the infringement raises the ceiling to a potential $150,000. Statutory damages are available in the alternative, i.e., a plaintiff can elect to seek actual damages, depending on which is higher. In a recent case involving a music downloader (*UMG Recordings v. MP3.com*), damages of $25,000 per CD uploaded onto the system were awarded with a the number of uploaded CDs being between 4,700 and 10,000 placing the total damages at an amount between $118 million and $250 million. *See* Enhanced Damages, Damages. *See* Registration, Copyright.

Staple Article of Commerce: a defense to contributory infringement [q.v.] under U.S. law patent is that the object, which allegedly contributed to the direct infringement, has a substantial non-infringing use. Such a product is known as a staple article of commerce.

Steps in the Shoes of: a dangerous cliché which expresses the idea that an assignee of intellectual property rights only receives what the assignor has to give, i.e., that an assignment [q.v.] is subject to any prior licenses or grants of IP rights. While this principle is normally applied in many jurisdictions, *__it is not universally applied,__* and in some instances an assignment of IP rights may defeat a pre-existing license, especially if that license either: (a) does not contain a clause providing that it survives an assignment; (b) if the law of the country that conveyed the underlying right requires recordation of licensee rights for them to be valid against a purchaser of the IP with or without notice. The cliché is more accurate when applied to licenses assignable by their terms—there the principle is widely upheld that all that can be assigned are the rights, as they existed under the license at the time of assignment, subject to any associated limitations and obligations. *See* Sub-License, *Bone Fide* Purchaser.

Stockholm Syndrome: strictly, the Stockholm Syndrome describes a psychological phenomenon first observed in a 1973 hostage incident in Stockholm, Sweden, where after six days of captivity in a bank, several hostages resisted rescue attempts, and afterwards identified with, and refused to testify against, their captors. However, the term is sometimes loosely used to describe the perceived problem that some agents, particularly in the entertainment industry, whose network of industry contacts and relationships is their main commercial asset, may identify more with those contacts in a deal than their own client, e.g., they may prove too flexible in negotiation for fear that being difficult may damage their own as opposed to their client's interests.

Strapline: term for an advertising slogan, such as "the real thing" for Coca-Cola. Straplines are occasionally trademarked.

Strawman, Straw-Man: a fictitious person (or entity) created to serve a legal purpose, but with no genuine substance, for example a shell company. The origin of the term strawman was in complex rules of pleading in the English courts, which meant that all cases had, by some contrivance, to fall within existing causes of action; thus someone seeking to bring a suit might need to arrange to be sued by a putative third party with a essentially specious claim (which would in fact be known by all to be invalid and without substance). Such third parties were known as strawmen, because individuals offering to serve in this role "hung around" outside courthouses displaying a symbolic strand of straw in their boot. Eventually the necessity to have an actual individual serve as the "strawman" fell into disregard and the strawmen became wholly fictitious. Subsequently pleadings reform led to an end to the need for such legal fictions and the term "strawman" came to be regarded as pejorative and generally implying some sort of chicanery.

Strict Liability: term applied to violation of third party rights (e.g., IP infringement), regulations and laws, where ignorance of the fact that one was breaking the rule or infringing the right, does not avoid liability, either for civil damages and fines (i.e., strict civil liability) or criminal offences (strict criminal liability—more rare). Fundamentally the concept is akin to saying that someone who drives a car is expected to know or inform themselves of the rules of the road—and cannot base a defense around for example, claiming not to know what a red light means, even if the assertion is true. It should be understood that strict liability usually only goes to the liability itself, ignorance can still usually be pleaded or argued to reduce the quantum of damages, fines or penalties.

Sub-License: a grant by a licensee of some or all of the rights it obtained from a licensor. In doing so the licensee can usually only confer the rights the licensee received. Whether a licensee has an automatic right to grant sublicenses varies from jurisdiction to jurisdiction and indeed in most legal systems is uncertain. To establish legal clarity, whether, and to what extent, a licensee has a right to grant sublicenses is usually specifically addressed in any license. By contrast licenses are usually presumptively assignable unless the facts or terms of the license make it clear that an assignment is impermissible; clauses addressing a licensee's right to assign and any conditions on assignment are also commonplace.

Submarine Patent, Application: until recent changes in U.S. patent law, patent applications were not published until 18 months after filing, as was and is the case in other patent systems. As a result, by deft filing of divisionals [q.v.], continuations [q.v.], and CIPs [q.v.], followed by abandonment of the original application, a patent applicant could keep a patent secret for decades, allowing it to surface as a patent only when an industry using the technology had evolved. Typically, the applicant also used the CIP process to steer the claims in the direction of industry trends. Further complicating this activity was the fact that U.S. patent terms used to be measured from the issue date of the patent (seventeen years) rather than from the application date. The most notorious user of submarine patents was Jerome Lemelson, who, with patents that appeared to cover bar codes, extracted over $1 billion in royalties before the patents were found unenforceable and indeed not enabling.

Substitute Technologies: technologies that are alternative approaches to solving a particular problem or manufacturing a particular product. The term is commonly used in the legal analysis of the legality of package licenses [q.v.] and patent pools [q.v.]. Combining substitute technologies in a single package license may raise competition [q.v.] or antitrust law [q.v.] issues of potentially illegal tying. *See* Complimentary Technology.

Success, Proof of: commercial success is acceptable in the United States as evidence of the validity (non-obviousness) of a patent, based on the premise that if there had been real commercial benefits to be gained from an invention, someone of ordinary skill in the art would have made it earlier.

Sui-Generis: Latin term meaning something is in a class of its own, i.e., different from the normal run of things. Since, in litigation, damages are often set at a "reasonable royalty," for which existing licenses are considered useful evidence, considerable effort is often employed by one side or the other to categorize such pre-existing licenses as *sui generis*.

Summary Judgment: *See* Motion, to Dismiss, Summary Judgment, Set Aside the Verdict.

Super-Royalties: a United States tax term, which refers to imputed royalties that the Internal Revenue Service (IRS) taxes companies on, under so called transfer-pricing provisions, when it believes that actual parent-subsidiary royalty payments are too low. This situation arises when a U.S. parent company establishes a subsidiary in a country that has a much lower corporate tax rate than the United States. Tax is only payable by the U.S. parent on repatriated profits (usually with a credit for foreign taxes paid) and the U.S. parent can defer paying the U.S. tax by holding the profits offshore, and using them, for example, to invest in other offshore businesses. However, tax is immediately payable on royalty payments to the U.S. parent, often without a deduction for foreign taxes; thus companies in such a situation may have an incentive to keep intra-group royalty rates artificially low. The IRS will, when it suspects such an arrangement, seek to impute a royalty rate or "super royalty," which it will then use as a basis for immediate taxation.

Supersedes Clause: *See* Integration Clause.

Supplementary Protection Certificate: term for the document conferring Orphan Drug rights in the EU.

Sweat of the Brow Doctrine: a copyright concept that the mere expenditure of effort in creating a work does not mean that it is entitled to copyright protection, rather the work must exhibit a degree of originality. The amount of originality required varies from country to country, with U.K. copyright law requiring very little, the U.S. in an intermediate position, and Germany and Italy requiring high levels of originality (excluding for example mere craftsmanship). The most famous recent instance of the term being used was in the case *Feist Publications Inc. v. Rural Telephone Service Co.*, 499 U.S. 340 (1991) in which the United States Supreme Court ruled that the "sweat of the brow" expended on organizing the entries in a telephone directory did not rise to a level of originality sufficient to justify extending copyright protection. One result of *Feist* is that the EU adopted the Database Directive [q.v.] creating a *sui generis* form of IP protection for databases justified primarily be the effort involved in creating them. A more interesting historic example is *International News Service v. Associated Press*, 248 U.S. 215 (1918); INS were the Hearst newspaper chain, which early in World War I took a pro-German position, which led to the British and French government prohibiting their use of transatlantic telegraph wires from England and France. As a result, the Hearst chain was unable to report war news easily; to partially solve this problem, INS took to reading news reports in AP newspapers and telegraphing salient facts to Hearst's west coast papers, which were several time zones later. AP brought suit for copyright infringement, but it was held that there was no copyright in the facts of the stories, which had resulted from AP newsgathering efforts (though INS' activities were held to be "unfair competition.") Although not a patent law concept, the term "sweat of the brow" is also sometimes used to explain that the expenditure of technical skill and effort, without an actual invention, but does not entitle a person to a patent.

Sweeper Clause: a clause designed to deal with rights or obligations not otherwise allocated under an agreement. For instance, in a development agreement, resolving who owns any intellectual property not clearly dealt with in more specific provisions of the agreement will usually be done by a sweeper clause.

Symbol, Copyright, Trademark: various symbols are used to indicate the legal status of copyrighted items and trademarks. The letters TM printed in a raised, superscript fashion after the brand name, i.e. Bubba™ indicates that the vendor asserts trademark rights in the name. It may usually be used even with a common law mark [q.v.] or unregistered mark [q.v.]; alternately for services a superscript SM for service-mark is sometimes used instead of TM. The R in a circle, i.e., ® means that a trademark has been registered in a trademark office—it is usually an offense to use this symbol if the mark is unregistered. The copyright symbol, i.e., © is a notice that an author asserts copyright in the work; it is usually followed by the year of creation. The advantage of the symbol © is that it is universally recognized as asserting copyright, even in countries where the English word "copyright" would not be normal usage.

Synchronization Royalties: royalties paid for music reproduced in a television program or radio drama.

Synergistic Merger: another term for a complimentary merger. The general justification for synergistic mergers is that the combined companies will achieve greater rates of return and thus increase shareholder value by either: (a) leveraging the combined assets to ensure better returns; or (b) eliminating cost duplication, usually by redundancies and layoffs. As (b) is the most common synergy, the more the word synergy is mentioned by management, the lower employee morale and the higher the merging companies' CVQ [q.v.] becomes. Contrast with consolidating merger, conglomerate merger, expansive merger, and diversifying merger.

Synthetic Currency: three related meanings:

(a) a currency unit derived by taking the value of a basket of currencies or other financial instruments used for accounting purposes in international and trans-national organizations. The best known such unit is the European currency unit (ECU) used in internal European Commission Accounting, which is based on a weighted basket of the currencies of the member states of the European Union. Note that the ECU is not the same as the Euro (€), which before its debut as a hard currency was also based on a similar weighted basket of the currencies of each of the countries that adopted it at its launch.

(b) a notional currency sometimes used in long-term international contracts where there is a risk of currency instability, or in international contracts where the parties each want the contract to be denominated in their domestic currency or principle currency of disbursement or revenue (i.e., the currency in which they pay for inputs or their customers typically pay them). Typically, the definitions portion of the contract defines the currency unit in relation to a basket of currencies, for example:

> "One Payment Unit = one United States dollar (US$1) plus one Euro (€1) plus one hundred Japanese Yen (¥100)."

A currency for the payment of amounts set under the contract is set (e.g., United States Dollars or Euros) and usually on the payment date, the amount in "Payment Units" is converted to a real currency amount in that currency of payment. The weighting of the currencies in the basket is usually varied in the negotiation of the contract. The advantage of using a synthetic currency is that the contract thereby hedges against fluctuations in hard or actual currency values; the disadvantage from an accounting perspective is that the sum to be paid and received under the contract is uncertain. One alternative to using synthetic currency is forward hedging of accounts receivable or payable. However this practice can be: (a) expensive; (b) require a high degree of sophistication; (c) present significant risks; and (d) be difficult to do beyond the medium term (i.e., more than six months to a year into the future). Indeed, the longer-term the hedging, the more expensive it becomes.

(c) a type of financial derivative created by options traders and used in hedging or by hedge funds. It consists of a basket of financial instruments that may be various real currencies, but may also include other asset instruments such as gold or other commodities, or option contracts.

Systemic Liability: a patent or intellectual property liability situation that most frequently arises in the context of non-infringement warranties or indemnities, where numerous customers have received such rights in a standard contract or license agreement. If the warrantor loses any infringement litigation, even with respect to a small part of its sales to a single customer, all of its sales may be subject to a damages claim for infringement. Thus losing even a small case can result in massive liability.

System Integrator: *See* Integrator, System.

T

Tacit License: a situation where a patent holder decides not to pursue an infringer, perhaps as a sleeping-dog license [q.v.]; because litigation would damage commercial relationships not related to the infringing activity; because the patent holder lacks the resolution or funds to pursue litigation; or because the infringing activity is on too small a scale to justify the cost of pursuing the infringer. The distinguishing feature of a tacit license is that no written or oral agreement exists and possibly there was no discussion between the parties. A Tacit License can be considered as acquiescence and after a sufficiently long period can allow the infringer to seek to avail of defenses such a *laches* and equitable estoppel.

Take-or-Pay Provision, Contract: a provision in a contract or agreement that requires a counterparty to take a specified amount of products or proportion of output at an agreed price or pricing formula. Usually such a provision is linked to a deep discount or is entered into to persuade a manufacturer to invest in production facilities for a product for which demand is uncertain. Take-or-Pay clauses can be very expensive to unwind, particularly if the supply price of the product drops or the subsequent purpose for which the buyer intended to use the product becomes uneconomic due to falling demand or price. Frequently, much of the cost terminating manufacture of a high technology product with custom parts results from take-or-pay provisions.

Tar-Baby License: in Tales of Uncle Remus, an anthology of children's stories compiled by Joel Chandler Harris, there is a tale of a doll, a baby made of tar, which Brer-Fox tricks Brer-Rabbit into touching. Brer-Rabbit then finds that the tar-baby is so sticky and contaminating that there is no way to get rid of it. A tar-baby license is usually a license of know-how or trade-secrets that is drafted in such a way that it is extraordinarily difficult for a company to develop a product, for example using a clean room, that is not subject to the license, its restrictions and provisions. A defining feature of a "tar-baby license" is the absence of a "residuals clause" or that clause's limited nature. One or two software and computer manufacturers are notorious for using a tar-baby license for access to technical information. *See*, Click License, Shrink-Warp License, Browse-Wrap License.

Tax-Treaty: sometimes referred to a double-taxation agreements, these international agreements establish the right of an investor in one country to offset with respect to repatriated profits, taxes paid in that country against taxes otherwise payable on those profits in the investor's home country.

Teach-Away: a patent teaches an invention. If a prior art reference teaches not to practice aspects of the claimed invention, it teaches away, which is a way of distinguishing that prior art reference as not anticipating the invention and therefore not being a bar to patentability. *See* Prosecution History Estoppel.

Tea-room Conferences: *See* Coffee-Pot Effect.

Technical Effect: term used in European software patents. Under the European Patent Convention, to be patentable an invention must be "susceptible of" industrial application, be new, and involve an inventive step. That is to say, an invention must have a "technical character," i.e., it must relate to a technical field and solve a technical problem. Article 52(3) of the EPC at present prohibits the patenting of "computer programs *as such.*" The term "as such" has been held to mean that a pure computer program cannot be patented, but if software achieves a technical effect it has a technical character and therefore may be patented. Technical effect has been defined as something that is more than the simple physical interaction between a program and a computer. In principle, this means that the software should enable the computer to do something it was unable to do, qualitatively or quantitatively, before. Thus it might include better performance from the computer, or might involve the carrying out of previously unknown computing processes. The views of the European Patent Office are set forth in a 2000 press release entitled Patentability of methods of doing business.

Technology Integrators/Developers: technology businesses can be divided into two broad categories (companies with multiple business lines can be in both camps): (a) businesses that develop new technology; and (b) businesses that integrate new or known technologies obtained from other sources. The former type of business is more likely to develop pioneer patents, the latter more likely to develop incremental patents (if it develops technology at all). Most businesses, as they mature, tend to become technology integrators, in part because the major technical problems for their sector are largely solved and in part because management tends to become conservative and technology integration as a business strategy is inherently low risk, if potentially less profitable, than new technology development. In the long term technology integration can be a more risky strategy as it becomes difficult to differentiate the integrator's products and they may as a result become essentially fungible [q.v.], making the integrator a commodity business [q.v.].

Technology License: usually denotes the provision of a package of intangible assets potentially including copyrights, know-how and technical information, copyrights and software, patents, and trademark rights.

Terminal Disclaimer: a disclaimer of some of the term of a patent. Usually terminal disclaimers are filed in the U.S. in continuations and CIPs to resolve double-patenting issues.

Terminator Gene, Seed: gene inserted in a genetically modified plant seed which causes it to cease reproducing usually after the first generation, thereby allegedly preventing contamination of extant strains of the plant with the genetically modified strain's DNA, and also ensuring that the farmer must buy the next year's seed from the seed vendor. The use of terminator genes is highly controversial.

Term License: a license for a fixed period of time, usually based on a fully paid up royalty. Term licenses can be very risky for a licensee, if renewal terms are not pre-agreed and the licensee is not absolutely certain that it will cease commercial activity using the IP right by the time the term is expired, since if the licensee does need to renew, it will usually have a very poor bargaining position vis-à-vis the licensor.

Testing Laboratory, Independent: a laboratory that has been authorized by the proprietor of a standard (i.e., a standards group or a company that has set a standard, or government agencies) to test products for conformance with the standard.

"That which would infringe if later in time, invalidates if earlier": an aphorism that illustrates the tension between prior art and infringement in patent law. If an item of technology falls within the properly construed claims of the patent, it is infringing, unless it existed before the priority date of the patent, in which case it serves to invalidate the patent on grounds of anticipation.

Thicket, the Patent: a thicket literally is a thick, thorny hedge. As compared to a normal thin hedge, which a person might force their way through, the same person would probably become entangled and trapped in a thicket, emerging, if at all, with many bloody scratches. In patenting a company's products, one objective is to develop a thicket or cluster of patents rather than a single pioneer patent, which standing alone is more vulnerable to a design around or invalidation. This is done both by applying for CIPs as the technology disclosed in the original pioneer application evolves and for numerous incremental patents that might prove essential or economically vital.

Threshold for Consolidation: *See* Consolidation Threshold.

Tickler: because patent applications, patents, trademark applications, and trademarks may lapse if, for example, fees are not filed on time, or a domestic application not converted to an international application, etc. and such deadlines are often spread out over months or years (and in the case of renewal fees decades) most intellectual property law firms, in-house IP departments and patent and trademark agents have multiple systems of reminders including computerized calendars, physical diaries, etc. to remind them not to miss such deadlines. These reminder systems are often colloquially referred to as ticklers.

TLA: three letter acronym—term used, usually despairingly, concerning the technology industry's love of such jargon, which many find confusing, especially because certain TLAs have multifarious uses and meanings. Based on a 26-letter alphabet, there are 17,576 potential TLAs, which makes the constant re-use of a limited number of only about 1,200 or so such combinations even harder to justify.

Toilet Talks: *See* Coffee-Pot Effect.

Trade-dress: refers to distinctive packaging, coloring etc. that has come to be associated with the goods it contains, for example the curvy Coca-Cola bottle. Distinctive trade-dress can be registered as a trademark or can be regarded as an unregistered mark [q.v.].

Trade Mark, Trademark: the right to prevent someone from affixing a mark to goods or using it in conjunction with goods or services without the permission of its holder. Trade Mark is primarily European English usage, Trademark North-American English.

Trademark (Trade Mark) Annuity Company, Agent: *See* Patent Annuity Company.

Trade Sale: refers to the sale of a business to another company operating in the sector. Trade sales are the most common exit strategy for startups, by contrast IPOs are in fact relatively rare.

Trade Secrets: usually consists of information used in manufacture or a process that is indeed secret, e.g., secret recipes, (though the secret can have been independently developed by more than one holder). *See* Know-How, Business Secrets, Bigot List.

Trading-while-Insolvent: English company law and the law of those countries who continue to have analogous law (e.g., Ireland, Australia, New Zealand, Singapore, Hong-Kong, etc.) makes directors of a company potentially liable to the company and/or to creditors for debts incurred if the company continued to trade while insolvent, i.e., unable to pay its debts in the ordinary course of business. Trading while insolvent is also sometimes referred to as wrongful trading or reckless trading. An analogous principle exists in French and Belgian law, *action en comblement du passif*, while German law permits an action for delaying insolvency proceedings, *Insolvenzverschleppungshaftung*, i.e., allowing a company to continue trading after the point at which the directors should have started bankruptcy proceedings. In some jurisdictions, directors can also face criminal liability for permitting a company to continue trading while insolvent, as well as other sanctions, such as a subsequent bar on becoming a director of another company. *See* Community of Interest when Bordering Insolvency.

Transfer of Undertakings Directive: the EU Directive on the approximation of the laws of the Member States relating to the safeguarding of employees' rights in the event of transfers of undertakings, businesses, or parts of undertakings or businesses, Council Directive No. 2001/23/EC of 12 March 2001 (OJ No. L. 82 p16 22.03.2001). In the U.K., this directive is implemented under "TUPE," the Transfer of Undertakings (Protection of Employment) Regulations 1981. Similar laws are present throughout the EU. The key provision of this directive and the applicable laws is that where an ongoing business or operation is sold or transferred, that sale or transfer cannot provide grounds for ending the employment of any of its existing employees and that in addition, the new owner becomes responsible for maintaining the employee continuity of employment, i.e., that substantial terms of the employees service such as salary and benefits, including those due because of the length of employment (both under the old and new owner) remain unchanged. The impact of the transfer of undertakings directive and its member state analogues on the liabilities a new owner faces when purchasing a business should be carefully considered as part of any acquisition. However, the directive does afford an acquirer advantages in that it is easier to purchase a business with its workforce and therefore its knowledge base, intact.

Treble Damages: *See* Enhanced Damages.

TRIPS: the World Trade Organization agreement on Trade-Related Aspects of Intellectual Property Rights, signed as part of the Uruguay GATT (General Agreement on Tariffs and Trade) round, which set minimum standards for intellectual property protection to be provided by members of the WTO.

Troll, Patent: term used to describe entities whose business plan is to buy up patents from bankrupt or defunct companies and then use them to pursue companies in various industries for royalties. The term is a play-on-words as it alludes both to the verb "trolling," which is a form of drag-fishing and the equipment used for such fishing, but also to an unpleasant Scandinavian goblin. The term was apparently coined between the late 1990 and 2001 by Intel's Assistant General Counsel for IP, Peter Detkin after the previous terms Intel used, such as "patent extortionists" or "patent terrorists" attracted accusations of libel and slander.

TTBER: acronym for the European Technology Transfer Block Exemption Regulation. *See* Block Exemption.

TUPE: *See* Transfer of Undertakings Directive.

Turnover Threshold: *See* Merger Regulation (European).

Two Syllable Rule: refers to a marketing theory that the best and most memorable trademarks have only two syllables when spoken. *See* Short Name Mark.

Tying: a practice that is illegal under most antitrust [q.v.] or competition laws [q.v.], it involves requiring a purchaser (or licensee) to buy a product that purchaser may not want as a condition of obtaining the product it does want, i.e., if you want A, you must take B as well.

Typo-Squatting: registering as a domain name a misspelled version of a company name (i.e., one with a typographical error or phonetically accurate but with a different spelling) and using it to redirect users to a competing Web site.

U

Ubiquity Principle, the: theory that, the more ubiquitous a product incorporating an item of intellectual property is, or has the potential to become, the more valuable the intellectual property.

UCC: abbreviation for the:

    (a)   Uniform Commercial Code, a code of commercial law developed by the National Conference of Commissioners on Uniform State Laws and broadly adopted by the constituent states of the United States. A useful index of the uniform laws enacted by this body is maintained on the Web by the University of Pennsylvania Law School. The UCC has been enacted as local law in whole or in part in all 50 states as well as the District of Columbia, the U.S. Virgin Islands, and Puerto Rico and thus has achieved substantial uniformity of commercial law throughout the U.S.

    (b)   Universal Copyright Convention an international agreement adopted under the auspices of UNESCO under which the signatories undertake to protect copyright in rights of authors and other copyright proprietors in literary, scientific and artistic works, including writings, musical, dramatic and cinematographic works, and paintings, engravings and sculpture.

UCC Filing: a way for a vendor or lender to register a security interest in property in the United States pursuant to the Uniform Commercial Code. The UCC allows a creditor to notify other creditors about a debtor's assets that are pledges as collateral against payment by filing a public notice (financing statement) with a particular filing office. Such a filing prevents reuse of the item as collateral for another debt or a purchaser claiming to be bone fide purchaser. The first step in making a UCC filing is to require the debtor to execute a UCC-1 financing statement, which is then filed with the appropriate filing agency. Filings are made either with the state(s):

(1) in which the organization is registered, e.g., the state of incorporation or where it is registered to do business;

(2) of the entity's headquarters if the entity is unregistered and has more than one place of business; or

(3) where an individual resides in the case of an individual or sole proprietor.

If a company should collateralize all of its assets in a "blanket" security statement, the assets cannot be sold or reused unless the creditor voluntarily releases parts of the secured collateral or the debt is to be paid in full. Four types of assets commonly used as UCC collateral: (a) accounts receivables; (b) inventory; (c) equipment; (d) anything else with recoverable value. However, the UCC-1 is a negotiable instrument. Thus if a company wants a small credit line but is owed substantial low-risk accounts receivable it could use just some of its accounts receivable as collateral, excluding the rest and its inventory and equipment available for future use as collateral. Companies regularly have multiple UCC-1 filings on specific pieces of equipment or vehicles.

Ultra Vires: an old legal concept of authority to act, that has never entirely departed in many jurisdictions. In essence, when an act or agreement is held to be *ultra vires* it is because either: (a) the person agreeing to the action on behalf of another, for example signing a contract on behalf of a company, did not have the power to do so; or (b) the party that was to be bound, for example the company, did not have the legal right to enter into such a contract or carry out the action. In general, where an action is *ultra vires* it is regarded as a legal nullity. The problem of *ultra vires* tends particularly to arise with respect to companies and trusts. In many systems a company has to be established for certain purposes and the shareholders grant management certain powers to act in pursuit of those purposes—actions outside the purposes and powers are in principle *ultra vires* (trusts are almost invariable established for limited purposes). Although most systems have broadened the scope of management powers in their corporate law, the problem of *ultra vires* remains in many legal codes for companies—and is ever-present in trusts. A person acting in a manner that is *ultra vires* may be personally liable to someone who relied on that action, for example, someone who, *ultra vires*, signed a contract on behalf of a company, may be personally liable to the other party to the contract. Obviously such a liability may be of little value to a claimant. An exception has grown up in most jurisdictions to the principle of *ultra vires*, known as apparent authority, where a counterparty was reasonable in its belief that the other party had the power to enter the contract. In order to avail of this exception, it is standard in international contract to include a representation and warranty of powers and rights to enter into the contract.

Umbrella License: a license that sets forth a broad standard set of terms for licensing between two organizations, with addendums covering clauses specific to particular items licensed or particular use. Thus for example, many key terms might be set forth in an umbrella license, but individual licensed items might be priced separately in license addendums as there are taken by the licensee.

Undertaking: two meanings: (i) a promise; or (ii) in European law, a synonym for a business, partnership, sole proprietorship, or company.

Unenforceability, Unenforceable: in U.S. patent law the lesser sanction for inequitable conduct or patent misuse is to render the patent unenforceable (essentially useless) and can be applied by the courts directly; the higher penalty and that applied in most system is outright cancellation of the patent. *See* Inequitable Conduct, Fraud on the Patent Office.

Unfair Contract Terms Act: U.K. legislation that prohibits the inclusion of certain types of provisions in contracts. The Act is most explicit in its protection of consumers from warranty and product liability disclaimers. However, it also explicitly prohibits exclusion clauses that would nullify the standard English contract law condition of good-title and right-to-sell, and unless the exclusion is "facially reasonable," the warranty of quiet enjoyment, (regardless of whether the condition or warranty is implied or explicit). However, the Unfair Contract Terms Act cannot be applied to contracts solely by virtue of a choice of law clause, if by ordinary application of choice of law rules the contract would not apply (i.e., if the contract would normally be under a different country or state's law, but English law has been imported by a choice of law clause). Similarly, a choice of law clause designed solely to exclude application of the Act is ineffectual, as is a choice of law clause that would limit the rights under the Act of a consumer habitually resident in the United Kingdom.

Unfair Trading/Competition: term that encompasses a wide area of activity and whose meaning varies from jurisdiction to jurisdiction. Generally it includes violations of Competition Law, Trademark infringement, false advertising, and predatory pricing. A few countries also include product comparisons in advertising as unfair competition. In some countries, particularly Japan, it may include "premiums," e.g., "two for the price of one" deals in retail stores. Also known as fair trade law.

UNIDROIT Principles: a statement of legal principles of international contract law, covering issues ranging from contract formation, validity, performance, breach remedies, and damages. In some jurisdictions, they may be referred to in the absence of an applicable law or choice of law clause, especially if the CISG is inapplicable. The principles are also sometimes made applicable by an explicit choice of law clause. The principles were drawn up by the Rome-based International Institute for the Unification of Private Law (L'Institut International pour l'Unification du Droit Privé), known as UNIDROIT. There are also a number of UNIDROIT Conventions that are sometimes relevant to international contracts. The organization has fifty-nine member states, most of whom have not acceded to the various conventions it has drafted. These are: Argentina, Australia, Austria, Belgium, Bolivia, Brazil, Bulgaria, Canada, Chile, China, Colombia, Croatia, Cuba, Cyprus, Czech Republic, Denmark, Egypt, Estonia, Finland, France, Germany, Greece, Holy See, Hungary, India, Iran, Iraq, Ireland, Israel, Italy, Japan, Luxembourg, Malta, Mexico, Netherlands, Nicaragua, Nigeria, Norway, Pakistan, Paraguay, Poland, Portugal, Republic of Korea, Romania, Russian Federation, San Marino, Serbia and Montenegro, Slovakia, Slovenia, South Africa, Spain, Sweden, Switzerland, Tunisia, Turkey, United Kingdom, United States of America, Uruguay, and Venezuela.

Uniform Franchise Offering Circular (UFOC): a standard franchise offering statement required to be filed and maintained with the state government in certain U.S. states known as Registration States. At the time of writing Registration States include California, Hawaii, Illinois, Indiana, Maryland, Michigan, Minnesota, New York, North Dakota, Rhode Island, South Dakota, Virginia, Washington, and Wisconsin.

Unintentional Copying: *See* Incidental Copying.

Unitary Tax, California: the state of California has enacted a highly controversial corporate tax system that treats as a single enterprise all of affiliates <u>worldwide</u> of multinational business groups engaged in so-called "unitary" business. The worldwide income is then allocated between California and the rest of the world using a three-factor apportionment formula based on property, payroll, and sales; California corporate tax is then charged against the California portion. The law was modified in 1988 to permit a multi-national corporate taxpayer to compute its California franchise tax liability on the basis of its U.S., as opposed to worldwide, business operations; the business in the U.S. is known as that falling within "the waters' edge." The U.S. taxpaying entity must include any other U.S. subsidiaries in its unitary business if those subsidiaries can be included in its U.S. federal consolidated tax return; certain foreign subsidiaries must be included if more than twenty percent of their average property, payroll, and sales are generated within the United States. However, for a foreign corporation to avail of this exception, the foreign parent company must take care to avoid substantial activity in California, i.e., activity should be by the U.S./California operating subsidiary. In practice this means that when a non-U.S. company has business activities in California, it should seek high quality tax advice; moreover, if it sets up a California subsidiary, it will need to closely monitor activities by the parent company in California, for example board meetings, management visits, and presence, etc.

Universal Copyright Convention: an international agreement adopted under the auspices of UNESCO under which the signatories undertake to protect copyright in rights of authors and other copyright proprietors in literary, scientific, and artistic works, including writings, musical, dramatic, and cinematographic works, and paintings, engravings, and sculpture. The main purpose of the convention was the inclusion of the United States, which then had not joined the Berne Convention, in a general system of international copyright. The UCC was signed at Geneva in 1952, was ratified by the United States in 1954, and came into effect the following year. The U.S. copyright law was modified to conform to the convention, notably by elimination of procedural steps for the establishment of U.S. copyright in works published in other signatory countries and of the requirement that works in the English language by foreign authors be manufactured in the United States to obtain U.S. copyright protection (the notorious "manufacturing clause.") Although the convention was amended in 1971, its importance was significantly reduced by the accession of the United States into the Berne Convention in 1989.

Unjust Enrichment: refers to the legal principle that someone should not be allowed to profit from their own wrongful actions, often expressed in the Latin maxim: *nemo debet locupletari aliena jactura* (no one ought to be enriched by another's loss). The principle lies behind the remedy of profit disgorgement, where an infringer can be required to pay to the victim all the profits that resulted from the infringement, which can often be interpreted to include convoyed sales as well as directors' and senior managers' salaries and bonuses. It is often applied in trademark and copyright cases as a remedy and in many jurisdictions to patents as well.

Unjustified Threats: *See* Wrongful Threats.

Un-named Inventor (Problem/Defense): from time to time, the name of an inventor may not be listed on a patent during the application, either as a result of vanity patenting or because the inventor is a contractor and not an employee, which is perceived as raising problems of "shop right." The problem with failing to name an inventor is that this may, if intentional, render the patent invalid and unenforceable. Alternately, since joint inventors are in principle joint owners, in a number of well-known U.S. patent cases, the defendant has approached the un-named defendant and secured a license to the patent, which the defendant then successfully raised as a defense in court.

Unregistered Mark: in many jurisdictions unfair competition or passing off cases can be brought for the misuse of another vendor's name or brand, even if it has not been registered as a trademark, provided the mark is well known and recognized. A mark which gives rise to such a right is known as an unregistered mark. Unregistered marks are usually designated using the symbol TM in raised superscript, i.e., Bubba™ or for services they can alternately use a raised SM for service-mark. In most jurisdictions it is an offense to use the ® symbol which designates a registered mark on an unregistered mark.

Unwarranted Threats: *See* Wrongful Threats.

UPOV: International Union for the Protection of New Varieties of Plants.

Urge-to-Merge: as merger discussions initiated between companies progress, it can be progressively more difficult to call off the proposed merger, as managements become increasingly politically committed to the deal and various advisors, some of which will often not be paid if the deal does not go through, press with increasing urgency to complete. The result is an urge-to-merge, which may outweigh one or both parties' better judgment. Resisting the urge-to-merge requires careful pre-merger due diligence as well as a pre-discussion identification of both "deal-killers" and hard criteria (value, price) for the deal to go through as part of a thorough business case.

User License: a software license that is tied to a particular user rather than a specific computer, core, or device.

USPTO: United States Patent and Trademark Office.

USP, Unique Selling Proposition: marketing term for the benefits most frequently conveyed by intellectual property—a feature of a product, process, or service that a competitor cannot reproduce either because of lack of know-how, patent license, trademark rights, or copyright licenses. *See* Economically Vital Improvement.

Utility Patent: also known as a "Petty Patent," a form of patent protection granted by some countries that requires a lower level of innovation than a full patent. Such patents are creatures of national law and vary greatly in terms of the quality and scope of protection they offer. Typically they are easier and cheaper to obtain than a normal patent.

Utility Requirement: §101 of the United States patent statute (35 U.S.C. §101) requires that to be patentable, an invention must be useful. The provision is most significant with respect to the patenting of chemical compounds where case-law has held that some sort of use for the invented compound or substance must be identified. Most recently the utility requirement has been held to preclude the patenting of specific gene sequences where no identified purpose or role of the sequence has been identified.

V

Validity: refers to whether an intellectual property right is properly granted and/or held. Invalidity is a defense to a claim of infringement, in particular of patent or trademark rights.

Value Added Reseller, VAR: a class of authorized distributor or reseller who is allowed to modify or combine a supplier's technology with its own or third-party products (adding value) before reselling the product. VARs can be "pure VARs" i.e., they can only resell the supplied goods after they have added value, or less frequently, they may also have distribution rights to sell or distribute the subject goods without adding value. VARs usually get wholesale goods at a deeper discount than an ordinary distributor: for this reason where VARs and standard distribution channels exist, it is important to prevent the VARs from reselling bare goods, i.e., goods without added value, which have been wholesaled to the VAR at the VAR price, since this would prove unfair to normal distributors. However, competition law may affect the manner in which VARs' reselling rights may be restricted and therefore mixed VAR/Distributor arrangements need to be approached with caution. *See* Channel Conflict.

Vanity Patent, Vanity Patenting: phenomenon where the names of mostly only senior managers in an organization appear on its patents. Because being a named inventor is regarded as quite prestigious, in some organizations, senior managers will pursue patents on their "pet ideas" often perhaps ignoring or at the expense (given limited budgets) of patents on commercially more valuable ideas. Vanity patenting is often also associated with a failure to name joint inventors, giving rise to the problem of missing or un-named inventors.

Vaporware: making false statements about a product or product feature that a company is developing, but which in reality will never be delivered, or if delivered will be very outside the predicted timeframe. Vaporware has allegedly been used in the software industry by manufacturers seeking to stop customers shifting to a rival's product, which offers the feature at issue or a less evolved version of the suggested vaporware. The tactic has been the subject of litigation, not only by commercial rivals for unfair competition and false advertising, but also by shareholders describing the vaporware as a "material misstatement" [q.v.] and, where the vaporware was a proposed future upgrade, class actions by disgruntled purchasers.

Venue: refers to the particular branch of a court where a case is brought. Thus in the United States for example, jurisdiction may lie in a whole state, but that state can be divided into districts, sometimes with multiple divisions, each with its own courthouses. The venue (and division) is the place of the suit. Different judges sit in different venues (and divisions) and jury pools vary, making venue as well as jurisdiction a key consideration in forum shopping.

Verification: literally means checking the accuracy of facts. In patent application can refer to a document filed by an inventor verifying key facts.

Versioning: a promotional practice allegedly inadvertently created by the rock group the Grateful Dead. In the 1970s, the group allowed fans attending its gigs to tape concerts freely. The result was a large number of poor-quality recordings circulating among fans, which encouraged the fans to buy higher-quality official recordings and attend concerts. The concept became known as versioning—giving away limited, imperfect, or incomplete copies of a product (for instance, a defeatured or demo version of a game) in order to encourage sales of the complete version.

Vexatious Litigant Order: a person who has been found to regularly file pointless cases may be declared a vexatious litigant in some legal systems. Such an order in essence uses the court's contempt power to threaten the person with a fine or short imprisonment if he or she files a suit without first stating his or her intent to do so to a court officer who will evaluate the case to determine if it is "vexatious." Such orders are rare and hard to secure, and usually the vexatious litigant is somewhat of a lunatic with little funds to pay fines and/or compensation.

Volenti non fit injuria: Latin maxim which literally means that to a willing person no injury is done. More clearly, it is an equitable principle that holds that where a party invites another or others to infringe on its rights, that inviting party may be precluded from then making a claim for any resulting injury (or infringement).

Volume Discount, Volume Step, Volume Break: refers to a change in a licensee's running royalty rate, usually downwards, when certain sales volumes are achieved by a licensee. Occasionally, but rarely, the royalty rate steps up, i.e., a low initial rate is charged to allow the licensee to partially amortize investments (e.g., specialized plant, training, and equipment) necessary to exploit the license, or no royalty might be due on a limited, specified number of prototype and demonstration units. *See* Escalator Clause, Kicker.

W

Waasenaar Arrangement (on Export Controls for Conventional Arms and Dual-Use Goods and Technologies): is an international organization established to coordinate various countries' export control regimes. Members of the Waasenaar Arrangement have agreed to control exports and sales of military goods and goods useful for the manufacture of chemical, nuclear, or biological weapons. In general, obtaining export licenses for dual use technology is considerably easier, or even automatic, if the trade is to be between the participants in the Waasenaar Arrangement, who are: Argentina, Australia, Austria, Belgium, Bulgaria, Canada, the Czech Republic, Denmark, Finland, France, Germany, Greece, Hungary, Ireland, Italy, Japan, Luxembourg, the Netherlands, New Zealand, Norway, Poland, Portugal, Republic of Korea, Romania, the Russian Federation, Slovakia, Spain, Sweden, Switzerland, Turkey, Ukraine, the United Kingdom, and the United States.

Waiting Period: the period between the filing of a firm's registration statement and its approval by the United States Securities and Exchange Commission (the "SEC.") During this period the firm may circulate a preliminary or draft prospectus, which is printed with a pink cover and known as a "red herring." The preliminary prospectus includes the information required by the SEC but omits an offering price.

***Walker Process* Counterclaim**: refers to a type of U.S. antitrust counterclaim based on §2 of the Sherman Act for wrongful efforts to enforce a patent obtained by fraud on the patent office or inequitable conduct. The term is derived from a seminal U.S. Supreme court case *Walker Process Equipment, Inc. v. Food Machinery & Chemical Corp.*, 382 U.S. 172 (1965). Although common and effective in the 1970s and 1980s, more recent court decisions have severely limited the effectiveness of *Walker Process* counterclaims.

Warning Letter: a letter warning someone that he or she is or may be infringing intellectual property rights. Such a letter should be carefully drafted and timed because of the risk of providing grounds for a declaratory judgment action, as well as the risk of a suit for wrongful threats. A typical patent warning letter will usually include a claim chart. It may also include a demand that the recipient "cease and desist" from infringing the sender's intellectual property rights, in which case it is also called a "cease and desist letter" [q.v.] or a letter of protest.

Warranty: is a guarantee of certain facts, e.g., the quality of a product, its fitness for a certain purpose, its legal status (e.g., non-infringing), etc. When included in a contract, breach of warranty allows the warrantee to sue the warrantor for damages. Warranties are frequently combined with representations in a contract. *See* Representations, Indemnity.

Warranty of Quiet Enjoyment: warranty often implied into contracts under common law, that a purchaser of goods (or land and buildings) will be able to use the goods without being harassed by third parties with claims against ownership or use of the goods. English case law has held that a buyer of goods that are subsequently subject to a claim of infringing intellectual property rights may have a claim against the vendor for breach of this warranty (*Microbeads AG and Another v. Vinhurst Road Markings Ltd.* [1975] 1 All E.R. 529).

Water-Cooler Channel: *See* Coffee-Pot Effect.

Watermark, Digital: code or messages imbedded in a digital file (containing, for example, an image, audio file, video software, or document). Typically the watermark is undetectable to the standard user, but can be read using the right equipment or algorithms. The watermark serves to identify the source of an image, for security purposes or for detecting copyright infringement. The watermark also can be used for license management, so as to enable licenses to be specific to individual copies of the digital file each bearing a unique watermark.

WGGM or Wiggums: Watching Grass Grow Mails—e-mails sent to various persons detailing in painful and frequent detail, incremental steps in a work project. Generally sent to persuade people that the sender is in fact working. Form of Epistolary Incontinence.

White List: *See* block exemption.

Willful Infringement: a term used to refer to intentional infringement of intellectual property rights, which may lead in the U.S. to enhanced damages.

WIPO: the World Intellectual Property Organization, an entity that administers a large number of international agreements regarding intellectual property for example the PCT.

Wire Fraud: *See* Mail Fraud.

Withholding Tax, Royalty: A number of countries require remitters of royalties, i.e., licensees, to withhold tax on royalties or technical assistance fees, particularly when paid to non-residents. Rates can be substantial, for example up to 25 percent. In most instances these taxes may be avoided under a tax treaty in place between the licensors country and the licensee/withholding country. However, avoiding such tax will usually require various permissions or certifications from the licensee country's government. In any event, liability for such withholding tax should be apportioned in any licensing agreement, as well as the obligation to obtain any necessary tax clearance documents.

Without Prejudice (Rule): because in most jurisdictions, it is public policy to encourage people and companies to resolve disputes between themselves, a principle of "without prejudice" has grown up that provides that the content and sometimes even the existence of settlement discussions and correspondence is not usable as evidence against the other party. In some jurisdictions this rule is strictly applied to all settlement discussions, regardless or whether the term "without prejudice" has been invoked. In other jurisdictions it is not automatically applicable, or barely applied at all. For this reason, all potential settlement discussions should be prominently marked (preferably on every page) "WITHOUT PREJUDICE— SETTLEMENT DISCUSSIONS" and may also invoke the relevant legal provision, for example Rule 408 of the Federal Rules of Evidence. If there is no formal legal "without prejudice rule" in a jurisdiction relevant to the dispute (e.g., where events took place or a party is situated), if there are intended to be wide-ranging discussions, or if the existence of a legal dispute sufficient to invoke the rule is unclear, it is wise to also negotiate and agree to a short "Without Prejudice Agreement," committing the parties to treat the discussions as a settlement negotiation and without prejudice. For a party, in particular a lawyer, to violate the without prejudice rule, is in most legal systems usually considered a major transgression. Occasionally, a party may want to make a proposal to resolve a dispute, or a statement that it wants on the record, if it serves to undermine the other party's future position. However, it may be problematic to succeed in putting such a statement outside the "without prejudice" rule.

Word Mark: a mark that is expressed in a word or words, as opposed to a symbol or drawing; also known as a lingual mark.

Work, a: commonly used word in copyright law to refer to the subject of copyright, i.e., the book, music, play, etc.

Work-for-Hire: U.S. copyright law provides that the creator of a work specifically commissioned by another may have transferred all rights to the commissioner. In general, for the work for hire rule to apply, the work must have been created after commissioning, not before. Musical composers and authors should approach work for hire clauses with caution. Most commercial software created by employees is a work-for-hire. *See* shop right.

Working Requirement: used for two purposes. First, the requirement that a trademark be used in countries where it is granted or risk cancellation for lack of use. Second, it refers to certain types of compulsory license provisions, which may be applied if the goods covered by the intellectual property are not made available in a given country or territory (this particularly applies to pharmaceuticals or medical equipment).

Wrongful Threats: in many European jurisdictions (and in parts of Asia) it is unlawful to make threats of litigation that lack a legal basis and a suit may be brought for damages based on such threats. Moreover, many patent and trademark laws (for example in the U.K.) also provide for parties threatened with spurious infringement claims to be able to recover damages for such threats. The greater economic strength of the party threatening litigation may also be a significant factor in such a suit. The existence of such statutes or statutory provisions should be considered when sending warning letters.

Wrongful Trading: *See* Trading while Insolvent.

X Y Z

X-Reference: a classification for prior art references established by WIPO in Standard ST. 14 for patent search reports. The X classification means that the reference entirely anticipates the invention. An X-reference is also called a knockout reference. *See* A-Reference, Y-Reference, E-Reference, and P-Reference.

Y-Reference: a classification for prior art references established by WIPO in Standard ST. 14 for patent search reports. The Y classification means that the reference, when combined with another Y-reference, anticipates the invention. Y references may preclude a patent in Europe and Japan, particularly if they are in the same field. The U.S. usually requires some impetus in the references themselves that would suggest combination. *See* A-Reference, X-Reference, E-Reference, and P-Reference.

Zangger Committee: an international organization named after its first Chairman Prof. Claude Zangger, formed following the coming into force of the Nuclear Non-Proliferation Treaty (NPT), to harmonize the interpretation of nuclear export control policies for NPT Parties. By interpreting and implementing article III, paragraph 2, of the NPT, the Zangger Committee helps to prevent the diversion of exported nuclear items from peaceful purposes to nuclear weapons or other nuclear explosive devices. The members are Argentina, Australia, Austria, Belgium, Bulgaria, Canada, China, the Czech Republic, Denmark, Finland, France, Germany, Greece, Hungary, Ireland, Italy, Japan, Republic of Korea, Luxemburg, the Netherlands, Norway, Poland, Portugal, Romania, the Russian Federation, Slovakia, Slovenia, South Africa, Spain, Sweden, Switzerland, Turkey, Ukraine, the United Kingdom, and the United States of America. The European Commission is permanent observer.

Zone of Expansion: the geographic area into which a trademark in use is presumptively likely to expand its use.

ZPO: Zivilprozeßordnung—the German Civil Procedure Rules, which govern litigation in Germany, including patent litigation.

About the Author

Colm MacKernan is a solicitor of the Supreme Court of England & Wales and in the Republic of Ireland, a member of the New York and District of Columbia Bars, and admitted to practice before various U.S. Federal Courts including the Federal District Court for the District of Columbia, the Court of Appeals for the Federal Circuit, and the United States Supreme Court, and is also a member of the Chartered Institute of Arbitrators. In addition to an undergraduate degree in physics from the University of Dublin, Trinity College, he holds a Juris Doctor (JD) degree from Georgetown University. After serving as a stagiaire in the European Commission's Competition Directorate (DG IV), he practiced law in a U.S.-based international boutique specializing in intellectual property litigation, international trade, and antitrust law for six years, spent three years in Tokyo at the leading Japanese international and intellectual property law firm Nagashima & Hashimoto, and was general counsel to two major international technology companies, Psion PLC and ARM Holdings PLC. He has represented and continues to represent high-technology companies based in Asia, the United States, and Europe on complex international matters including transactions and litigation, and has written and been published on issues relating to intellectual property law and competition and antitrust law. He is a director (principal) of the London technology boutique law firm Origin Ltd. and of counsel to Nagashima & Hashimoto in Tokyo and lives, mostly, in London and Washington, D.C.

Origin Limited is a London-based law firm specializing in advising and representing companies on novel issues at the interface of technology and law. Origin's clients include Arm, Symbian, Psion, Unilever, Royal Liver, SpinVox, Inside Contactless, TomTom, ING Bank, Nokia, and a large number of other technology companies, big and small, as well as venture capitalists.

Nagashima & Hashimoto is a Tokyo law firm regularly and independently rated by Japan's leading business magazine, Nikkei Business, in its annual survey of the top-ten law firms in Japan, as in the upper half for intellectual property and international commercial law, and indeed, from time-to-time as the top firm. Clients include Oki, Ricoh, Tosoh, Sharp, Organo, Sojitsu, Sanofi and a large number of Japanese and non-Japanese companies.

International Legal Strategies Reference Collection

Country-by-Country Legal Snapshots for Corporate, Patent, IP, Product Liability, Litigation, Arbitration, M&A, Tax, and Labor Law

$1999.95

The International Legal Strategies Reference Collection: is an unprecedented set of books designed to aid attorneys in helping clients conduct business around the world. The collection features five books that together will provide readers with a comprehensive guide to the fundamentals for conducting business in major markets around the globe. Within these 3,000+ pages lies a wealth of critical information that every global businessperson and attorney should have at their fingertips.

- *International Product Liability Law* centers on risk analysis, insurance, theories of recovery, and strategies for product liability litigation.
- *International Corporate Law* includes information on mergers & acquisitions, forms of incorporation, taxation, real estate, corporate governance, competition, transfer of capital and more.
- *International Intellectual Property Law* covers topics such as trademark, copyright, patent, technology licensing, and other relevant aspects of intellectual property protection, as well as tips for capitalizing on available protections and remedies from the registration process to IP dispute resolution.
- *International Patent Law* includes information on registration requirements and enforcement, patent litigation, industry-specific regulations, piracy & counterfeiting, infringement, data protection, and important legislation
- *International Labor Law* covers hiring and firing, unions, employee benefits, and other important aspects of labor and human resources, from sending employees overseas, acquiring an already-staffed company, or building a new workforce.
- *International Litigation* provides readers with information on specific regulations and practices relating to discovery, trial, settlement, the appeals process, and other important aspects of litigation.
- *International Arbitration* lays the foundation for a broader understanding of arbitration procedures and practices around the world.
- *International Mergers & Acquisitions Law* covers the regulations and procedures that govern mergers, acquisitions, joint ventures, takeovers, and other types of cross-border transactions.
- *International Tax Law* covers tax on stock, exemptions for businesses, issues in corporate transactions, choosing forms of incorporation, and more.

As well as country-by-country analysis of the current legal climate and accepted business practices by local attorneys, these books include a wealth of sample documents and other appendix materials designed to familiarize the reader with the practical aspects of doing business in foreign jurisdictions.

In purchasing these detailed reference guides as a collection, readers will realize savings of 75% off the retail price for each book.

Call 1-866-Aspatore or Visit www.Aspatore.com to Order

Legal Best Sellers

Visit Your Local Bookseller Today or www.Aspatore.com for More Information

- Winning Antitrust Strategies - Antitrust Chairs from Latham & Watkins, Wachtell, Lipton and More on the Laws that Regulate, Promote, and Protect Competition - $79.95
- The Art & Science of Patent Law - Patent Chairs from Vinson & Elkins, Foley Hoag, and More on the Laws That Regulate, Promote, and Protect Competition - $37.95
- Inside the Minds: The Art & Science of Bankruptcy Law - Bankruptcy Chairs from Perkins Coie, Reed Smith, Ropes & Grey, and More on Successful Strategies for Bankruptcy Proceedings - $37.95
- Inside the Minds: The Corporate Lawyer - Corporate Chairs from Dewey Ballantine, Holland & Knight, Wolf Block, and More on Successful Strategies for Business Law - $37.95
- Inside the Minds: Firm Leadership - Partners From Dykema Gossett, Thatcher Proffitt & Wood, and More on the Art and Science of Managing a Law Firm - $37.95
- Inside the Minds: The Innovative Lawyer - Managing Partners from Bryan Cave, Jenner & Block, Buchanan Ingersoll, and More on Becoming a Senior Partner in Your Firm - $37.95
- The Art & Science of Antitrust Law - Antitrust Chairs from Proskauer Rose, Weil Gotshal & Manges, Wilson Sonsini, and More on Antitrust, Trade Regulation, and White Collar Defense - $37.95
- Inside the Minds: Leading Deal Makers - Leading Venture Capitalists and Lawyers Share Their Knowledge on Negotiations, Leveraging Your Position, and Deal Making - $37.95
- Inside the Minds: Leading Intellectual Property Lawyers – Intellectual Proerty Chairs From Foley & Lardner, Blank Rome, Hogan & Hartson, and More on the Art and Science of Intellectual Property Law - $37.95
- Inside the Minds: Leading Labor Lawyers - Labor/Employment Chairs from Thelen Reid & Pries, Wilson Sonsini, Perkins Coie, and More on the Art and Science of Labor and Employment Law - $37.95
- Inside the Minds: Leading Lawyers - Managing Partners from Akin Gump, King & Spaulding, Morrison & Foerster, and More on the Art and Science of Being a Successful Lawyer - $37.95
- Inside the Minds: Leading Litigators - Litigation Chairs from Weil Gotshal & Manges, Jones Day, and More on the Art and Science of Litigation - $37.95
- Inside the Minds: Leading Product Liability Lawyers - Product Liability Chairs from Debevoise & Plimpton, Kaye Scholer, Bryan Cave, and More on the Art and Science Behind a Successful Product Liability Practice - $37.95
- Inside the Minds: Privacy Matters - Privacy Chairs from McGuireWoods, Kaye Scholer, and More on the Privacy Strategies and the Laws that Govern Privacy - $27.95

Buy All 14 Books (Excluding International Product Liability Law) and Save 40% (the Equivalent of Getting 4 Books for Free) - $339.95

-Or-

Buy All 15 Books INCLUDING International Product Liability Law and Save 50% (the Equivalent of Getting 6 Books for Free) - $419.95

Call 1-866-Aspatore or Visit www.Aspatore.com to Order

Other Best Sellers

Visit Your Local Bookseller Today or Go to www.Aspatore.com for More Information

- <u>Corporate Ethics</u> – The Business Code of Conduct for Ethical Employees - $14.95

- <u>Term Sheets & Valuations</u> – A Line-by-Line Look at the Intricacies of Term Sheets and Valuations - $14.95

- <u>Software Agreements Line by Line</u> – How to Understand and Change Software Licenses and Contracts to Fit Your Needs - $49.95

- <u>10 Technologies Every Executive Should Know</u> – Executive Summaries of the Ten Most Important Technologies Shaping the Economy - $17.95

- <u>The Board of the 21st Century</u> – Board Members From Wal-Mart, Philip Morris, and More on Avoiding Liabilities and Achieving Success in the Boardroom - $27.95

- <u>Deal Teams</u> – Roles and Motivations of Management Team Members, Investment Bankers, Professional Services Firms, Lawyers, and More in Doing Deals (Partnerships, M&A, Equity Investments) - $27.95

- <u>The Governance Game</u> – Restoring Boardroom Excellence and Credibility in America - $24.95

Call 1-866-Aspatore or Visit www.Aspatore.com to Order